CLAIMING OUR TRUTH

REFLECTIONS ON IDENTITY
BY
UNITED STATES WOMEN RELIGIOUS

Nadine Foley, OP, editor

Leadership Conference of Women Religious
Washington, D.C.
1988

© 1988 Leadership Conference of Women Religious
Library of Congress Catalogue Card Number: 88-080851

Published by the Leadership Conference of Women Religious
8808 Cameron Street
Silver Spring, MD 20910

TASK FORCE MEMBERS AND THINK TANK PARTICIPANTS

LCWR TASK FORCE ON RELIGIOUS LIFE

Constance Fitzgerald, OCD
Nadine Foley, OP
Janet Mock, CSJ
Anne Munley, IHM
Carmelita Murphy, OP
Marilyn Thie, SC
Mary Daniel Turner, SNDdeN

With the assistance of

Rita Hofbauer
Margaret Nulty, SC
Lora Ann Quinonez, CDP
Janet Roesener, CSJ

from the staff of the LCWR National Secretariat

PARTICIPANTS WITH THE TASK FORCE MEMBERS IN THE WRITERS' SEMINAR

Sheila Carney, RSM
Anne Clifford, CSJ
Shawn Copeland, OP
Mary Elsbernd, OSF
Margaret Gannon, IHM
Valerie Lesniak, CSJ
Patricia Jean Manion, SL
Catherine Osimo, CSC
Margaret Page, OP
Elaine M. Prevallet, SL
Patricia Wittberg, SC

ACKNOWLEDGEMENTS

In editing this book I have been supported and assisted by members of my Adrian Dominican Congregation. The design of the book is the creative work of Carol Fleming, OP, currently the Associate Vice President, Corporate Communications, at Mercy Health Services, Farmington Hills, Michigan. For transferring the manuscript from the typewritten page to the word processor, and for meticulous attention to detail, I had the indispensable assistance of Carol Bollin, OP. Proofreading was done with expert care by Marion Goeddeke, OP, Ann Thomas Griffin, OP, Carol Bollin, OP, and Lois Spear, OP. Lois also coordinated communications with the printers. In many other details I was aided by Una Deasy, OP.

With these women and others I have experienced uniquely, in editing this volume, the meaning of religious community. I am grateful to them for their special expression of this living reality we claim as truth in our vowed commitment.

Nadine Foley, OP

CONTENTS

Introduction

After the Second Vatican Council the institutes of religious life were directed by Pope Paul VI to engage in a process of renewal. The directives given to them at that time were three: 1) to hold chapters of renewal within three years; 2) in the preparation, to consult all of the members; and 3) to introduce some experimentation where it was deemed appropriate to the institute's renewal. The religious life of United States apostolic women religious has not been the same since. One of the reasons is that the process of consulting the members once begun has become a continuing feature of dialogue and decision making within the congregations. It is no longer possible to hold a chapter of a religious institute without the consultation of the members. Consultation, in fact, is built into the forms of governance currently being adopted by increasing numbers of U.S. women's congregations.

Processes of consultation, to draw upon the individual and collective experiences of members of religious institutes, have been employed with great expertise by apostolic women religious in the United States. They have been developed through relying upon the competence of their members who have adapted techniques from the behavioral sciences, and who have reflected upon modes of decision making uniquely appropriate to women for eliciting responses from the members. Such processes honor and respect the individual experiences of women religious in the variety of their ministries and the awareness they have developed in carrying them out. Some of their insights are theological and specifically ecclesiological; some are the insights of women rendered acute in this age of rising women's consciousness; some are the cultivated insights and analyses of women religious who have been educated in specialized disciplines; but above all, they are the insights drawn from experiences in ministry with the people of God at home and abroad.

The essays in this volume are uniquely products of consultation and reflection by women religious who have responded at different times to issues and questions put to them by the Leadership Conference of Women Religious. Through the years of the renewal period since 1966 LCWR has acted as facilitator and synthesizer of what may be called a second level of consultation, that among the congregations of women religious that takes place at regional and national levels of the organization. From time to time special surveys and studies have been undertaken in order to assess the self-understanding that is emerging among apostolic women religious in the United States.

Since 1976, when LCWR identified envisioning the future of religious life as a priority, a particular effort has been made to articulate the emerging theology of religious life.

One phase of this exploration was marked by the publication of the book *Starting Points* in 1980. The contributors to this volume wrote their essays as reflections upon data collected over a period of four years from members of LCWR congregations. At the time of publication one of the members of the Task Force that had directed the project noted two important conclusions to be drawn from their work: that the women religious were beginning to trust their own experience and that the uniqueness of the project for the participants lay in their realization that it was not the end.

The exploration of contemporary religious life by U.S. women religious has in the meantime continued. Clearly they do trust their own experience. And there is an evident convergence around their sense of identity, particularly their claiming themselves as women and their grappling with God images and symbols to fit their emerging self-awareness. These are important developments that fit into a larger context of understanding and of implementing mission and ministry in the contemporary world. Lines of convergence are becoming clearer and the impulse toward an integrated God-centered worldview consonant with the Christian feminism of U.S. women religious is gaining momentum.

This volume, *Claiming Our Truth*, represents another step along the path of continuing reflection in the effort to articulate a contemporary understanding of the apostolic religious life of women in the United States. It has been produced as part of a process directed by an LCWR Task Force appointed in 1984 to further the effort begun in 1976. Some recent developments have helped to focus the effort at this time, notably the document *Essential Elements of Religious Life* issued from the Congregation for Religious and for Secular Institutes in 1983, and the work of the Quinn Commission established by Pope John Paul II in the same year to facilitate the pastoral work of the American bishops in helping the U.S. religious to live their ecclesial vocation to the full.

In carrying out their mandate, the Task Force members first reviewed the areas identified by the Quinn Commission as problematic in U.S. religious life: community; consecration and mission; structures of authority; religious obedience; religious identity and public witness. From these they chose three areas for focus: apostolic community, apostolic prayer, and mission and consecration. To explore these areas the Task Force developed three comprehensive questions: What is the world? Who do we say God is? Who do we say we are? These questions were proposed as the foundation for scholarly papers, content analysis and stimulus pieces.

The work of the Task Force in pursuing its agenda has been multifaceted. The questions were first posed to LCWR members for their initial response. From data collected in this way descriptive statements were developed and these formed the basis for the paper "Reflections upon the Religious Life of U.S. Women Religious" (Appendix, p. 173), prepared by the Task Force for the Fifth Inter-American Conference on Religious Life. Anne Munley, IHM, a member of the Task Force, established a sub-committee to do a sociological content analysis of congregational documents. The results of her two year study are summarized in the paper, "An Exploratory Content Analysis of Major Themes Present in Selected Documents of United States Women Religious" (Appendix, p. 183).

In the fall of 1985 the Task Force produced a videotape, "Exploring Religious Life," modeling conversation around the three questions among a group of women religious from a variety of ministerial backgrounds. The videotape was then used in regional meetings to stimulate further dialogue. Data from these conversations were summarized in the piece, "Images of God" (Appendix, p. 193).

In 1985 LCWR members were asked to recommend possible writers of papers to be based on the accumulated data. From the proposed list writers were chosen to represent a spectrum of disciplines. They were women who also brought interdisciplinary perspectives and who had a developed consciousness of women's issues. In addition, in order to broaden the expertise of the group, several other women religious were invited to participate with the writers and the Task Force members in a Think Tank Writers' Seminar held at Weber Center in Adrian, Michigan, in August, 1986. Prior to the convening of the seminar all the participants were asked to read the background materials in order to familiarize themselves with the results of the data gathering phase.

The Think Tank Writers' Seminar was conducted in a mode of collaboration. Each writer had the benefit of two or three consultants from the group in developing her paper. The entire group at regular intervals served as reflectors as ideas were generated, refined and given context. Valerie Lesniak, CSJ, used her artistic gifts to help the group internalize their experience and ritualize it. The manner in which the papers were developed symbolized the faith-inspired values of relationship and collaboration that are central in the lived reality of U.S. women religious today.

The papers were completed by the individual writers in the months following the seminar. During this time they had the further benefit of responses from those who had originally cooperated in the papers' development. As they are presented here, then, they are the products of a unique process. At the same time, however, the individual writer's insights, plan of development and style have been respected.

The papers in *Claiming Our Truth* represent one more step along the way as U.S. women religious attempt to give voice to their perception of contemporary religious life from their experience of living it in apostolic mission and ministry. The members of the Task Force hope that readers will be stimulated to think further about the issues raised and conclusions suggested. For this reason questions are included so that, having arrived at this point, the process may continue toward a more fully articulated grasp of the apostolic religious life of women in the United States.

Nadine Foley, OP

Some Learnings About a Collaborative Process of Learning

Anne Munley, IHM

This book is not merely an interdisciplinary collection of essays. It is in the fullest sense an outcome of an interdisciplinary collaborative process. From the initial meeting of the Task Force, the effort to continue the process of articulating the contemporary experience of religious life in the United States has been shaped by several key awarenesses:

> How women religious understand themselves and their world is to be grasped not by abstract theorizing or by "outsider" interpretations, but by exploring the subjective viewpoints, interpretations and meanings that flow from direct "insider" experience of contemporary religious life.

> The phenomenological experience of religious life is multifaceted. Although women religious in the United States to some degree share a "culture" of religious life that transcends congregational differences, the lived reality of contemporary religious life is interpreted from multiple perspectives.

> Besides subjective experience of religious life, the reality of contemporary religious life is also an intersubjective reality, a reality of shared meanings.

> Shared meanings are generated and uncovered in face-to-face interaction.

These awarenesses were the root of the decision to gather a group of women religious with academic training in theology, philosophy, psychology, history, spirituality, literature and sociology to reflect on data about religious life and to collaborate in the development of interdisciplinary papers about emerging themes in the present day experience. The process design for this seminar provided for five days of intensive interaction among writers and members of the Task Force. Along with roles as coordinators and facilitators, the Task Force divided itself into a content team to track the threads of ideas to be developed in the papers and a process team to focus on the dynamics of collaborative learning. To recognize needs for attentiveness to mind, body, and spirit, at given points each day, an artistic interpretation of what was taking place in the group was reflected back to participants.

In the course of the five days participants moved from an initial stage of sharing personal perspectives and hermeneutical frameworks to one of generating collective insights and interdisciplinary refinement of ideas. This process was facilitated through a variety of group dynamics: large and small group discussion, one-on-one work of writers and reactors, and small and large group presentations, critiques and refinements. Throughout the entire process, commitment to a collaborative style of thinking, working and relating was maintained.

What observations about the nature of the learning process in a collaborative environment are to be gleaned from this experience? Gathering a group of women religious to ponder about their way of life proved to be a rich experience. Rather than being boxed in by their particular disciplines, participants in the seminar exhibited an ongoing willingness to re-shape ideas as well as a capacity to create new learnings. The process of collaborative learning that took place was characterized by a high degree of receptiveness to input from one another, sensitivity to the concrete and particular, awareness of and concern for the effect of structures on people, openness to learn from the experience of others as well as a willingness to recount one's own experience, and a great deal of mentoring between older and younger participants.

In contrast to a spirit of academic competitiveness in which one holds on to an idea and massages and develops it until it can be published, a fascinating phenomenon of letting go of ownership of an idea characterized the dynamics of the group. At several points in the seminar a participant relinquished an original thought or observation to be incorporated into one or other of the papers. An ambiance of trust and reciprocity fostered a willingness to experience the sense of vulnerability that accompanies exposing one's thoughts or ideas. A general climate of acceptance and the active listening stance of participants facilitated critical questioning. Personal identity did not appear to be attached to the work being criticized.

To some extent the design of the seminar provided a fertile context for observing how women experience a collaborative learning process. There are striking parallels between a collaborative learning process and the experience of natural childbirth. Though breaking beyond the confines of a specific discipline was initially somewhat of a struggle, commitment to interdisciplinary collaboration gradually turned the work of refining ideas into a process of labor. As writers labored to bring forth outlines, other participants assumed roles of friend, coach and team. In the process of clarifying ideas there were even times when the language used was a language of birthing. Conscious that she was on the brink of grasping a core focus for her paper, one writer defined her situation this way: "Nothing has come to birth yet, but I suspect I'm pregnant." Toward the end of the seminar another writer quoted from *Herland* by Charlotte Perkins Gilman to express appreciation for the non-competitiveness and fruitfulness of interdisciplinary collaboration: "Everybody is a mother to every child. Be glad to give your child to the group so someone else can help it develop. Lack of competition is good for the child."

How did seminar participants experience their roles in the learning process? Their reflections specify various roles: listener, questioner, encourager, learner, weaver, midwife, reflector, cheerleader, buffer, organizer, challenger, brainstormer, tension-releaser, affirmer, stimulator, integrator, and catalyst. What were some of the specific learnings they derived from the collaborative process? One writer succinctly stated: "I learned that collaboration regarding substantive ideas is possible. It is energizing and hard work. Its success depends on the willingness of each person to enter into the process. Leaders of the process who are willing to be flexible are very important." Others left the experience convinced that interdisciplinary study has a critical importance. They came to know that process-generated work is efficient, but also that, through the effort to appreciate differing perspectives, backgrounds and experiences, their own awareness was enhanced. Their horizons were expanded through intellectual exchange in a warm, gentle and non-competitive environment. Through shared creativity they became more deeply aware of how God's revelation is expressed in a human process. One writer listed as an important additional learning that she did not ever feel in the course of the seminar "threatened, put down, unaccepted, talked down to or over."

What aspects of the process could have been better? For several of the participants five days was too brief a period for such an inclusive collaborative process. In such a group-oriented context, more attention needed to be given to meeting the needs of introverts for quiet time for individual thought and reflection. A third learning is that future seminars based on a similar collaborative design would benefit from a follow-up gathering of participants to review and critique collectively the first drafts of papers. Once papers had to be exchanged by mail and critiqued in writing or over the telephone, the richness of the collaborative process tended to lessen.

An important conclusion can be drawn from this experience of collaborative learning. At times during the seminar it became painfully apparent that women religious hunger for opportunities for ongoing development of scholarship through interdisciplinary collaboration. Interdisciplinary collaborative seminars are not a luxury; they are well worth the expenditures of time, energy and money. If scholarship among women religious is not sufficiently enabled and fostered, a rich and unique Gospel-oriented perspective will be lost to the Church and to United States society.

Women's Center: Incarnational Spirituality

Catherine Osimo, CSC*

Once upon a time, in the beginning, a labour of love was undertaken.

Introduction

The center holds things together. "Being centered" means one has a focus and direction, a characteristic way of living. The center integrates and energizes the activities of the self and relates the self to others and to the universe as a whole. Paradoxically the center from which we act is both familiar and ultimately unknowable. When our world begins to "fall apart" or is assaulted, we cannot always explain the truth we have experienced, but "we know that we know."

The pastoral and theological renewal that followed the Second Vatican Council has thrown the Church off balance, and we have experienced the disorientation and shock that accompany the coming of God's Reign among us. The last twenty years have been hard and demanding ones for United States women religious seeking to center themselves according to the vision and praxis of Jesus. Despite the enormous efforts of women religious to follow the direction set by the Council, Archbishop John R. Quinn of San Francisco observed an unprecedented level of misrepresentation and attack directed at them from both right and left:

> Sisters who had for so long lived as the object of an almost uncritical awe within the Church now were exposed to two implacable critics: shrill accusations that their catechetics were destroying the Church, that their every change was a betrayal of their heritage, that they had become worldly, compromised women who deserve their own decline. Or from the left came the arch suggestions that religious life could only attract the sexually stunted, the socially and economically insecure, an unenlightened and declining remnant from a dated church . . . There are circles in which to be a woman religious today is to walk into an atmosphere of the joke half-told, of suspicion of unconscious arrogance sometimes on the part of clerics, of the question that waits for no answer, of the unrelenting demand for justification.[1]

*I wish to acknowledge the assistance of Anne Clifford, CSJ, Mary Elsbernd, OSF, Nadine Foley, OP, Valerie Lesniak, CSJ, and Mary Daniel Turner, SNDdeN, who affirmed my initial insights but challenged me to greater clarity.

Have United States women religious lost their center? They have endured great personal and institutional costs during the years of renewal and adaptation, but is there a center that "holds things together?" Archbishop Quinn concludes that women religious have passed through a profound experience of the paschal mystery and have risen with a fundamental focus on Jesus Christ:

> There is a clear and profound sense of identity in many American religious born of prayer, faith and a deep love for the Church, which has enabled them to live through these years of deflated expectations and even searing personal disappointment. And that identity lies with their configuration to Christ.[2]

U.S. women religious welcome Archbishop Quinn's insight that Jesus Christ is the source and "justification" for how they understand themselves and their mission within the Church and the world. Nevertheless, the general public, Catholics and others, have missed the christological foundation for renewal within the contemporary historical and cultural situation of U.S. women religious.

Church officials too often miss the christological foundation in the life of U.S. women religious. Cardinal Ratzinger, Prefect of the Congregation for the Doctrine of the Faith, for example, agrees with the theory that men and women religious are trying to solve an identity crisis through "liberation." He concurs with the view that, while many men religious have tried to solve their identity crisis by seeking an exterior liberation in society and politics, many women religious are pursuing an interior liberation through psychology. Fearing that many women religious have turned to psychology rather than theology, Cardinal Ratzinger concludes that the minds of many women religious seem to be "working in a void, without a discernible direction any more."[3] Women religious are confused, says the prelate because:

> A feminist mentality . . . [has entered] into women's religious orders. This is particularly evident, even in its extreme forms, on the North American continent. On the other hand, the cloistered contemplative orders have withstood very well because they are more sheltered from the *Zeitgeist*, and because they are characterized by a clear and unalterable aim: praise of God, prayer, virginity and separation from the world as an eschatological sign. On the other hand, active orders and congregations are in grave crisis: the discovery of professionalism, the concept of 'social welfare' which has replaced that of 'love of neighbor,' the often uncritical and yet enthusiastic adaptation to the new and hitherto unknown values of modern secular society, the entrance into the convents, at times wholly unexamined, of psychologies and psychoanalyses of different tendencies: all this has led to the burning problems of identity and, with many women, to the collapse of motivations sufficient to justify religious life.[4]

Whether or not one supports Cardinal Ratzinger's views or Archbishop Quinn's more positive assessment, there is a need for U.S. women religious to clarify the shift in their theology and spirituality that has taken place since Vatican Council II. No full-scale theology of postconciliar religious life has to date been authored by a woman. To do so may not be even a desirable goal in the near future. Sandra Schneiders observes:

> . . . [The] content, the method, and the results of the theological efforts of women religious have changed radically in the years since Vatican II. The primary subject matter upon which religious have trained their reflective energies has been their own lived experience rather than theoretical or legal formulations concerning their life. The method of reflection has been inductive rather than deductive and widely collaborative rather than hierarchical. The results have been highly articulate but provisional formulations of the meaning and directions of various forms of religious life in the contemporary situation rather than systematic treatises defining the unchanging nature of religious life as such.[5]

The Leadership Conference of Women Religious (LCWR) has had an ongoing interest in stimulating the type of theological reflection that Sandra Schneiders describes. The most recent document from LCWR indicates that women religious in the United States have not engaged in the renewal of their communities because of an uncritical adaptation to values of modern secular society or because of "a feminist mentality." Still less is there a shift among U.S. women religious from theology to psychology. The data gathered from the LCWR membership for the Fifth Inter-American Conference on Religious Life acknowledges the positive and negative influence of a variety of cultural forces, but identifies a "shift in consciousness: toward incarnational theology as the primary factor explaining the identity and mission of women religious today."[6]

This essay will describe the incarnational theology at the center that "holds things together" in the lives of more and more U.S. women religious, despite an unprecedented level of change over the last twenty years. In the words of Archbishop Quinn, the experience of "configuration to Christ" characterizes the lives of women religious during these years. Yet the configuration to Christ takes on a different shape depending on *who* experiences God as incarnate, *where* one "looks" for God in the flesh, and *how* one proceeds to articulate and act on those experiences that result in an "incarnational theology."

The following development begins by summarizing the main elements of the incarnational theology emerging from the data gathered by the Leadership Conference of Women Religious. It then proceeds to uncover the underlying christological approach reflected in the data as well as the understanding of the incarnation and the theological implications that follow.

The Good News of the Incarnation

Who do United States women religious say Christ is? Jesus Christ addresses women and men of every age with the question and he always waits for an answer, even though the answer may be tentative and the result of a long struggle for integrity. After twenty years of change in church and society, U.S. women religious are responding:

> You are God in the concrete circumstances of our society, history and culture. You are God immanent in creation, in the midst of the web of life. You are the one who has shown us that the human environment is a sacred place. You are God suffering with us and you see in our womanhood a capacity to participate in the painful process of birthing a future in which all life is revered. You are the God of the poor and marginalized who did not cling to your divinity, but emptied yourself out of a desire to be with us. You are the depths of humanity itself and you restore our gifts so that we might name ourselves for the first time. You are the reconciling energy who overcomes sinful dualisms and leads us to ultimate wholeness. We stand with you, Jesus Christ, and identify with the goodness, holiness and beauty of this world and reject the powers of sin even to death. Yes, you are God's sacrament, God incarnate, God-with-us.[7]

This short confession of faith is the basis for a longer exposition or "theology" that flows from the direct experience of Jesus as God-with-us. When Peter first expressed his faith in Jesus as the Christ, he did so based on his "spirituality"—on the concrete way he had already experienced Jesus. U.S. women religious are in a similar situation as they experience Christ in their contemporary culture. New experiences of God in daily life, that is, in one's "spirituality," lead to new articulations of who God is—to "theology." Unlike theology, spirituality is more unconscious and implicit, since it is the characteristic pattern or response to the experience of God in the totality of one's life.

Twenty years after the Second Vatican Council, U.S. women religious are calling their spirituality "incarnational," indicating that they are coming to new theological insights on the basis of their spirituality. Peter at Pentecost did not have a fully developed theology about Jesus as the Christ. He had experienced more than he could express in human words. Faced with new experiences of Jesus as God incarnate, women religious today also know more about God's ways among them than they can adequately explain. Like Peter, they are eager to announce the Good News of the incarnation as revealed in Jesus Christ. The LCWR material implies that the identity and mission of U.S. women religious will center on a theology of the incarnation that will evolve from this proclamation of the Good News of the incarnation:

That God entered decisively into human history
    by embracing the goodness of humanity

and the burden of its sin
in the person of Jesus
whom we now experience as the Christ
in the concrete circumstances of
our society, history and culture.
That Jesus is God-with-us revealing
that women and men are images of God
who are called to manifest
the divine presence and compassion.
That God continues to be in solidarity with humans,
especially with the poor, the oppressed
and those who stand with them.
That God desires our freedom
so that, like Jesus, we will cooperate in the
co-creation of the world
and resist the powers of personal sin
and structural evil,
even to death.
That the Spirit of the Risen One fashions us
into a people called to be church
to continue the mission of Jesus
in order to birth a future
where the world will be God's dwelling place
and a fit place for humans.
That until God's reign comes we shall live "in-between"
sinful structures and their transformation,
alienation and actual conversion,
the vision of incarnation and its accomplishment . . .
When, finally, God will be "all in all."[8]

The Experience of a Cultural and Theological Shift

The data gathered by the Leadership Conference of Women Religious seems to indicate that recent developments in apostolic religious life are part of, as well as a response to, broader trends in the Church and world. The shift in consciousness toward an incarnational theology by women religious also appears to emerge, at least in part, from the experience of shifts occurring in contemporary culture and theology. Before analyzing what U.S. women religious understand as an incarnational approach, we need to acknowledge the shift toward an historical or evolutionary consciousness in the culture at large, and the impact of this shift on biblical criticism and theology.

Historical Consciousness

The Pastoral Constitution on the Church in the Modern World observed in December, 1965, that "Today's spiritual agitation and the changing conditions of life are part of a broader and deeper revolution" in the human and technological sciences. Somewhat optimistically, the Council's participants note that human beings are gaining more control and autonomy in their lives:

> To a certain extent, the human intellect is also broadening its dominion over time: over the past by means of historical knowledge; over the future by the art of projecting and by planning . . . History itself speeds along on so rapid a course that an individual person can scarcely keep abreast of it. The destiny of the human community has become all of a piece, where once the various groups of [peoples] had a kind of private history of their own. Thus, the human race has passed from a rather static concept of reality to a more dynamic, evolutionary one. In consequence, there has arisen a new series of problems, a series as important as can be, calling for new efforts of analysis and synthesis.[9]

These signs of the times are, according to the Council, normal difficulties that accompany any "crisis of growth."[10]

Without saying so directly, the Church leaders at the Council imply that theology itself will move away from the classical philosophical worldview that reality (truth) is essentially static, unchanging and unaffected by history. A classical consciousness finds the good and true in universal laws and propositions whose meaning is fixed and expressed in the same way in every age, irrespective of the particular historical or cultural situation. The slow rate of change in the classical world made such a view tenable. It did seem that what was essential was stable and that change simply indicated imperfection. Without the historical knowledge of the past, one could assume that "the way things are" is the way they always were.

On the other hand, an evolutionary or historical consciousness expects change as the possibility for growth. Modern science and technology now enable us to change what we find undesirable and allow us to create alternatives for ourselves and others. The human sciences have increased our awareness of concrete persons and the process of growth and maturity we find in individuals and groups. Not "human nature" in the abstract, but actual human persons in specific situations are our concern. From this perspective, one sees that human institutions are the product of our making and also subject to change.

Historical Conditioning of Dogma

Raymond E. Brown, in the preface to an historical review of the Church's biblical renewal in the twentieth century, concluded from the perspective of 1975:

> The Roman Catholic Church spent the first third of this century in opposition to biblical criticism; it spent the second third of the century accepting biblical criticism; only now, in the last third of the century, is it really facing the problem of how to live with the impact of biblical criticism.[11]

Twelve years later Brown's judgment rings true. Despite magisterial endorsements of biblical criticism by popes and pontifical biblical commissions, biblical scholars still are struggling to convince Church leaders and Christian faithful that the books of the Bible express the word of God in the words of human beings who were themselves culturally conditioned. In order to discover God's revelation one must take into account the historical situation, the philosophical worldview, and the theological limitations of those who wrote the Scriptures, as well as the technical considerations associated with literary *genre* and texts.

The same struggle exists in relation to Church dogmas. Pope John XXIII, in opening the Second Vatican Council, affirmed the Church's need to take "a step forward toward a doctrinal penetration" of traditional teaching, using the "literary forms of modern thought." As Pope John explained, "The substance of the ancient doctrine of the deposit of the faith is one thing, and the way in which it is presented is another."[12]

As Raymond Brown predicted, the Church currently is "facing the problem of how to live with" the results of biblical criticism, especially as we begin to apply its insights to further our understanding of Church doctrine. Just as the tools of historical criticism have enriched our knowledge of the Scriptures, the same methods alert us to the historical situation, the philosophical worldview, and the theological limitations of those who developed the dogma.

U.S. women religious in 1987 express their understanding of the incarnation very differently from that of the Church Fathers at the Council of Chalcedon in 451. In the last third of the twentieth century this development is in keeping with what the Church itself admits. A different language and symbol system, different theological issues, different experiences of self and world call for a more complete expression of the faith than one finds in an earlier age.[13] Quoting Pope Paul VI, the Congregation for the Doctrine of the Faith reiterated in 1973:

Nowadays a serious effort is required of us to ensure that the teaching of the faith should keep the fullness of its meaning and force, while expressing itself in a form which allows it to reach the spirit and heart of the people to whom it is addressed.[14]

Because of the shift from a classical consciousness to an historical consciousness, a shift that has had an impact upon our understanding of Scripture and our theological tradition, we must expect women religious in the United States to approach the experience of the incarnation in a manner that addresses the spirit and heart of people in these times.

The Shift in Christology

An awareness of the shift taking place in christology, due to the shift from a prior classical consciousness to the contemporary historical consciousness, explains the way in which U.S. women religious center their lives in Christ as God incarnate. Christology, as a theological discipline, is the continuing reflection on the person and meaning of Jesus Christ for the believer. Whether or not they are theologians, all serious Christians theologize or seek to explain who God is in their lives. Whether or not they are theologians, each one also centers the self according to a personal christology that nourishes the Church at large. The task of theologians is to articulate how each generation experiences the ongoing presence of Christ as God incarnate. Thus spirituality precedes theology; the immediate experience of Christ precedes the interpretation of that experience. Some may argue instead that theology comes first, and that our spirituality and way of being in the world follow the formation of a well-established theological foundation. Whatever the position one holds, the point is that spirituality and theology are related to one another. They should not run on two separate tracks, standing independently from one another.[15]

Though christology is approached in various ways, Karl Rahner's distinction between a "descending" and an "ascending" christology is the one theologians cite most frequently to describe two different methods of christology.[16] The alternate christologies explain some of the tensions the Church and religious communities now experience in following Jesus Christ. Contemporary theology and spirituality are oriented toward the ascending christology, having shifted away from the descending christology of tradition and official Church teaching. Anyone born prior to Vatican Council II was shaped undoubtedly by a spirituality and theology from the descending perspective. Some current preaching and piety still reflect only a descending christology. An understanding of the two dynamics in christology is critical to what follows.

A descending christology begins with dogmatic affirmations of the divinity and messianic election of Jesus, and then moves to a consideration of his earthly, historical existence and its meaning for us. One reads the Gospel accounts about Jesus, already knowing that he is the pre-existent Word of God, the Second Person of the Trinity, who came down to earth from heaven. The Gospel according to John is the preferred lens for viewing the mission and ministry of Jesus as the divine Logos. From this perspective, we focus on the Son of God coming down to earth to assume human flesh in order to redeem us by dying on the cross. As we read the Scriptures, we know that Jesus will rise from the dead and return to heaven as exalted Lord. Scholars sometimes call this approach a "high christology" or a "christology from above" because its pattern is from heaven to earth.

An ascending christology, however, as distinct from this approach "from above," begins with an awareness of the historical development of the Gospels. As the 1964 instruction from the Pontifical Biblical Commission points out, there are three stages behind the Gospels as we know them today.[17] The original words and deeds of the historical Jesus comprise the first stage. Jesus expresses himself according to the world-view and reasoning process of his time, one that is limited from our twentieth century perspective. The second layer of tradition is that of the oral proclamation by the apostolic witnesses of the life, death and resurrection of Jesus. The instruction recognizes that the christology of the early church was post-resurrectional in origin. In other words, a fuller understanding of the words and ministry of Jesus, revealed in the experiences of the Resurrection and Pentecost, is read back into the events of Jesus' life prior to his death. The presence of different literary forms within this second stage of tradition also indicates an evolution and development in the early Church's faith in Jesus as found in its catechesis, narratives, testimonies, hymns, doxologies and prayers. The third stage marks the selection, synthesis, further explication and editing of the primitive preaching about Jesus into written form, according to the particular purpose of each evangelist. As one can see, the Gospels are not literal or chronological accounts of the words and deeds of Jesus but a testimony of the Church's faith. An ascending christology will thus attend to the gradual revelation of Jesus' identity and mission.

Beginning with the Jesus of history, who is like us in all things except sin, an ascending christology focuses on the historical testimonies concerning the man Jesus, and what Jesus reveals about the meaning of human existence. Primarily through the Gospels of Matthew, Mark and Luke, we experience Jesus as did his first followers, who struggled as we do for wholeness and integrity in the search for God. Jesus evokes wonder from his contemporaries who see him speak and act with authority. Growing in his self-awareness, Jesus claims a unique relationship with God and a special intimacy. Yet Jesus does not preach about himself but about the Reign of God. Nevertheless, his life of service leads him to the cross and to death from which God raises him up and exalts him. Gathering after the resurrection, the followers of Jesus gain clarity about his identity and mission. Then empowered by the presence of the Spirit, they proclaim Jesus as the Son of God, the Christ who was sent by God. This approach to Christ's life has a pattern that moves from earth to heaven, and is called accordingly a "low christology" or a "christology from below."

Both of these christological approaches can be exaggerated, but reputable scholars emphasize the distinction between them rather than their opposition to each other. Both approaches are present within the New Testament, and one sees the adherents of each debating at the Council of Chalcedon. The Alexandrian school, defending the true divinity of Christ, operated out of a christology from above. The Antiochene school, safeguarding the human identity of Jesus, espoused a christology from below.

The Council of Chalcedon rejected the extreme positions of both the Alexandrines and the Antiochenes. While affirming the integrity of both the divine and the human natures in Jesus, the Council described the union of the two natures existing in the one person as a union "without confusion or change, without division or separation." In other words, Christ is not a divinized human, but God-with-us in the flesh, God revealed in a human being. Jesus does not have a double identity. Rather he is one person, the divine Logos, incarnate. While his human nature has its existence in the Logos, it is not overtaken by it. The divine does not overwhelm the human. The Council did not explain *how* this is true, only *that* it is true, and that the fact of the incarnation has saving significance for us.

The Council of Chalcedon dealt with the tensions between the two christological approaches that complemented and corrected one another. Unfortunately, the theology of the following centuries oriented itself toward a descending christology alone. An ascending christology, beginning with the Jesus of history, must ground descending christology's affirmations of divinity if Jesus Christ is to be other than simply a mythological figure. On the other hand, an ascending christology is not sufficient if the Jesus of history is not related to the Christ of faith.

Along with many in the Church, women religious seem to be turning away from a descending christology as a beginning point for their reflections on the experience of Jesus Christ today. The data gathered by the Leadership Conference of Women Religious appears to document that shift. U.S. women religious are no longer bypassing the historical Jesus in favor of the Christ of faith. Chart "A" summarizes the alternate christologies.

By highlighting the theological implications derived from the two christologies, we can appreciate better the theological framework out of which U.S. women religious are acting. Christology centers all the other theological and spiritual questions of our lives. What follows is schematic and generalized in order to indicate dominant trends and themes suggested by the alternate christologies. The purpose of outlining the theological implications is heuristic, a means of stimulating further discussion and clarifying positions.

CHART A. Alternate Christologies

	Descending Christology	*Ascending Christology*
Starting Point	from above with pre-existent Logos (Word) of God; start with divinity	from below with historical Jesus; humanity as starting point
Pattern	heaven to earth	earth to heaven
	Second Person of Trinity comes down to earth, takes on human flesh in order to redeem us by dying on cross; rises from dead and returns to heaven as exalted Lord.	Jesus is seen in historical situation of his time; struggles with human questions as we do, but is sinless. He preaches God's Reign, not himself. He acts with authority and claims a closeness to God. His life of service leads to cross and death. God raises him up. Followers experience his risen presence and proclaim him as God's son.
Scriptural Sources	John	Synoptics (Matthew, Mark, Luke)
Mission	to save us from our sinful humanity	to initiate the Reign of God, thus liberating human beings

Theological Implications of a Descending Christology

The center of activity in a descending christology is heaven. What is important begins in heaven and is prior to history. Thus God's will is eternally preordained apart from human involvement.

One comes to know God's will by turning to the Bible. As the revealed word of God the Bible sets forth clearly God's intentions and the reader discovers them. Coming down from heaven, revelation is external to human experience and is understood as a divine "deposit of faith" handed on intact to human beings, as the words of God not of human origin.

Though the Scriptures present God as both immanent and transcendent, God's distance from creation and the creature predominates in a descending approach. Characterizations of the deity as all-powerful and all-knowing reflect Hellenic metaphysical perfections projected onto God. The portrayal of God as perfection itself, the supreme being who is not subject to change or limitation, then overwhelms the biblical witness that God bears the burdens of human beings. A remote and utterly transcendent God would not suffer because suffering implies imperfection. A descending approach does not address sufficiently the paradox of God's nature.

By emphasizing God's distance from creation, it follows that creation and the creature abide in a different and separate realm. The material world stands in sharp contrast with spiritual reality. While the biblical worldview understands the two worlds as existing harmoniously in the beginning, the subsequent dichotomy is attributed to the disobedience of Adam and Eve. Through them all creation is now disordered, out of balance, due to an original sin "back then." Human nature, weak and by itself incapable of redemption, needs to be rescued.

What does Jesus Christ reveal about the relationship of the divine to the human? There is no direct access to God because divinity far transcends humanity. The Son of God arrives as an intermediary between the supremely holy God and the utterly sinful human race. The humanity of Jesus is useful, but his divine identity overwhelms his humanity. The doctrinal affirmations of the Council of Chalcedon sharply contested any dualism between the divinity and humanity of Christ, but subsequent Church teaching did not devote much attention to the saving significance of the humanity of Jesus. Thus, by default, Christ's divine qualities of omnipotence and omniscience overwhelm his human care and compassion. The divine Word, in "assuming" a human nature, leaves the human nature extrinsic to the mission of Jesus. Ultimately, human nature must be elevated to the supernatural level to attain its end.

Jesus Christ reveals the supreme activity of human freedom. He shows us that human beings must submit to divine authority. God, who is all-knowing, has already ordained the plan for our salvation. By following the teaching and example of Jesus Christ, clearly indicated in the Scriptures, one only need obey.

The mission of Christ is one of redemption. The focus of his life is geared toward the cross, to save us by dying on the cross. St. Anselm's theory of satisfaction, developed in the medieval period from the perspective of a descending christology, sought to explain why God became human. He argued that the incarnation was necessary in order to make restitution for human sinfulness and to repair the injustice done to God's honor by our offenses. On the one hand, because sinners are humans, a human must make satisfaction; on the other, because God is offended, no one less than God can make adequate amends. Thus justice is done and God's love is clear. Anselm's rationale for the incarnation has many weaknesses, not the least of which contributes to the image of God as vengeful. Even though Anselm emphasized that God did not exact the punishment due to sin, explaining that the punishment was an exigency of the natural order, the image of a merciless God persists in some popular piety. Unfortunately, this tradition can justify victimhood. Anselm, and the descending christology out of which he wrote, slight the saving significance of the public ministry of Jesus as well as the resurrection. What is important is crucifixion.

Pauline christology, with its attention to Christ's death on the cross, would seem to justify Anselm's approach, but Paul sees the crucifixion in antithesis to the resurrection. He does not mention one without the other. Furthermore, Paul presents Christ's whole life as one of obedience and submission, from incarnation to death on the cross. Paul is more interested in the self-emptying of the incarnate Son of God in the form of a servant, than stressing his divine prerogatives as Lord. The starting point for Paul's soteriology is the death and resurrection, with the incarnation as the road toward the resurrection.

After Paul, the patristics will view the incarnation as the saving event, an enrichment of human nature by union with the Logos. The Logos became human in order that humankind might be made divine. Paul's approach was: a) Christ was born of a woman, b) so that he would be able to die in a human body, c) and thus obtain for all people the dignity of children of God. The patristics dropped the middle part of this formula and saw the incarnation itself as the cause of our divinization, or at least a subordinate cause.[18]

Early Church Fathers, like Gregory of Nazianzus and Cyril of Alexandria, safeguarded belief in Jesus' divine identity by arguing that unless the incarnate Son of God had assumed an integral human nature, his redemptive grace could not have healed and divinized human life in all its dimensions. One can see how Anselm pushes the conclusions of the classical descending christology still further. Descending christology's preoccupation with ontological questions (the personal identity and nature of Jesus, how the human and divine nature are related in him) imply soteriological questions (what Jesus did and does to save us). Anselm takes up the soteriological questions more directly but with the limitations of his model of redemption.[19]

A critical issue for a descending christology is the significance of the resurrection. As stated above, the resurrection appears as an afterthought, an outcome of the incarnation. Because the divine identity of Jesus is certain, the resurrection is assured. It is possible even to imagine Jesus raising himself up in order to prove his divinity one more time.

The Church in relationship to Christ is a divine institution with divine authority, based on its historical founding by Christ. Before his resurrection, Jesus, knowing all things, handed over his divine authority to the man Peter and his apostolic successors. Because the Church's hierarchical structure rests on the divine will, the influence of human, historical and cultural factors is minimized. Ordained clergy, who assume the role of other Christs, become guardians of the deposit of faith under the guidance of the Pope and bishops. The sacramental system, controlled by the apostolic successors, assures one of salvation and more immediate access to the divine. The non-ordained are recipients of the salvation ministered to them by the ordained, to whom they are subordinate.

The logic of a descending christology extends to the relationship between the Church and the world. Mirroring the dualistic extremes of the informing worldview as the divine opposed to the human, the Church stands in direct contrast to the world. The laity have a lesser call to holiness since they remain in the world. Ordained clergy and members of religious communities, having separated themselves from the world, have a higher call to holiness.

The question of when, where and how Christ will come again has an answer consistent with the dualism. Since earthly existence is a time of trial and testing in preparation for the *real* world that is heaven, salvation will come in the next life. Christ's coming is at the end of the world, this world. Characteristic of this approach to eschatology is the value placed on passive endurance of injustice and suffering in this life. The Church, concerned with individual salvation, enables its members to attain salvation through the sacramental system. Followers of Christ give little thought to the communal dimension inherent in the promise of ultimate liberation, and less attention to social and material well-being. The cycle of a descending christology is now complete. What is important begins in heaven and ends in heaven, bypassing the earth.

A descending christology has both strengths and weaknesses. It affirms a strong belief that God has made salvation available to us in and through Jesus Christ. We have the assurance that God has become one of us in Jesus, one who shares our pains and makes sense of them by showing the redemptive power of suffering. This approach also offers stability and security because human life has ultimate meaning and there is a basis for hope. An all-knowing, omnipotent God guides the events of the world and assures all people of what is true and good. If they only have faith, they can transcend whatever turmoil exists in life. While there is a sacred and mysterious dimension in life, this approach clearly identifies the reality of sin and evil and the human need for salvation.

The primary weakness of a descending christology is that it appears too sure, too secure about God's designs for human beings. This approach risks being rigid and controlling, closed to new expressions of faith. Only passive intellectual assent to a collection of clearly defined doctrines is required with no ongoing conversion. A tacit acceptance of social injustices and human suffering naturally results when little is made of Jesus' public ministry. By limiting salvation to the next life, believers can avoid efforts to extend the Reign of God in this life. Lastly, an individualistic or privatistic spirituality is associated with the extreme expressions of a descending christology.

Theological Implications of an Ascending Christology

The synthesis on pages 12 and 13 of this essay summarizes the Good News of incarnation based on the data gathered by the Leadership Conference of Women Religious. It is obvious that the approach underlying the synthesis, when compared to a descending christology, is different. It clearly exemplifies the theological implications of an ascending christology. References from the paper prepared by LCWR and CMSM for the Fifth Inter-American Conference on Religious Life will illustrate the correlation between the spirituality characteristic of many U.S. women religious and an ascending christology.

The center of activity in an ascending christology begins with earthly reality in concrete history and experience. Those who prepared the LCWR paper for the Fifth Inter-American Conference on Religious Life began with a reflection on the experience of change in Church and society over the last twenty years. They acknowledge that they look for "the movement of God in concrete circumstances of society, history and culture," for "it is by being immersed in culture" that they are "led to a deeper experience of the sacred" (Appendix, p.174).

How does one know God's will? An ascending christology does not focus on a divine plan but on "an awareness of and identification with a particular need in society" (p. 175). "[Aware] of God's presence incarnated in all reality, but especially manifested in activity that transforms and liberates from oppressions" (p. 176), women religious rely on "an ongoing reading of the signs of the times" (p. 179). When one reads the Scriptures, one finds a long religious history that reflects universal questions and longings. To the extent that the Scriptures address and do not violate "our experience of ourselves and even our experience of Jesus," they will prove liberating. Any interpretations of the Gospel that do not support an immersion in the world the women religious judge as inauthentic (p. 180). Thus an ascending christology begins with contemporary human experience and relates that experience to what we know from the religious history of humanity. But women religious believe that revelation, God's self-manifestation, is mediated to them as women and through the manner "that they perceive, think, act, feel and experience" God (p. 174).

An ascending christology expects that God will act anew in history, an approach that is compatible with the development of an historical consciousness. Change indicates God's life and creativity. Women religious identify themselves as "leaven, agents of change, catalytic . . . forces for conversion and cultural transformation in light of

Gospel values" (p. 174). Laboring "for the ongoing conversion and continual transformation" of society and culture (p. 178), U.S. women religious also realize that technological progress makes massive violence and destruction possible (p. 173). "[Seeing] the world in women-centered ways," they work to create alternatives rather than to maintain existing structures (p. 178).

An ascending christology operates out of an awareness that God is immanent within history, in the concrete circumstances of life. Women religious know God to be involved in human affairs, ready to take on human suffering because justice is "the cry of God's being." They find God immanent in creation, "in the midst of the web of life," "incarnated in peoples of color, in women, in the homeless and battered, the victims of violence and oppression of all kinds" (p. 177). Women religious are also imaging God with a woman's consciousness. God is therefore "mother and father; creator and nourisher; patient and compassionate" and "a woman struggling to give birth" (p. 177). The data gathered by LCWR suggests that women religious are shifting away from images of God that come primarily "from above."

What then are creation and the creature in relation to God when the material world no longer exists in sharp contrast to spiritual reality? If God is immanent in creation, then "the secular world has become the place to encounter and to reveal the sacred" (p. 177). Rootedness in United States culture (p. 178) shapes one's consciousness in both positive and negative ways, yet women religious seek to be "vulnerable to God's presence in all of reality. Creation is good; the human is a sacred place" (p. 173).

An ascending christology does not focus on an historical fall in paradise, but calls attention to present personal and communal experiences of alienation and oppression. In contrast to a descending christology that characterizes sin as disobedience against God, an ascending christology stresses that sin is the result of our present human failures toward self and others, failures to make responsible choices. Dichotomies such as "sacred/profane, faith/action, consecration/mission" promote disintegration, rather than incarnational wholeness (p. 174). The data gathered speaks of structures of evil in the world order that induce and perpetuate oppression, exploitation, domination and violence (p. 180). Instead of referring to sin in the abstract, U.S. women religious more readily identify the victims of sin in daily life: immigrants, the homeless, battered, and imprisoned; the unemployed, unemployable, and retired; Third World peoples; women, children, elderly, sick, etc. (p. 177).

In an ascending christology Jesus Christ reveals that, in the relationship of the divine to the human, divinity never overwhelms his humanity. Jesus' human presence, compassion, and undermining of oppressive attitudes and structures reveals God's way of being in the world. From the life of Jesus we know that God's presence will make us "vulnerable" but will not overwhelm us (p. 173). God's presence among us is not manifested in subordination of the human to the divine, of women to men, but found in those who live incarnational values of interdependence, integration, cooperation, collaboration, bonding, enablement, and reconciling wholeness (p. 175). Above all, Jesus is an effective sign of God's own self-emptying of divinity (p. 176), rather than a figure who comes "from above" to "assume" a humanity defined as male.

Jesus Christ exercises his human freedom and, like us, he must also struggle to achieve identity and autonomy. He discovered transcendent depths and possibilities in his humanity, and experienced God as the author of his human freedom. From the perspective of an ascending christology, we see that Jesus had no divine foreknowledge, but that God actively promoted his human freedom as a sign of God's Reign. Divine and human freedom interact; they do not compete. Risk-taking, developing new values, and speaking and acting for peace and justice are, for U.S. women religious, responsibilities they assume as indications of a maturing conscience (pp. 176–7). They are committed to changing parent-child relationships in religious organization and to acting instead from a peer relationship with Church leaders (p. 178). Personal growth, every effort "to name ourselves," and "responsible dissent" are a "manifestation of the freedom with which Christ has made us free," and sources of empowerment making mission possible (p. 178). After twenty years of renewal, women religious know that there are no "clear and safe answers" when one follows Christ (p. 175).

The redeeming mission of Jesus is to preach God's unconditional love for all people, and to work to initiate and extend God's Reign on earth and in human hearts. An ascending christology does not skip over the public ministry of Jesus and rush to the cross as the descending approach tends to do. U.S. women religious realize the redemptive aspects of their ministries and identify with Jesus as "the suffering servant" who sees in womanhood "a capacity to participate in the painful process of birthing a future in which all life is reverenced" (p. 174). Responding freely to Christ who includes women in God's Reign, they describe their mission as walking with "a Christ who walked with the poor, who identified with the marginated" (p. 176). Because the majority of the poor are women, women religious know that the more they stand with poor women, they will see and experience the sinful structures that oppress all women in Church and society (p. 176). Just as Jesus did not seek crucifixion or victimhood but experienced them as a consequence of his ministry, women religious also anticipate being drawn more deeply into a "dynamism of dispossession" as they identify more closely with the oppressed (p. 175). Even now, "Religious find themselves in a 'dark night' " (p. 177).

The resurrection of Jesus in this view has an altered significance. Jesus' death is not a ransom to satisfy the punishment due to sin, but an enduring sign that love, carried to such limits, will not be vanquished. God raises Jesus from death and vindicates his mission and prophetic witness. The resurrection does not reveal Jesus' omnipotence, but the salvific meaning of his entire life and mission. Hoping in God's promise, religious face "the painful and intense moments of disintegration" with confidence that God will break through the barriers that inhibit the incarnational process (p. 177). The liberating effects of dispossession and ongoing conversion make "transformation of our society and our Church" possible (p. 178). Apostolic religious life is geared toward mission that is "co-creative and incarnational" (p. 179). In other words, the resurrected life is one of new creation, of ongoing incarnation in the midst of the world.

An ascending christology is aware of the historical nature of the Church. Jesus Christ "founded" the Church and he is the cause of its existence and its ongoing vitality and effective action. Those who look back at the development of the Church after the resurrection can say that Peter was the first "pope," though Peter did not have that precise awareness at the time. It is not the apostolic succession, narrowly defined in terms of the first apostles who assumed authority for the Church, but the ecclesial community's ongoing manifestation of Jesus Christ's vision and praxis that guarantees this community's identity as Church, in continuity with Jesus the Christ.[20] The many biblical images for the Church recalled by Vatican II indicate a variety of ecclesiologies in the early Church as does recent biblical scholarship.[21] It follows that the future Church need not perpetuate present hierarchical structures that are historically conditioned.

It is important to preserve the foundational experience of the resurrection that unleashed a profound sense of freedom among the followers of Christ. Understanding themselves as the *basilea* of God, members of the Jesus movement in Palestine modeled themselves according to Jesus' own manner. As an egalitarian discipleship of equals, energized by the memory of Jesus as the child and prophet of Sophia, the community manifested prophetic and charismatic activity on behalf of God's poor. The Christian missionary movement beyond Jerusalem welcomed the leadership of women and emphasized baptismal equality over patriarchal domination. Fear of persecution by civil and religious authorities, however, soon motivated the Church to justify the restoration of patriarchal household codes as a model for its way of life.[22] An ascending christology makes it more possible to retrieve Jesus' radical vision and praxis of equality before God.

Throughout the material prepared for the Fifth Inter-American Conference, women religious identify themselves in terms of Christ's transforming and liberating mission. Acting *as* the Church itself, women religious understand themselves as "agents of change" who work in concert with all the baptized (pp. 178-9). Religious communities especially witness to the prophetic dimension of the Church's way of being in the world and remind the Church of its mission to be "a sign/sacrament of freedom and hope" (p. 180). As one reads the material, one finds a pronounced openness to new structures, forms and ways of being Church. Incarnational values of mutuality, equality and collaboration have more significance for U.S. women religious than patriarchal hierarchical expressions deriving from the former descending christology. The Church that women religious envision is, like Christ, a Church suffering with the world's people, rather than asserting its control over them. Though the Church promotes God's Reign, "creating a dwelling place on earth characterized by justice, mercy and love," the Church is not itself the fulfillment of God's Reign because of its ongoing need for conversion (p. 181).

What is the world in relationship to Christ's Church? An ascending christology affirms that the world has its own sacred dimension, and that the role of the Church is to call attention to the signs of God's movement within the world. As the Church incorporates all that is "good, just, beautiful in human and cosmic experience," the Church will learn from the poor, the suffering, the marginalized "and itself [become] a poor, marginalized community" (p. 181). By immersing itself in the experience of the world, a world that is "the locus of God's revelation and activity," the Church will confront the powers of sin and build on the liberating elements within each culture (p. 180).

When and where and how will Christ come again? The question appears with a different emphasis from the perspective of an ascending christology. Just as Jesus did not preach himself but the coming Reign of God, we might better ask, "What are the signs of the Reign of God that we hope for as Jesus did?" Both the contemporaries of Jesus and twentieth century Americans may be characterized by their apocalyptic expectations of the future. "The end of the world" is a clear and present possibility in the nuclear era when the superpowers daily risk global holocaust. Rather than passively await the coming of God's Reign, as the early Church itself was tempted to do, the followers of Christ instead lived as if God's Reign were already present. The early Church lived with the tension between the experience of God's presence now and yet to come, but in the midst of the "now" they lived out the liberating vision of Jesus.

U.S. women religious characterize themselves as living "in-between" the vision of incarnation and its accomplishment (p. 177). Knowing that "the Reign of God has not yet fully come," women religious commit themselves to creating "lifestyles and structures that fit us to be a leaven of transformation and a witness to the values of Jesus' Gospel" (p. 180). Rather than worry about their personal immortality, women religious expend their energies "birthing a future in which all life is reverenced" (p. 174). And what do they actively hope for? They dream of a world and Church marked by incarnational inclusivity—"the embracing of peoples, cultures, male-female, the poor" and the celebration of the full diversity of their gifts (p. 181).

What are the relative strengths and weaknesses of an ascending christology compared to a descending christology? A major benefit of this approach is that it preserves the strengths of our past descending christology, while avoiding or lessening its weaknesses. An ascending christology affirms our traditional belief that God has made salvation available to us, in and through Jesus and the Reign of God which he initiated among us.

Furthermore, this approach addresses the contemporary issue of freedom and autonomy, for individuals and for peoples. The stress on our human involvement and participation in our own liberation fits our modern psychological consciousness. Yet this

CHART B. Theological Implications

	Descending Christology	Ascending Christology
Center of Activity	before time and history	in concrete history and experience
Revelation	deposit of faith directly from God	God's self-manifestation mediated in human experience
God	perfect, remote in heaven	involved in human affairs, affected by suffering
Creation	what God is not	where God is
Sin	disobedience against God in the past	present alienation and irresponsibility toward others
Divine/Human Relationship	divine assumes, overwhelms human nature	God's self-emptying through humanity
Human Freedom	obedience to divine plan, little human involvement	interaction of human and divine creativity amid uncertainty
Redemption	salvation through death on the cross	public ministry as solidarity between God and humans; cross as consequence of ministry
Resurrection	outcome of incarnation, Jesus raises himself and proves his divinity	revelation of ongoing incarnation and creativity; God vindicates Jesus' mission
Church	historically founded by Christ as divine institution	body of believers gathered by Holy Spirit, gradually "founded" as members act on charisms
World	object of salvation by Church	subject of salvation, potential dwelling place of God
Eschatology	salvation in next life	salvation begins in this life

approach does not deny that God's presence enables us to do what we could not accomplish alone. By attending to the public ministry of Jesus, this approach also provides a sound theological basis for the Church's ministry of social justice.

An ascending christology welcomes ecumenical dialogue and the possibility of sharing with other religious traditions as we seek God together. In an approach that begins "from below" a triumphalistic ecclesiology is not possible although an ascending christology has confidence in the abiding presence of God.

Lastly, an ascending christology is more open to women's experience of God. Both the descending and ascending christologies are to date the result of male theological reflection. This essay relies on the fruits of that prior theology, although it is not necessarily bound by it. Women religious in the United States are finding an incarnational theology, within the framework of an ascending christology, more suited to their contemporary questions and needs.

Obviously an ascending christology does not provide the security of certitude and stability. But since appeals to divine authority are less convincing in the contemporary world than are exercises of human authority, the strength of an ascending christology is that it does lead to the sacred dimension within ordinary human experience. The danger of the approach is that it always risks collapsing the sacred altogether.

If one is a member of a privileged group, the ascending approach challenges more than it comforts. No divine mandate exists for justifying "things as they are," as one can so easily claim according to an approach "from above." On the other hand, if one is a member of a marginalized or an oppressed group, the ascending christology offers more potential for change. Perhaps this is why U.S. women religious are expressing their experience of an incarnational consciousness "from below." They hope for change.

Chart "B" summarizes the theological implications of the alternate christologies.

Incarnational Spirituality Today and Tomorrow

Our tradition proclaims that "Jesus Christ is the same, yesterday and today, yes, and forever" (Hebrews 13:8). Jesus Christ transcends human articulations of both a descending and an ascending christology. As Pope John XXIII warned, the substance of the ancient doctrine is one thing, and the way in which it is presented is another. Whatever shifts take place in time and history, the Church holds true to the central message revealed through Jesus the Christ: God is with us.

The purpose of this essay has been to clarify how U.S. women religious understand their identity and mission in relationship to Christ as God incarnate. This clarification was necessary because of concerns within the Church that women religious today appear to be centered on secular values, psychology, feminism or professionalism, rather than centered according to the mind and heart of Jesus Christ. The Leadership Conference of Women Religious, at the same time, has had an ongoing interest in sponsoring opportunities for women religious to reflect on their experiences of renewal. The material gathered by LCWR indicates that U.S. women religious have been eager to share their experiences and reflections with the larger ecclesial community.

The shift from a classical consciousness to an historical consciousness with its impact on christology provides an explanation for how U.S. women religious understand their identity and mission. From the perspective of an ascending christology, they find validation for their experiences of God-with-us. The public ministry of Jesus Christ coupled with a contemporary reading of the Gospels by women experiencing God in the present cultural and historical situation account for the direction women religious are taking as they follow Christ today. Secular values, psychology, feminism and professionalism surely have influenced members of women's religious institutes in the United States. Many could acknowledge this reality without apology because openness to the positive values of one's own time reflects an incarnational spirituality. Yet more to the point, the liberating vision and praxis of Jesus is the primary motivation for the way women religious are choosing to embody the mission of Jesus today.

It is difficult to know what kind of spirituality will emerge from the present incarnational spirituality of United States women religious. Karl Rahner, looking into the century ahead from the perspective of 1981, advised that:

> Spirituality is a mysterious and tender thing, about which we can speak only with difficulty. As intense self-realization of the Christian reality in the individual person as individual, it is inevitably very different in every Christian, according to the natural disposition, age, life-history, cultural and sociological milieu, the ultimate free and never wholly comprehensible uniqueness of the individual. For that very reason our theme [spirituality of the future] is an exacting one and difficult to cope with.[23]

Even more difficult to project is a spirituality that will characterize an entire group like United States women religious. Based on the incarnational spirituality expressed in the data gathered by the Leadership Conference of Women Religious thus far, one can expect a shift from those spiritualities that render women's experiences of God invisible or negligible.

A descending christology has proven problematic when its patriarchal assumptions are not faced. Such a christology can legitimate unjust social structures and ignore women as images of God.[24] The maleness of Jesus, because of patriarchal cultural assumptions, has reinforced the ideas that maleness is normative for humanity and that men are superior to women. Male privilege and primacy, based on questionable interpretations of Genesis 2, pervade every aspect of life today.[25]

The data gathered by LCWR indicates that United States women religious, reflecting upon their faith experience, propose a variety of images for God as alternatives to patriarchal forms. An incarnational spirituality "from below" can more readily transcend the metaphor of the "fatherhood of God" and not be limited by it. One forgets that the theological tradition has never assigned actual sexuality to God whom Scripture affirms as pure Spirit (John 4:24). "In other words, God is neither a father nor a son but the first person of the Trinity is related to the second person as origin is related to that which is originated."[26] Women religious are not denying the traditional image of God as father but affirming that God is also mother and woman incarnate among the poor and marginalized.

There is nothing in the material from the Fifth Inter-American Conference on Religious Life that addresses the question of the ordination of women to the ministerial priesthood. The underlying assumption of these reflections synthesized by LCWR is that women religious do bear a natural resemblance to Christ by embodying the mission of Jesus within their very selves. Like Jesus they have not generated children but they have embraced the world's sons and daughters. They, too, have wept and suffered with the oppressed. At the bed of the sick in long vigils and sleepless nights, they have felt the agony of Gethsemane. Just as Jesus handed over his body and laid down his life for his friends, women religious are physically spending themselves for the sake of the Church. Such prophetic gestures keep alive the memory and activity of Jesus, God-with-us. These women religious are signs of the Church's call to sacrificial love. Apart from their ministry of service and that of the whole Church, no sacrament is efficacious.

An ascending christology has the potential to legitimate women's experience of God and the following of Christ with a woman's consciousness. This does not mean that a descending christology has no potential salvific significance for women, but that a descending christology could be enriched if it were purged of its patriarchal interests.[27]

Though the experience of God is "a mysterious and tender thing," one can project that United States women religious will continue to experience God in women-centered ways. What "new heaven" and what "new earth" do women religious anticipate due to their incarnational hope? The whole of creation waits with eager longing for these signs of God's Reign coming near:

> The center of activity will include the poor and the marginalized. The concrete history and experience of women and subjugated peoples will find a voice.
>
> Each generation will experience God's self-revelation as Good News of liberation. Charismatic and prophetic activity will energize the ongoing tradition.
>
> Creativity will order all things rightly, day by day. Women and men together will assume responsibility for the world and all that is in it.

The mystery and incomprehensibility of God shall lead us into the future.

The world shall recover its identity as matrix of life, sustaining humanity. Neither shall there be enmity between our bodily existence and our life in the spirit.

Sin will be unmasked as the cause of dualisms that violate human integrity and God's presence in women and men.

The incarnational unity of the human and divine natures will model liberating relationships among peoples.

In the world to come, the freedom of one group will not threaten that of another.

Salvation will arise as a participation in one's own liberation as God's Reign nears.

Women will continue to herald resurrection so that they might be freed of their fear and risk what they treasure.

The Church will be a discipleship of equals, signifying God's effective coming among us.

As a prophetic community the Church will witness to the presence of God in this world and its history, and its members will resist the forces which threaten life.

Those who hunger and thirst for justice will hasten God's future on earth as it is in heaven.

The center holds things together but its energy moves outward. It is Alpha and Omega. God is with us at the center, yesterday and today, yes, forever but as a provoking presence. The Word is made flesh amid crisis and decision. The world of the past is gone—now all things are made new.

ENDNOTES

1. Archbishop John R. Quinn, "Extending the Dialogue about Religious Life" (Address to the Leadership Conference of Women Religious Assembly, August 16, 1983), Robert J. Daly, *et al.*, eds. *Religious Life in the United States: The New Dialogue* (New York: Paulist Press, 1984) 26.

2. *Ibid.* 27.

3. Joseph Cardinal Ratzinger with Vittorio Messori, *The Ratzinger Report: An Exclusive Interview on the State of the Church* (San Francisco: Ignatius Press, 1985) 100.

4. *Ibid.* 99–100.

5. Sandra M. Schneiders, *New Wineskins: Re-imagining Religious Life Today* (New York: Paulist Press, 1986) 5–6.

6. Leadership Conference of Women Religious of the USA and Conference of Major Superiors of Men of the USA, "Synthesis: Reflection Questions for Fifth Inter-American Conference on Religious Life" from Leadership Conference of Women Religious, *Apostolic Religious Life in a Changing World and Church* (Silver Spring, Maryland: Leadership Conference of Women Religious and Conference of Major Superiors of Men, 1986). See Appendix p. 173.

7. This is my own synthesis gathered from the conference data from LCWR.

8. Again, this is my own synthesis of the data.

9. *Pastoral Constitution on the Church in the Modern World #5*, ed. Walter M. Abbot *The Documents of Vatican II* (New York: Herder and Herder/Association Press, 1966) 203.

10. *Ibid.* #4, 202.

11. Raymond E. Brown, *Biblical Reflections on Crises Facing the Church* (New York: Paulist Press, 1975) vii.

12. Pope John XXIII, "Pope John's Opening Speech to the Council," in Abbot, 715.

13. Sacred Congregation for the Doctrine of the Faith, *Mysterium Ecclesiae*, ed. Austin Flannery *Vatican II: More Postconciliar Documents*, II (Grand Rapids, Michigan: Wm. B. Eerdmans, 1982) 433.

14. *Ibid.*, quoting Pope Paul VI, Apostolic Exhortation *Quinque iam Anni*, AAS 63 (1971) 100 ff.; 435 in Flannery.

15. Agnes Cunningham, "Ten Questions on Spirituality," *Chicago Studies* 25 (November 1986) 279–91.

16. Karl Rahner, "The Two Basic Types of Christology," *Theological Investigations*, XIII (New York: Seabury, 1975), 213–23. What follows is indebted to Rahner but is used according to my own purposes.

17. "The Biblical Commission's Instruction on the Historical Truth of the Gospels" can be found in Joseph A. Fitzmyer, *A Christological Catechism: New Testament Answers* (Ramsey, New Jersey/New York: Paulist Press, 1982) 97–140.

18. L. Cerfaux, *Christ in the Theology of St. Paul* (New York: Herder and Herder, 1959) 161–72.

19. See Gerald O'Collins, *Interpreting Jesus* (Ramsey, New Jersey: Paulist Press, 1983) 19–21, and 133–69 for a fuller treatment of redemption.

20. Karl Rahner, *Foundations of Christian Faith: An Introduction to the Idea of Christianity* (New York: Seabury, 1978) 322–35.

21. Raymond E. Brown, *The Churches the Apostles Left Behind* (New York: Paulist Press, 1984) and Elisabeth Schüssler Fiorenza, *In Memory of Her: A Feminist Theological Reconstruction of Christian Origins* (New York: Crossroad, 1983).

22. Fiorenza 99 ff.

23. Karl Rahner, "The Spirituality of the Church of the Future," *Theological Investigations*, XX (New York: Crossroad, 1981) 143.

24. Sandra M. Schneiders, *Women and the Word* (New York: Paulist Press, 1986) 1–7.

25. See Phyllis Trible, *God and the Rhetoric of Sexuality* (Philadelphia: Fortress Press, 1978) 72–143.

26. Schneiders, *Women and the Word* 3.

27. See Patricia Wilson-Kastner, *Faith, Feminism, and the Christ* (Philadelphia: Fortress Press, 1983).

REFLECTION QUESTIONS

1. Jesus addresses every age with the question, "Who am I?" Who is Jesus for you?

2. Osimo describes what she believes to be "a confession of faith" for U.S. women religious. Write your profession-confession of faith. What does this confession reveal to you about your spirituality?

3. Osimo also describes "signs of God's Reign coming near." What are the signs of God's Reign within your own life? within your congregation? within the Church as you experience it? What attitudes of mind and heart, what deeds, will foster the "coming near" of God's Reign? What are the obstacles to this coming?

RECOMMENDED READING

Cone, James H. *God of the Oppressed*. New York: Seabury Press, 1975.

Ruether, Rosemary Radford. *Sexism and God-Talk: Toward a Feminist Theology*. Boston: Beacon Press, 1983.

Women Missioned in a Technological Culture

Anne Clifford, CSJ*

It started with a sign, to show that something was about to happen.
Light came forth from the deep darkness, bright, clear and unmis-
takable.
And it was very good.

Orientation

Theology of apostolic religious life for women religious in the United States is in its infancy. This is the case because theological reflection properly follows upon, rather than precedes, lived experience. The contemporary lived experience of U.S. women religious is marked by a re-interpretation and a re-appropriation of what it means to be Christian women missioned in the world. The social world in which United States women religious are missioned is a technological society. Our theology of religious life, therefore, needs to incorporate a critical understanding of the relationship of technology to our understanding of mission. This essay contends that such a theology needs, at one and the same time, to reflect our experiences of ministry in a technological culture and to provide appropriate expressions of our experience which will stimulate a creative fidelity to the spirit of the Gospel and to the unique heritage of each community. In this regard I propose that the summary expression "mission as consecration" identifies both the present experience common among us and the challenge of the future.

The major premise of this essay is that a focus on mission is redefining the meaning of apostolic religious life lived in many women's communities today. Since this is the case, we find ourselves impelled to engage in theological reflection on experience. An important aspect of our experience is the increasing awareness of the dynamic interrelationship of major changes in religious life lived in women's communities in the United States and those changes occurring in our society. This awareness is evident in the LCWR paper about our mission in the world prepared for the Fifth Inter-American Conference on Religious Life. The paper referred to the developments in apostolic religious life over the past twenty years since Vatican Council II as *part of* or a *reaction to* broader social and cultural trends."[1] This recognition of the impact of social and cultural

---

*The author wishes to thank all who contributed support and ideas for the writing of this paper, particularly Shawn Copeland, OP, Nadine Foley, OP, and Mary Daniel Turner, SNDdeN, who offered substantive criticism and helpful suggestions.

change on religious life has contributed to our increasing engagement in analysis of the social structures of the society in which we participate. In conjunction with social analysis it is also important for us to engage in cultural analysis. For beneath the political, social and economic structures that affect us lies the less accessible, but powerful, world of myth and symbol that is the substance of our cultural life. Cultural analysis is a difficult task, because we cannot simply disengage ourselves from our culture and find a neutral perspective from which to view it.

The LCWR paper for the Fifth Inter-American Conference on Religious Life notes the role of technology as a major force that shapes the social structures of our society.[2] Advanced technology and the centralization of economic and political power that accompany it are important parts of our everyday life and are worthy of our critical attention.

In this essay I will engage in an exploratory reflection on apostolic religious life as it is developing in women's communities in the United States with explicit attention to our cultural situation as it is impacted by technology. As is clear from the data gathered by the LCWR Task Force on Religious Life, it is important for us to attend to technology as a dominant force in our society and culture. Its effects on our daily living and our evolving life stories are becoming increasingly pervasive. Moreover, the influence of technology on our culture shows no signs of abating, as we find ourselves rapidly entering a postindustrial age.

The following theological reflections on the mission of apostolic women religious in our technological culture will at best be exploratory and tentative. In their reflections theologians for the most part have ignored the world of technology and its effects in our cultural situation.[3] We do not have, therefore, many guide posts to assist us in finding our way in this area. But this fact need not prevent us from beginning to engage in theological reflection on apostolic religious life with a critical awareness of the impact of technology on our cultural situation. In this essay I will analyze some of the major changes in apostolic religious life lived in women's communities and in our culture due to the advance of technology in terms of major "paradigm shifts." It is my hope that this analysis will serve both as a stimulus for further reflection on our present experience and as an aid for discernment about possible directions for the future.

The Paradigm Shift in Apostolic Religious Life

While the essence of Christian commitment is apostolic, the expression "apostolic religious life" needs some initial clarification. Christianity with its incarnational self-understanding is rooted in the belief that the Wisdom of God entered our world as a full human being. To be a Christian is to exercise concern for this world in which Jesus

Christ was and is enfleshed. In the sense that having a commitment to our world and its well-being is implicit in the very meaning of Christianity, every Christian has a call to be apostolic, to be a disciple of Jesus in our world. The term "apostolic women religious" refers to communities of women who have publicly committed themselves to and for the mission of the Church. The apostolic commitment is not necessarily more complete that that of other Christians, but it is more explicit and visible.

This perspective on "apostolic life" as encompassing the commitment of the Christian follows from the focus of the Second Vatican Council (1962–65) on the mission of the Roman Catholic Church. In its sixteen conciliar documents the Church sought to clarify its mission in a way that was responsive to the signs of the times. Thus the Church publicly incorporated the culture of modernity into its self-understanding. This fact is worthy of note in the light of the Church's vigorous condemnation of "modernism" and "Americanism" at the turn of the century. These condemnations do not have a direct bearing on communities of women religious in the United States, but they do have a bearing on the Church's understanding of its mission at a time when women's communities in the United States were multiplying and flourishing.[4]

It is at the turn of this century during the anti-modernist era, that congregations of women living under simple vows and without strict enclosure were formally recognized as canonically "religious" in the eyes of the institutional Church. *Conditae a Christo*, a Bull issued by Pope Leo XIII in 1900, served as the "Magna Charta" for congregations of women who were actively involved in the works of the Church, primarily the education of youth. This document is worthy of note because it marks the departure from the requirements of strict enclosure and solemn vows for women's communities to be "religious." These requirements for women religious can be traced to 1298 and Boniface VII (*Pericoloso*), which was further refined by Pius V in 1566 (*Circa Pastoralis*) and in 1570 (*Lubricum Vitae Genus*), and restated in 1869 by Pius IX (*Apostolicae Sedes*).[5]

Conditae a Christo applied to almost all of the communities of women religious in the United States, including communities with monastic roots, such as the Benedictines.[6] This was the case because women in North American communities were engaged in works, primarily the education of children, which made strict enclosure impossible. The needs of the immigrant Church and the lack of financial endowments that would have made strict enclosure possible contributed to the apostolic adaptation of many communities of women who lived under solemn vows and strict enclosure in Europe.[7]

Conditae a Christo and the *Normae* (1901), which provided guidelines regarding partial cloister and simple vows, served as major sources for the 1917 Code of Canon Law governing consecrated life for women. It is this Code, and the theology of religious life for women that is implicit in it, that determined the constitutions and daily life of women religious prior to the Second Vatican Council.

Since the Second Vatican Council and its call to renewal of religious life in response to the conditions of the times and the requirements of the culture women religious have entered decisively into the culture of modernity. We have engaged in a process of discerning what it means for us to live an apostolic life faithful to our distinctive charisms. The many corporate stories unfolding among communities of women give a distinctive form to each community's apostolic commitment. In our stories we recognize that a basic intuition of modern culture in which we participate is an awareness of the historicity of humanity, of human attitudes and institutions.[8] The very nature of our movement into modernity lends itself to analysis of our evolving histories as apostolic women of the Church in terms of a "paradigm shift." Such an analysis can serve to make the historical developments we are experiencing more intelligible.

A paradigm represents a coherent structure of meaning that creates a community's or a society's self-understanding. It provides a group with a shared symbolic framework or net of meaning for interpreting reality.[9] The data gathered by the LCWR Task Force on Religious Life clearly indicates that its members recognize that they are participating in a major paradigm shift in religious life. The internal rules of our communities have been adapted to express a new paradigm, with particular attentiveness to the changes that are occurring in our society and culture.

A shift in paradigms, the surrender of once life-giving and people-bonding experiences and events, occurs only when the accepted paradigm no longer adequately copes with significant dimensions of experience. A paradigm shift is a transformation in meaning that amounts to a multi-leveled conversion through which a community or society can relate to experience and events with a radically different perspective. Apostolic women religious are participating in a new paradigm through conversion to a new understanding of apostolic identity.

I propose the metaphor "mission as consecration" to name the new paradigm shared by apostolic women religious in the United States. In the reflections to follow I will indicate, first of all, why I believe "mission as consecration" is an appropriate metaphor for naming the fundamental experience of U.S. women religious. Then I will explore some of its implications for ministry in a highly technological culture.

Apostolic Religious Life: Mission as Consecration

"Mission as consecration" attends to the reflections contained in the LCWR paper for the Fifth Inter-American Conference. In reflections on the shift in consciousness among women religious the paper noted that there is a growing tendency among us to reject a dichotomy between consecration and mission.[10] This shift is occurring because during the past twenty years we have begun to interpret our consecration with a heightened sense of mission.

For apostolic women religious mission is the governing principle because we perceive that our consecration does not set us apart from the world. Rather, through it we are sent into the world to listen to the call of God in our sisters and brothers. Our consecration signifies a personal relationship with God in Jesus Christ that we share with all the baptized. As members of religious congregations we affirm our graced relationship with God through a public pronouncement of the evangelical counsels whereby we make the Gospel our primary rule of life. While at its core our consecration is the same as that of all the baptized, that is, full participation in the mission of Jesus Christ, the difference lies in the manner of our consecration. Our public "yes" made in response to God's grace commits us to the mission of Jesus in accord with our community's ongoing appropriation of its founding charism.

"Mission *as* consecration" names the nature of this discipleship and participation in the mission of Jesus by apostolic women religious. The emphasis given above to the word "as" is to draw attention to the claim that consecration by the women religious is not just *for* the mission of Jesus. We do not enter a religious community in order to perform apostolic works for the Church. "Mission as consecration" does not connote apostolic religious life in functional terms; rather it expresses the self-identity of the woman religious as a participant in an apostolic community.

The metaphor "mission as consecration" conveys this basic assumption about apostolic religious life: carrying out the mission of Jesus in our world is the primary locus for experiencing a heightened awareness and love of God. Prayer, life in community, and ministry compenetrate each other. The recognition of this compenetration is clearly expressed in the LCWR paper for the Fifth Inter-American Conference:

> There is among American religious a growing tendency to reject dichotomies such as . . . *consecration/mission* (sic, emphasis is my own). Apostolic spirituality is a dynamic spirituality that involves continuous efforts to integrate contemplation and action, commitment to a religious life style and to practical deeds of compassionate love . . . It is by being immersed in culture and living an integrated life of prayer and service that one encounters and is led to deeper experience of the sacred.[11]

Our consecration depends on God and draws its life and strength from God. The consecration we make as members of a religious community, therefore, is a consecration to all that God loves and for which Jesus laid down his life. Through consecration in community we seek, together with others, to embody the mission of Jesus to humanity as his co-disciples. Mission is not something merely added on to our consecration, but a reality at the heart of who we are. It means that we immerse ourselves in our culture with an incarnational faith. Together as members of communities gathered in faith we stand with Jesus Christ in identification with the goodness and beauty of this world and with him against the powers of sin.[12]

In proposing "mission as consecration" to name our present paradigm, I do so with some caution. I recognize that some of my readers may associate "consecration" with the paradigm we have left behind. In pre-Vatican II theologies of religious life consecration was commonly associated with being set apart from the world. These theologies reflect the definition of "religious life" for women which centered on cloister, whether it was complete or partial. The stricter regulation of the life of women religious by ecclesiastical authority manifests dualistic philosophical assumptions about male and female that can be traced to classical Greek thinking and its appropriation by highly influential theologians for the tradition, such as Augustine and Thomas Aquinas. In the Greek dualism of rational spirit and irrational matter, the male is closely associated with the superior rational aspects of being human and the female with the inferior sensual and emotional aspects. This philosophical dualism gave the male the advantage in the spiritual life. By contrast, the female was disadvantaged in her quest for holiness and required rigorous discipline, such as cloister, and supervision by ordained males.[13]

The metaphor "flight from the world" used to describe the nature of consecration was supported by the dualism in Catholic spirituality between the supernatural and natural realms. Thus, it was not unusual for pre-Vatican II constitutions for apostolic communities of women to express the primary end of their congregations as the personal sanctification of the members or as "saving one's soul." Given our disadvantaged state, withdrawal from the world seemed to be a requirement for achieving that supernatural end. The secondary end was to bring others to salvation through apostolic works.[14] The concept of "flight from the world" was combined with the notion of religious life as "a state of perfection" which put women religious in a class that separated them from their non-vowed brothers and sisters whose salvation they were to promote.

My proposal for "mission as consecration" radically shifts the emphasis away from consecration as "flight from the world," and all that is associated with it, to communion with God *in* the world. Underlying this shift in emphasis are two very different understandings of eschatology. The notion of "flight from the world" was associated with traditional theological interpretations of "the last things": death, judgment, heaven and hell. Today our focus on "mission in the world" reflects a reinterpretation of eschatology rooted in insights gained primarily from the biblical studies of recent years. Eschatology refers above all to the mission of Jesus that centered on his eager expectation of the coming of the Reign of God (Mark 1:14–15). Our recognition that the Reign of God is come in Jesus, and is ever coming, forms and informs our spirituality. Through our consecration we, as his disciples, play an active role incarnating the Reign of God revealed in Jesus. Therefore, we cannot stand apart from the world's groanings for justice and peace.

Factors Contributing to the Shift in Paradigms

The shift in paradigms among U.S. women religious originated in the years that followed Pius XII's "World Congress on States of Perfection" held in 1950 and the foundation of "The Sister Formation Movement" in the United States.[15] A major outcome of this movement was an emphasis on education in order to prepare women religious adequately for apostolic works. Education brought increasing numbers of us to expand our horizons on many levels, to grow in self-reliance, and to begin to question many of the assumptions we had heretofore accepted.

The major historical event that precipitated the shift in paradigms in apostolic religious life for women was the Second Vatican Council held in the 1960s. The mandate given to religious congregations by the Council for renewal and adaptation was taken up by women's communities. For many communities the way had already been prepared by the education and networking in the 1950s. In *Perfectae Caritatis* the Council called all communities of religious to renew and adapt their lives to fit the mission of the Church in the twentieth century. The processes of renewal were to be guided by a return to the sources of Christian life in the Gospel and to the original inspiration of each institute (#2).

In implementing *Perfectae Caritatis* we engaged in an intensified search for institutional authenticity. Research into our foundations led many of us to become aware for the first time that our history had been one of conflicts in the Church over our role. Our research has uncovered the ways in which the ministries of the women who went before us were often constricted by Church legislation that required us to adopt a papal interpretation of the monastic tradition. Critical appropriation of the essence of our founding spirits provided women's communities with a prism through which we could take a fresh look at the Church and at our place in it.

Through work for general chapters women religious in the United States entered into the complex process of renewal. In conjunction with this process many of us also read and discussed other Vatican II documents. Key ideas from *The Dogmatic Constitution on the Church*, such as the notion of Church as the "People of God" (9–17) and that of the universal call to holiness shared by that people (39–42), served as a basis for critiques of formerly held notions about the nature of religious life and the place of women religious in the Church. The understanding of religious life as a call to a state of perfection that made us members of an elite group set apart from our lay sisters and brothers was rejected. The nineteenth and early twentieth century theology of religious life that laid emphasis upon the differences separating vowed religious from other Christians was reevaluated. We came to see religious life as situated within the life of baptismal communities, all of which are called to the fullness of discipleship in different ways.

For some of us the most significant document of the Second Vatican Council was *The Pastoral Constitution on the Church in the Modern World.* This document's emphasis on the Church and mission as integral to each other led women religious to grapple with the meaning of the Church as a people missioned in the modern world. Reading the signs of the times in the light of the Gospel (4) became an axiom that informs our on-going discernment about how we can best live our mission in the world.

Attentiveness to the Church as a community in mission, and not as an institution with a mission, has profoundly affected the self-understanding of apostolic women religious. Mission is integral to the identity of the apostolic religious. Our response to the perceived needs of people in the light of the Gospel has been informed by the recovery of the original inspirations of our congregations' foundations.

In the years of renewal since Vatican II apostolic women religious in the United States have abandoned enclosure and emphasis on common life as constitutive of religious life. Incarnational spirituality has replaced an other-worldly emphasis on saving one's soul. Not flight from the world, but apostolic involvement in society is viewed as constitutive of religious life. Apostolic women religious are no longer removed from society because we recognize it as a primary locus of salvation.

Integral to the paradigm shift is the fact that U.S. women religious are coming to believe and deeply value our experience as women.[16] Our recovery of the original spirit of our founding women, who bonded together through the inspiration of the Holy Spirit to respond to particular needs of society, has taken place in the context of the evolution of the position of women in society, a position that has changed in an extraordinary way in the past twenty-five years.

As we look back at the decade of the 1960s we recognize that it was marked by much more than a call for renewal in the Church. During these same years the rise of concern for the rights of women in U.S. society burst forth with new vigor. In 1966 the National Organization for Women, the largest organization active in the work of lobbying for women's rights, was founded. This movement for women's liberation evolved from the civil rights and anti-war movements of the sixties. Recognition of socially and legally sanctioned injustices by racial minorities led women to critique the disparities that they too were experiencing in society. Increasing numbers of women began to identify themselves as feminists and call attention to the need for liberation from the same patriarchal and hierarchical social structures that led to both the male dominance over females and the white dominance over blacks and other people of color.

In the process of renewal that brought women religious into dialogue with modern culture many of us have participated in the women's movement. Concern for women in the Church and society is given explicit attention in our general chapter documents, in our constitutions, in goal and mission statements.[17] These statements reflect our consciousness of societal issues such as the feminization of poverty, economic inequity and domestic violence. Our documents indicate that our concern for women extends to the Church as well. We are attentive to the dualisms in ecclesiastical legislation about our lives as women and in magisterial teachings about human sexuality. We are critical of patterns of Church life that are contrary to the doctrines that both males and females are created alike in the image of God and that all Christians are baptized into the same Spirit.[18]

Women Ministering in a Technological Culture

A major way in which active apostolic women religious embody "mission as consecration" is through ministry.[19] Ministry is a dynamic process of response by a congregation to the signs of the times, particularly to those persons most in need of the Good News of Jesus Christ. Increasingly, ministerial choices are being made in accord with how the members of congregations, both corporately and individually, envision the redemptive mission of Jesus in continuity with their own developing traditions. In discerning how best to embody the mission of Jesus in today's world we find the question "by whom are we being called?" ever before us. It is in addressing this question that the call of God is heard and that the God to whom our consecration is made is revealed.

From the data gathered by the LCWR Task Force it is clear that United States women religious are listening to this call by attending to the changes in our society and culture. Many of these changes result from the acceleration of growth in technology. We recognize that the rapid growth in technology makes positive contributions to the quality of our lives in countless ways. Technological developments, however, also have considerable negative impact on people by contributing to the dehumanization of their lives and to a mounting concern about the possibility of mass destruction. Our embodiment of mission through ministry in the United States demands a critical appraisal of the possibilities for liberation that technology offers and of the contradictions to Gospel values it holds. Commitment to the mission of Jesus in the world requires that we engage in critical analysis of our technological culture.

What is technology? We use many terms for which we may not have precise definitions. Technology is one of them. It is a polyvalent and pervasive concept whose broadest meaning expresses humanity's purposeful mastery of nature's forces and resources through the application of science. In many respects science and technology cannot be totally separated. Technology is consequent to science insofar as new technology is made possible through scientific research and at the same time it precedes science because it provides science with the instruments it uses in its research. Technology, in addition, is not a single reality. It is made up of many kinds, of many trends and of many instances. Over all, its basic function is to expand the realm of practical human possibilities.

The current acceleration in the growth of technology constitutes a paradigm shift, as we witness the movement from emphasis on heavy industry to high technology in our economy. An apt metaphor for naming the technological paradigm emerging in the United States which I would like to suggest is "megastructure" because increasingly complex technological networks are dramatically changing our societal patterns and our cultural world. An obvious example of new technological megastructures can be found in the related areas of communications and information processing. So great is the change in these areas that in recent years we find ourselves witnessing a shift in our economy from manufacturing goods to processing information. Complex computer networks are making information a new form of wealth.

The ambiguity of the historical reality associated with major developments in technology is evident to North American religious.[20] The social patterns that result from the emerging paradigm shift to high technology make possible both potential enrichment and potential danger. On the one hand technology offers expanding possibilities for the liberation of human beings from the forces of nature that diminish human life. It lessens the drudgery of routine tasks in countless ways. But on the other hand, it has the capacity to dehumanize people because megastructures can easily determine and limit personal creativity and satisfaction. Once a megastructure is in place the number and variety of work patterns attached to that technology are fixed. A social pattern forged by the megastructure becomes set without a great deal of thought given to its human and societal consequences.

As a society we seem to place great faith in the power of technology. Many of us are impressed by the might of technology that revolutionizes our lives. It is humanity's own product, a child of the human spirit. Through it we have succeeded in setting free and using for our own purposes the hidden forces of nature. But we have not succeeded in controlling the results of the process. Technology presents us with a formidable potential for the destruction of humanity.

In order to sort out the ambiguity surrounding the emerging technological paradigm it is important to engage in a critical appraisal of our culture. To do this we must look carefully at the patterns of meaning our society uses to interpret itself. Language patterns are an important part of our culture and require our attention. The impetus for developing megastructures through the "grand designs" of technology draws power in our culture from accompanying myths.[21] Our cultural myths provide us with a frame of reference or a set of assumptions that operate in us as members of our society whether or not we are conscious of them. Their power is immense because they tend to create the boundaries of our societal imagination. They provide us with a cultural net of meaning.

A very important facet of our being missioned in the world is to attend to the cultural myths of the society in which we are missioned and critique them in the light of the Gospel. To carry out this agenda we must begin with the premise that we are affected by our culture and cannot simply disengage ourselves from it. As we reflect on our own attitudes, we recognize that our culture and its myths are deeply within us—in our ways of thinking, doing and being. To assess critically the assumptions operative in our technological culture is, first of all, to raise the question: what are the myths which shape our cultural imaginations? And secondly, are these myths open or closed to the Gospel of Jesus Christ?

One of the most pervasive myths of technology in our culture is that of progress. This myth fits well with the symbol of "The Great American Dream" with its components of unlimited freedom, unlimited possibilities, unlimited growth and unlimited power, that have long been a part of our cultural fabric. This dream has been applied in a variety of ways in the course of our history. It adds persuasiveness to our technological myth of progress whose promise is that all the problems worth solving will be solved in due time by science and technology. Diseases of the body, the scarcities of vital consumer goods, problems with communications, concerns about national security—all these qualify as the problems eligible for scientific-technological diagnosis and cure. For our technological society these are the basic problems, the "evils" we face, and we can solve them.

The technological myth of progress is a modern day secular salvation myth claiming that the healing power of objective knowledge discovered through science and guided by the process of technological advance will bring about a new and better world. This progress-salvation myth plays a major role in the symbolic structure that unites and directs our society's life. It serves as a kind of faith outside the pale of Christianity.

The myth may receive some legitimation in our society from a working assumption that the research carried out in the university is ethically neutral and value free. This assumption is integral to the acceptance of the premise that what can be envisioned as scientifically possible should be done. A critical assessment of this myth reveals that arguments for the advances of technology are not so much "value free" as "human context free," and that the grand designs of technology often ignore the impact they may have on people and their lives. The development of technology is a social phenomenon and, therefore, is far from value free.

We can gain insight into technology as a social phenomenon affecting the mythos of our culture, if we attend to the role played by metaphors used in the formation of the values, aims and goals of the scientific-technological enterprise. From the dawn of the Enlightenment science has been conceptualized and defended by the language of control and domination. The goal of science, the subjugation of nature by penetrating its secrets applied in technology, became the mode of exercising control over nature.

Critically to assess this aspect of the mythos of our scientific and technological culture requires that we trace the linguistic patterns of control and domination to their roots.[22] In the seventeenth century Francis Bacon, a major architect of modern science, equated scientific knowledge with power.[23] In describing this power Bacon often invoked sexual imagery, with nature given the image of a female to be controlled and dominated. Bacon's central metaphor—science as power, a force virile enough to penetrate and subdue nature—has provided an image that permeates the rhetoric of modern science and technology.

The androcentric linguistic patterns that can be traced to Bacon provide patriarchal interpretations for the role of science and technology in society. Subsequent history of science provides ample evidence that the values articulated by Bacon and other early scientists were effective in promoting the kinds of knowledge that would lead to the mastery, control, and domination of nature. Gender symbolism provides resources for the moral and political advancement of science. Through scientific understanding and technological control "man come of age" is sovereign over the forces of nature and master of his own destiny.

Our culture seems to have swallowed Francis Bacon whole. Empirical knowledge, we believe, is power to control and dominate the forces that run our world. Through such knowledge and the technologies that develop from it we can make our life infinitely better. Given the beginnings of this tradition of thought, there is good reason to argue that the pursuit of objective knowledge about nature for the purpose of dominating it through technology is a manifestation of patriarchy that is pervasive in our culture. Patriarchy and the technological myth of progress seem to go hand in hand. They manifest themselves in an ethos of competitiveness and technological mastery over the earth and its material and human resources.

A prime example of the technological myth of progress at work in our society is the Strategic Defense Initiative popularly referred to as "Star Wars," proposed by the current Reagan administration. Its nickname is revealing, because it conveys the assumption that "the force" is with us as it is with the heroes of the popular movie by the same title. Through technological advances the United States will dominate our enemies rendering their forces harmless. SDI symbolizes a promise of "salvation," an invitation to believe that we will be invulnerable to harm through the progress of our technology. The "Star

Wars" initiative holds out the hope that the United States will not only dominate planet Earth, but outer space as well. The scientific research for this project is under way at our major universities under the guise of ethical neutrality due to the "pure research" proper to these institutions. The government moneys channeled to universities for this purpose establish areas of scientific research and patterns of technological development for generations to come.

One of the most noteworthy facets of the SDI research is that it is designed to protect our deterrents. This means that its objective is the protection of our missiles in their silos. The SDI megastructure in outer space is not being designed to protect large population centers. SDI is a case of technology protecting other products of technology with all parts linked in a grand design. While the research continues at considerable taxpayer expense, the poor in our cities and rural areas suffer the escalation of the loss of human services that tax dollars given to the defense of missiles could provide.

The Strategic Defense Initiative illustrates well one of the major problems with a culture driven by the myth of technological progress, that is, its insensitivity to the human cost of its grand designs. The myth of progress underlying the United States' drive for technological growth, that reaches even beyond the limits of our earth and its resources into outer space, ignores the pathos in human history to which it contributes. Although many oppose the "Star Wars" proposal, there is no outcry by the majority of U.S. citizens against it, something difficult to assess. One reason may be that the relationship between technology and religion in our society is characterized at best as peaceful co-existence and, more often, as two mutually exclusive ways of perceiving the world. Thus, religion is treated as a matter of personal preference with morality centered on questions of personal ethics.

The separation of technology from religious concerns is incompatible with the mission of apostolic religious. We recognize that religious commitment is not only a positive, joyful affirmation of our openness to the Divine, but a struggle to recognize and protest against evil, both personal and societal. The experience of a relationship with God in Christ at the heart of the identity of the apostolic women religious seeks modes of response to all forms of evil, including those that result from the advance of technology.

Our mission is a call to engage in the transformation of the culture in which we are immersed.[24] We recognize that this transformation must begin with our own conversion. In a cultural context governed by a myth of unlimited progress through technology, we must ask ourselves how this myth and its assumptions may play a role in our own doing and being. Does the ethos of competitiveness and mastery find a place in our lives?

One major way our conversion finds expression among women's congregations is the emphasis we are giving to the "preferential option for the poor" in our ministerial directions.[25] With this as our conscious focus, we attend to the pathos in human history and the suffering of people around the globe that results from it. The "preferential option for the poor" is a matter of making the Gospel of Jesus our rule of life in our own historical situation. Although "option for the poor" is not a biblical phrase, it does capture the mysterious choice on God's part—God's preference for the poor revealed in Jesus. In the option for the poor we find an emphasis on the full meaning and function of the incarnation: transcendent love is made visible in Jesus who, though rich, became poor for our sake. Jesus' preference for the poor is manifested in his identification with the poor and the outcast. The message he preached out of his experience of God as "Abba" centered on a God who blesses the poor and the oppressed. Jesus brought these people the Good News that they would be set free and that the coming Reign of God would belong to them (Luke 4:16–22). To make the Gospel our rule of life is to look at Jesus' response to the poor and marginalized of his society and to ask what we are called to do in our own.

In discerning how we are to live the mission of Jesus in our times solidarity with the poor and service to the poor have become major forms of commitment among U.S. apostolic women religious.[26] Ministries with the poor are receiving increased attention as apostolic women religious engage in the struggle to eliminate the causes of poverty or to alleviate the results of poverty. A growing number of women religious are undertaking social work ministries that bring them into direct contact with the sick, the elderly poor and with women bearing the burden of heading single parent households. Although many of us may not think of these ministries as posing a critical stance to the myth of technological progress, they are an implicit critique of it. For we find ourselves ministering to those persons who, if judged on the basis of their contribution to our technological progress as a nation, are making no positive contribution.

Apostolic women religious also respond to the increasing numbers of the poor due to the economic inequity in the process of technological advance. The growth process is selective as to whom it benefits and, by and large, it is biased against the low-skilled worker. The movement from a labor intensive economy of the industrial past to the capital intensive economy of high technology contributes to the increase in the number of the poor. The shift to high technology is evident in many manufacturing industries, as computer-run robots replace workers. People who are ill equipped to respond to the demands high-technology places on them become the marginalized people who are finding their way in increasing numbers to soup kitchens and shelters for the homeless.

The many forms of ministry in which women religious work directly with the poor cannot be separated from the ministry of peacemaking. The critical stance taken by many of the congregations of women religious against the proliferation of nuclear weapons and projects is a form of advocacy for the poor.[27] It is quite obvious that each of the billions of dollars being spent on technologies for the war-machine could be spent to relieve the misery of the poor in our own nation and in the Third World where the need is acute. To take a stance as peacemaker is to engage in the struggle to overcome the deadly leviathan Pentagon of Power whose transformation is necessary if the hungry of the earth are to be fed. In this transformation true human progress lies, for it contributes to human liberation from starvation and early death.

Although many women religious have assumed new forms of ministry in recent years, many of us continue our commitment to the traditional ministries of health care and education. In both cases these ministries had their beginnings in this country as responses to the basic health and educational needs of the immigrant poor. Women in these ministries continue to struggle with complex questions about how to live the mission of Jesus in today's world. Women in health care recognize that medical technology has lessened the threat of many diseases. The momentum in medical technologies, however, warrants careful monitoring, as technology offers a broad spectrum of biological innovations such as the artificial heart, in vitro fertilization and genetic engineering. Technological progress in medicine often raises ethical questions of great complexity. Women religious in health care institutions, therefore, are engaged in discernment about how to make the best apostolic use of science and technology in service of the health needs of the ill, particularly the poor.

Women religious in education are engaged in the ministry of the Word, endeavoring to bear witness to the freeing truth of the Gospel. This ministry calls for and challenges women religious to relate faith and praxis. Although the ministry of education transcends the activities of the classroom, the schools in which we teach do provide us with a forum for our students to address the impact of technology on society and to critique our cultural myths. In many respects the underlying myths associated with science and technology have become the unifying "religion" of our society. It is common for North Americans to look to science and technology as the sources of truth and of "salvation" from sickness, pain and fear of our enemies. Through critical cultural analysis combined with peace and justice education women involved in the ministry of education can heighten the awareness of our future citizens and leaders to the potential for good and evil that technology bears.

In each of these major ministerial areas women religious find themselves in a critical stance *vis a vis* technology and its capacity for dehumanization and destruction. While accepting many technologies as gifts that enhance our quality of life, the question of responsibility to the human community remains. The primary criteria for judging the value of evolving technologies must center on their effect on the human family.

I have noted that many of the ministerial directions taken by women religious today contain an implicit critique of the cultural myths stemming from the predominance of technology in our society. To further the mission of Jesus it seems advisable to make some of our implicit critiques of our cultural myths more explicit for the sake of future direction setting. We need to redefine progress in a way that is rooted in the Christian mythos, that is, at the center of who we are. Thus we can come to greater clarity about a vision that will provide us with directions for the future.

A Vision for a Preferred Future

In the book of Proverbs we read: "Without a vision the people perish" (Proverbs 29:18). This is a harsh saying that challenges us to articulate a vision for our time. We need such a vision to guide us as we continue to seek out ways to embody the mission of Jesus in our world. A necessary preliminary step in articulating the vision is a critical analysis of our cultural myths with their inherent assumptions. I have drawn attention to what may be the most obvious and pervasive myth that legitimates the United States drive for technological advance, that is, the myth of progress with its inherent patriarchal assumptions. These assumptions validate the drive for mastery over the world's resources, both material and human.

The recognition of how women religious are already embodying a critical stance *vis a vis* the myth of technological progress is one important step toward addressing the question: "What is our vision for a preferred future?" It remains for us to make our implicit critiques of our culture more explicit for the sake of bringing the message of the Gospel to bear on our society, for it is a simple fact that both our faith and the technological myth of progress deal with the future. A fundamental aspect of our effort to articulate a vision is the reality that apostolic women religious are not a group set apart with specific solutions for the problems of the people of the world. We are missioned in co-discipleship with our lay brothers and sisters, many of whom are better equipped to effect needed cultural transformation than we are. Therefore, both the vision and its implementation must be carried out in collaboration with others who recognize the dehumanizing effects of many of our technological developments.

What is the fundamental source of a vision for a preferred future? It is faith in the God of Jesus Christ. Because we share in the life of God in human history through our baptism, we believe that the horizon of the future is open. The envisioning of a preferred future is rooted in the hope that we have in Jesus Christ. It is a hope in the Reign of God, already active in history, never fully embodied in any society, always coming in justice and love. Awareness of the presence and absence of the Reign of God that Jesus proclaimed in his life is basic to a vision for the future. The Reign of God is at once now and not yet. Fidelity to the mission of Jesus requires that we envision the Reign of God yet to come.

It is obvious that a vision for a preferred future to inform our apostolic discernment cannot be simply a romantic anti-technological primitivism. To withdraw into primitivism is to become drifters in the sea of technological progress. Rather, we need an evangelical vision, one that looks to the Gospel of Jesus with its preference for the poor, to provide a basis for thoroughgoing transformation of the technological megastructures that are determining the future of our globe. The poor of the world, the beneficiaries of the Good News of Jesus Christ, require this of us.

The evangelical perspective that we bring to our cultural situation must be a global vision rooted in this saving mission of Jesus. It cannot be limited to our own society because no society can be isolated from the global reality of our contemporary world. Our hope rooted in the Gospel of Jesus with its preference for the poor tells us that a new era for our world is in prospect. Justice will reign and peace will be established. It is in the light of this future that we must shape our present, our individual, congregational and societal here and now.

ENDNOTES

1. The Fifth Inter-American Conference on Religious Life, *Apostolic Religious Life in a Changing World and Church,* November 17–22, 1985. See Appendix p. 173.

2. *Ibid.* See original unpublished document, pp. 4–5.

3. Resources on the interface of theology and technology include those of Jacques Ellul, the French sociologist/Protestant theologian, particularly *The Technological Society* (New York: Knopf, 1964 [1954]); Langdon Gilkey, *Society and the Sacred, Toward a Theology of Culture in Decline* (New York: Crossroad Publishing Co., 1981); and Carl Mitchan and Jim Grote, eds., *Theology and Technology, Essays in Christian Analysis and Exegesis* (New York: University Press of America, 1984).

4. For an analysis of the history of the forms of religious life and for statistics on this period, see Bro. Raymond L. Fitz, SM and Bro. Lawrence J. Cada, SM, "The Recovery of Religious Life," *Review for Religious* 34 (1975) 690–700.

5. The restriction of enclosure was not placed on communities of men who were engaged in apostolic service; they applied only to women. For a history of the development of ecclesiastical legislation for women religious see either Lynn Jarrell, OSU, *The Development of Legal Structures for*

Women Religious between 1500 and 1900 (Unpublished JCL dissertation, The Catholic University of America, 1984) or James R. Cain, "Cloister and the Apostolate of Religious Women," *Review for Religious* 27 (1986) 243–280, 427–448, 652–672, 916–937; 28 (1969) 101–111. [This series of articles is part of Cain's doctoral dissertation in canon law.]

6. The history of the "unenclosed American Benedictine women" is told by Mary Collins, OSB, "American Benedictine Women in the Roman Catholic Church," in *Climb Along the Cutting Edge, An Analysis of Change in Religious Life* (New York: Paulist Press, 1977) 99–101.

7. Mary Ewens, *The Role of the Nun in Nineteenth Century America* (New York: Arno Press, 1978). In this study the author notes the tension about enclosure as an essential part of "religious life" for women in the nineteenth century. Members of women's communities in the United States were not permitted to take solemn vows because they could not keep the cloistral prescriptions and staff the growing number of schools (Five Visitandine communities are the exceptions). See pp. 202–209.

8. For more on the emergence of historical consciousness and its relationship to apostolic spirituality see Catherine Osimo, "Women's Center: Incarnational Spirituality," in this volume.

9. For a more thorough understanding of the concept of "paradigm shift" see Thomas S. Kuhn, *The Structure of Scientific Revolutions* (Chicago: University of Chicago Press, second edition, 1970).

10. The Fifth Inter-American Conference on Religious Life, *Apostolic Religious Life in a Changing World and Church*. See Appendix p. 173.

11. *Ibid.*

12. *Ibid.*

13. For this analysis I am dependent on Mary Collins, OSB, *op. cit.* 104–105.

14. Mary Milligan, "Charism and Constitutions," *The Way Supplement* 36 (1979) 48.

15. For some excellent personal reflections on the "Sister Formation Movement," see Elizabeth Carroll, "Reaping the Fruits of Redemption," in *Midwives of the Future*, edited by Ann Patrick Ware (Kansas City: Leaven Press, 1985) 53–68.

16. Appendix, p. 174.

17. Anne Munley, IHM, "An Exploratory Content Analysis of Major Themes Present in Selected Documents of United States Women Religious." See Appendix p. 183.

18. For a more thorough treatment of this aspect of the paradigm shift in communities of women religious, see Mary Elsbernd and Marilyn Thie, "What's at Stake: Women Religious Naming Ourselves Women," p. 143 in this volume.

19. For a clear articulation of the relationship of mission and ministry, see Doris Gottemoel-

ler, RSM, "The Changing Mission of Religious Life," in *Starting Points* (Washington, D.C.; LCWR, 1980) 25–26.

20. Cf. Endnote 2.

21. "Myth" is obviously not being used here in the sense of a fable. Rather, it is being treated as a certain perennial mode of language whose elements are multivalent symbols and whose meanings concern assumptions about our human destiny.

22. It is not possible to engage in a full examination of the roots of the linguistic patterns of science and technology here. I recommend the following works, which address this topic from a feminist perspective: Sandra Harding, *The Science Question in Feminism* (Ithaca: Cornell University Press, 1986); Evelyn Fox Keller, *Reflections on Gender and Science* (New Haven: Yale University Press, 1985); Carolyn Merchant, *The Death of Nature. Women, Ecology and the Scientific Revolution* (San Francisco: Harper and Row, Publishers, 1980).

23. Evelyn Fox Keller, *op. cit.* 33.

24. Appendix p. 180.

25. Anne Munley, IHM, "An Exploratory Content Analysis of Major Themes Present in Selected Documents of United States Women Religious," Appendix, p. 183 and Fifth Inter-American Conference, Appendix p. 173.

26. Anne Munley, *op. cit.*, Appendix p. 183.

27. This point is well made in the U.S. Catholic Bishops' Pastoral, *Economic Justice for All: Catholic Social Teaching and the U.S. Economy.* See #91 and #320.

REFLECTION QUESTIONS

1. Have you experienced that the centrality of "mission" in apostolic spirituality has shaped both personal and corporate decision making? If so, how?

2. What are some of the ways in which women religious can and do offer an alternative vision to the "myth of progress"?

One Perspective on Change

Patricia Jean Manion, SL

At the second time, the waters were broken. At first, they gushed, then they dried to a trickle, and a space was created. It was exactly the right size. By now, the creation was well under way. And it was very good.

Communities of women religious in the United States are claiming responsibility for their own corporate lives, no longer depending without question upon others to define them. Like individuals who come to realize that what they repressed in trying to conform to collective expectations must be reclaimed, these communities are in a new phase of development. It seems to me that, by looking at C. G. Jung's theory of the process of individuation as it applies to the individual, we can gain some perspective on what is happening in communities of women. Based on the assumption that a community, like an individual, can go through psychological maturation and learn to trust its own innate potential, my belief is that what we see happening today in many communities of women religious is substantial movement in the direction of responsible awareness that Jung describes with reference to persons.[1] This new awareness has been gradual and, as with individuals, often painful. Altering "authorized" ways of being creates feelings of guilt for the one changing and often draws criticism from those who prefer the familiarity of the known.

We can gain some insight into the changes in awareness and the accompanying pain that we observe in communities of women religious by looking first at Jung's theory of individual development, called "the process of individuation." Then I will suggest some parallels to this process that seem to be reflected in the data gathered by the LCWR study of congregation documents. And finally, I will suggest that the outcome of the process will mean that communities of women religious in the United States will be fundamentally alike in their processes but substantially different in their ways of being.

Jung's Theory
Simply put, Jung's theory of individuation describes development of the person as having two distinguishable phases. The first reaches a kind of culmination as ego identity sometime before or during mid-life. During the process of forming an identity from childhood to adulthood, one accepts in oneself, even when resisted, what the outer

world of family and culture affirm, while unconsciously repressing and consciously denying what is not affirmed. This process creates an identity, but an identity that does not embrace the full potential of the individual. Much of what is unique may disappear, partially formed, into the unconscious of the person where it resides with other unrecognized possibilities. This Other, Jung named *the shadow*.[2] The shadow begins to surface, to claim its place, in the second phase of the individuation process. Often triggered by some experience of loss or trauma that shocks the individual into disequilibrium, this second phase requires a kind of self-consciousness wherein the person begins to question what has been assumed to be one's real identity. When this process is operating, the individual pulls forth, often painfully, what was repressed in conforming to outer expectations and tries to reclaim those dimensions that are an essential part of being true to one's own inner core. It becomes a humanizing experience of recognizing one's own vulnerability as well as one's own strengths, making participation in the human condition one of shared struggle with others in the human community. Jung says, "It follows that the process of individuation must lead to more intense and broader collective relationships and not to isolation."[3]

While isolation once typified congregations of U.S. women religious, today many are forming intense and widening relationships with persons and groups formerly outside their ranks. Communities are recognizing the value of broadening their membership to include both men and women as lay associates and what is called, for the Loretto Community, co-membership. These extensions or inclusions involve persons of a variety of backgrounds not necessarily like those of the members of the core community. Many communities of women religious have left behind a kind of ghetto or isolationist attitude and have begun networking with others even on a global basis. We see, for example, growing connections between the world peace movement and the human rights efforts that have come to expect, and do have, the support and involvement of women religious. Realizing that we share a common humanity makes it less and less possible to take an elitist attitude that views ourselves as exempt from prejudice and injustice either as sources or as recipients.

Before dealing with some ways the individuation process is reflected in communal development, let me return for the moment to an illustration of how what is lost in the individual's ego development may surface to be claimed in the second half of the individual's life. It is easier to understand community individuation if first we see clearly how it works for the individual person.

A person reared in an environment where feelings are not given much credence, where it is understood that only logical reason matters, eventually dismisses feelings and perhaps even loses touch with them. That person comes to be seen and to think of her/himself as logical and unemotional. Basing decisions solely on logic may even seem to work for years, but the time comes when the individual has to claim feeling as another form of knowing. Such a person, for instance, may continue for years doing work that she experiences as a violation of her own desires, but because personal feelings are to be disregarded, she ignores the first thrusts of discontent. If she continues to ignore them and remains in the situation, ignored feelings can become physical symptoms or negative attitudes. Eventually she could be thrust into exhaustion or begin to have fantasies, unwanted ideas about how she could get herself fired. To move beyond the limitations of ego identity, the repressed dimension, the shadow, needs to be claimed and used.

We could take any number of characteristics and look at them in the same way. Any characteristic that gets "lost" in the process of ego development continues to exist unconsciously as part of the individual. According to Jung, those dimensions act even though they may not be conscious to the person. They act in crude and unexpected ways. The logical non-feeler mentioned above can find herself overcome by emotion in surprising ways when, for example, a fairly insignificant event elicits a disproportionate outbreak of emotion. What is unconscious acts in spite of us. It is in the second half of life, if the individual is to move beyond ego, that she/he must deal with these unconscious dimensions. The shadow is all the undiscovered, the forgotten, and the denied dimensions of a person.

Jung's Theory and Communities

Let me move to what I think are parallels in the life of women's communities. In the "first half of life," U.S. communities were given and took their definition of themselves from outside: from older communities in Western Europe and from canon law, which very specifically delineated the parameters of congregations of women religious. In the process of developing a sense of identity, the "parental" stance of the Church was primary. Like individuals who develop an ego that conforms to outer society, communities got their sense of value from what was approved. Communities of women, like women generally, were allowed particular roles. Designated as "daughters of the Church," like good daughters, they looked to "father" for permission to be contemplative or apostolic or monastic within clearly defined lines. Like individuals who lose touch with some dimensions of themselves by conforming to outer expectations, some communities, through adhering to the tenets of canon law, relinquished fundamental aspects of their original charism unique to their beginnings.

Like the individual who has received identity from others, U.S. communities of women religious came to identify themselves by what they were expected to be. Much of the potential for being unique was lost. Much potential, like that of the individual, came to reside in the shadow, namely, the community unconscious. Unrecognized, this potential was capable of erupting in unexpected and often unwelcome ways in the behavior, desires and insights of individuals. Like the unrecognized feeling dimension of the person of my earlier illustration, some "maverick" would arise who did not fit the pattern. While circumstances varied, often those who wished to live the community's original commitment to a radical poverty in the midst of educators of the middle and upperclass were suspect. Or artists in a health care community were told to pray for an obedient spirit or were tolerated without real affirmation. Even today members of apostolic communities who desire lives of contemplation are often viewed, not as signs surfacing a need for the integration of reflection into the community, but as problem persons who do not fit the conventional definition of the community as described by themselves or by the Church. The possibility that the nature of the community might evolve in healthy new directions by attending to these promptings is out of the question, something to be avoided.

Until religious communities of women began to revise their constitutions, every apostolic community, at least on paper, was a near carbon copy of a blue print designed by outer authority. The size of the book and the style of print may have been different, but the wording with a few changes here and there was the same. And for all the ways communities of women religious viewed themselves as distinct, thousands of them all over the country rose at the same hour and kept the same great silence at night. During their waking hours, most worked long hours in careers chosen for them by someone else.

As John Sanford says in *Healing and Wholeness*, "Individuation always means being healed of something, but we cannot be healed unless we have been forced to recognize where we are injured or wounded."[4] With many individuals the wounding is experienced as loss—loss of position, loss of a significant relationship, disillusionment with past achievements. An individual is forced to ask serious questions about who one is and what one has abandoned in the efforts to conform to outer, collective expectations. In looking at the data gathered from communities, it is clear that religious congregations of women over the past twenty years have experienced a whole series of experiences that have acted as shocks or traumas, woundings of the corporate ego sufficiently important to cause the same kind of questioning that individuals must do. "We know what it is to be dispossessed . . . we know a more conscious oppression and marginalization."[5]

Communal Wounding
Events that first affected some religious communities did not initially touch others, but

it is fair to say that over the years outer events affected most communities. One of the first blows to corporate identity (ego) came by way of the studies done in the late 1940s and early 1950s that led to the founding of the Sister Formation Conference. When religious teachers learned that the very data they themselves supplied indicated that they were acting unjustly by not being educationally and professionally prepared for the work they were doing, many were stunned. That realization was a blow to the way teaching communities, for instance, viewed themselves since they had to face the fact that perhaps they were hiding professional incompetence under the veil of dedication. Dedication was not enough. It was time to look honestly at the possibility that in some communities women religious were teaching without the necessary educational background and preparation. It was painful to realize that what they had been doing in the name of service was in many ways inferior. The pain of recognition for them included the pain of outside criticism as some communities decided not to fill future openings in classrooms with their educationally unqualified members. Pastors and bishops were critical and even abusive. For teaching religious the guilt of recognizing their own shortcomings as educators was augmented by the guilt projected upon them by the people for whom they worked.

For some communities, a shock to their belief system occurred when their own members who had responded to the Church's call to work in South America returned to the States to challenge the political naivete of their North American counterparts. It was painful to hear and hard to believe that their staunch belief in their own country's politics and policies made them a party to the exploitation of people they wished to help. Like individuals first faced with unwelcome new information about themselves, religious communities of women did not want to believe these voices rising in their midst. If they accepted them, they would be faced with the need for painful change. Perhaps they would even lose some of the support from "good people" associated with U.S. domination in Latin America. Ultimately they would have to recognize the Church's part in keeping people poor. Women in communities were becoming conscious in ways that were to disturb their very sense of security.

Each time a community's self-image was or is put in question by some new awareness, initial reactions of pain and disbelief follow. Pain follows from knowing that what was thought to be positive is in question; and disbelief arises about the implications of this new information for the future. Then comes depression which has the potential to move the community into a time of serious reflection. If community fears of change do not take over and block movement, a release of creative energy, comparable to that which occurs with an individual, can ensue to bring into being new possibilities, a fresh sense of vitality.

For some communities the first battering (for others, a new round of battering) to the corporate ego came during the early years of the civil rights movement and during the period when, by law, schools had to be integrated. Some communities had not known that they were racist until they had to face how separatist they were. While some communities refused permission for their members to march at Selma or later, to attend Dr. Martin Luther King's funeral, all communities had to ask themselves where the blacks were in their schools and neighborhoods. Where were their own black members?

For yet other communities, the intrusion of the Vietnam War through the evening news became a source of tension. As some communities took anti-war stances, the sense of an harmonious identity was shattered. Doves and hawks arose. Some communities were embarrassed by other communities whose members took up signs and were shown in newspapers being arrested. It was painful to see the "good sister" image eroding. As public affirmation seemed to evaporate, some communities, like individuals who wish to change, came to realize that approval is not always an indication that one is doing the best one can do. To grow may mean being other than one has known oneself to be. A community, like an individual, can experience feelings of guilt when some long-held way of being is set aside. This is especially true if the outer authorities in one's situation refuse to honor the newfound sense of direction.

Most recently, the impact of the women's movement has acted as a painful and sometimes shocking experience for communities. As much as communities of women religious did not like to hear themselves described as uneducated or as politically naive or as racists or as oppressors, they have liked less to hear that they are oppressed. U.S. women religious have not wanted to admit the possibility that they have been used by the very Church they love. For some it has been as painful as it would be to learn that one's own father had sold one into bondage. It is painful but like any dimension of one's truth that gets beyond the initial shock and moves into realization, it can be a source of energy. The energy that kept the awareness below the level of consciousness is released for possible creative use.

Self and Community

Another of Jung's concepts about individual development that offers some parallel in the life of communities is that of the Self. Although a highly complex phenomenon, one dimension of it, that of an inner instinct toward wholeness, seems relevant here. Jung speaks of the Self as a source of energy that urges the person to become what one is, that is, as an archetype that provides a sense of order and meaning.[6] "The Self can be defined as an inner guiding factor."[7] There seems to be within the corporate life of a community also a similar reality that informs its existence and development. Just as with the individual, this process of becoming goes on through inspiration from within and suggestion from outside. As with the individual, both resources can be helpful. Neither has the whole truth.

Just as a person, recovering from the first shock of disillusion, turns within to find what will complement the wounded ego, so too, the information communities gave about themselves suggests that there has been an awakening and a discovery of creative dimensions not previously tapped. Reconnecting with the roots of identity in the unique charism of the founders and rediscovering forgotten initiative have been sources of new life and energy for some communities. Ironically, however, doing what was asked by the Second Vatican Council has sometimes made U.S. women religious displeasing and suspect to the very authorities who initiated renewal. The effort to change worked and women have gone far beyond what was envisioned.

Before leaving this analogy of individuation as it seems to apply to communities, it is important to look at some of the possible pitfalls. Just as the individual can assume exaggerated self-importance, so too the community always faces the possibility of inflation. The new energy that comes from recognizing what has been unconscious can lead to a sense of importance, of having conquered some powerful adversary. The possibility that a person, or a community in this case, may take on a stance of righteousness is dangerous. In seeking to become more conscious, the individual is always cautioned to remember that there is no arriving. Individuation is an ongoing process. Today's state is up for re-evaluation tomorrow as other dimensions of reality to which one has been blind become apparent. It is possible to get stuck at any stage and to atrophy. As an individual can think that she/he has "done the whole thing" so, too, can a community come to see itself as having "made it" into the modern world and fail to keep listening to both the inner promptings and the outer circumstances of the collective situation. Complacency is a tendency in human nature that lurks just beyond the next accomplishment.

In addition to inflation, there is always the pitfall of projecting on to others what one still needs to do. Just as individuals often blame others for what they themselves do not do, so is it possible that communities may act similarly. Religious communities of women might ask themselves whether the oppression of women they see in society and in the Church is in any way a part of their lives as well. Do religious women oppress their own members by insisting that they do works for which they are not suited? Do we put institutions ahead of individuals? "You have to take this assignment because the school or the hospital cannot survive without your service." Do we, like the rest of society, see women as suited for only particular works or careers? Do we disenfranchise some of our members by the processes we have developed or failed to develop? What we may find wrong in our country's government or in our Church may also need attention in our own communities.

As we decry violence in society, do we perhaps run the risk of not seeing how violent we are at times within our communities? There is violence or manipulation by silence. There is the violence of control by withholding appreciation or information. There is the violence of hurry and rush, an unconscious way of conveying to others that they are not important or do not matter. There is the violence of the work ethic that honors the addicted workaholic and pressures both subtly, and not so subtly, those who would take time and space. There is the violence of strong opinions expressed forcefully that leave no space for discussion or helpful disagreement.

As we consider what we see happening with religious communities of women, we must raise questions about yet another form of control. There is a delicate difference between evolving in ways congruent and true to one's inner promptings against the backdrop of collective needs and simply falling into yet another kind of conformity. Each religious community of women, like each person, if responding to the deepest Self in light of the setting where one is and the tradition from which one comes, will be unique. The Mercy community will be different from the Josephites and the Lorettines will not have a charism like that of the Notre Dames. Dominicans will not be Franciscans and Charities will not be Benedictines. Each community will be similar in a sense of awareness, of responsiveness, of searching, seeking its own truth, but the results will in many ways be different.

As communities of women religious in the U.S. claim responsibility for their own corporate lives, no longer depending without question upon others to define them, the community of communities will be as varied as was initially intended when each came to be in a unique time and place. And the richness will be in the variety of our being as we are companions on the road to the future.

ENDNOTES

1. The term "individuation process" occurs for the first time in Jung's book *Psychological Types* (originally published 1921), but the idea of it can be found in his doctoral dissertation. It was a guiding idea that was to hold him in its grip all his life and reached its culmination in his last major work, *Mysterium Conjunctionis* (1955–56), 12. See Jolande Jacobi, *The Way of Individuation* (New York: Harcourt, Brace & World, Inc., 1967).

2. Carl G. Jung, *Man and His Symbols* (New York: Doubleday & Company, 1964) 168.

3. *Collected Works* VI:448.

4. (New York: Paulist Press, 1977) 33.

5. p. 38.

6. Jean Shinoda Bolen, *The Tao of Psychology* (New York: Harper & Row, 1979) 21.

7. *Man and His Symbols* 162.

REFLECTION QUESTIONS

1. What forces inhibit us from acknowledging our personal and communal shadow?

2. In what ways do we project on the Church and others what we still need to do for ourselves? What processes might be developed to foster our personal and communal liberation?

From the Inside Out

Elaine M. Prevallet, SL

At the third time, a cradle was made ready. It was comfortable and beautiful and waiting. And food was prepared, issuing sweetly and warmly and in precisely the right measure from the being of the labourer.
And it was very good.

Introduction

The past twenty years have been tumultuous for apostolic communities of women religious. But they have also been decisive. During these twenty years, we have been developing along certain identifiable lines. I want to single out two among the many currents of thought that have, I believe, influenced the course of our development: awareness of life as "process," and emphasis upon the importance and uniqueness of the individual. That we should have been affected by these currents is not surprising. They are strongly present, in both positive and virulent form, in our society. We did not, I think, very consciously or deliberately adopt them. Rather, we *lived* them intuitively, and only now can begin to see their effects, and perhaps avoid their dangers. If now we can get a clearer understanding of our experience in these twenty years, we can go forward with greater ease and purposefulness.

If it is true that there was a period of time when we felt ourselves undergoing an "identity crisis," that period is passing. We have a growing sense of what it means to be members of an apostolic religious order in the United States today. We are conscious of being "in process," that is to say, aware that change and adaptation are *ongoing* components of our lives, individually and collectively. Further, after removing many of the collective features that previously secured our identity—habit, horarium, a highly regulated life-style—we have come face to face with the remainder: ourselves, each other as individuals, each called by the Gospel to a life of service in faith. When that "identity" disappeared, we found ourselves. As women, we are keenly aware of the strength we have in and from the relational dimension of our lives; we are not inclined to give questions of structure primacy of place or interest. Structure and collectively held values and beliefs are indeed essential, but we recognize that they are not permanent and fixed. Rather, they can be allowed to emerge as we, in continuity with our past, make way for the future. We are learning to trust that our identity can be grounded less in uniformly recognizable collective features, than in the work of the Holy Spirit who draws unique individuals together to share their lives with each other in faith, through a vowed commitment. We are learning to trust that a unity consciously forged from individual integrity has marvelous potential for deep and genuine community.

Because we have been learning to affirm diversity and continuing change, allowing them to become integral to our lives, our identity may therefore be difficult to articulate and even to recognize. Like life itself, it will elude precise definition. We can only sense it and learn to trust it. Moreover, even if we are allowed to develop along these lines without outside interference, it will be some time, I believe, before we ourselves understand these developments well enough to be completely comfortable with them and able to facilitate them consciously. In any case, it will be evident that the notions of life-process and individual responsibility have been influential in forming the perceptions that I will be articulating in this article.

We have changed. Some of the changes—our dress, our life-style, new forms of ministry—are visible from the outside and much about us now would not have been recognized even twenty-five years ago as appropriate for a woman religious. There have been many factors influencing the changes: a subtle but pervasive awareness of a societal paradigm shift, a new global consciousness of the human family, awareness of economic and social injustices, the challenges of technological culture. All of these had their impact on Vatican Council II as it directed the whole Church to attend to "the joys and the hopes, the griefs and the anxieties of the (people) of this age, especially those who are poor or in any way afflicted . . ."[1] As women religious have tried to respond to these new challenges, however, we have become increasingly conscious of ourselves as women in a patriarchal Church and society. It would be impossible to separate the strands that have led to this awareness. But in the end, what has been decisive in our experience is a new sense of our own capacity for self-determination and the release of energy that this particular awareness has effected.

The changes in our outer life are evident, visible for all to see. The changes in the inner life, the "spirituality" that undergirds the changes, are more difficult to articulate. We have found, since Vatican II, that former ways of naming and systematizing our religious impulse no longer seem to speak to our experience. Further, as we have tried to talk with each other about our underlying beliefs and values, we have often found ourselves at variance with one another. We have been challenged to incorporate into our lives two skills or disciplines that we experience as inseparable: to trust our own experience, and to trust and respect the experience of each other. Ordinarily we find ourselves much more comfortable explaining ourselves in terms of what is visible. And yet, at times we ask ourselves about what has kept us steady and faithful through all the change. We try to probe beneath the surface, to find words to express the *source* of the passion for life, the energy and creativity we experience.

Because there are always intimate, personal, and ultimately mysterious, inner realities in the life of the Spirit they are not easy to bring to expression. Further, they are constantly changing, as they are affected by our active engagement and our dialogue with the world about us. Still, in the first part of these reflections I want to speak about the religious dimension of our experience. I will look first at what effect the recognition of the incarnation has upon spirituality and try to articulate something of how we experience *the process* of our relationship with God. In a second section, I will draw on some insights from Jungian psychology that I believe may shed further light on some facet of our experience. In a final section, I will consider how the vows serve as channels for our energies. It will be clear that I cannot speak for everyone. My hope is that there are enough commonalities in our experience to enable us to recognize one another, even in the dark.

The Significance of an Incarnate God

"Incarnation" is probably the central Christian concept that underlies the dramatic shift we have experienced in how we view our world and our lives. Incarnation means that in Jesus Christ, God is irretrievably committed to presence in our world. It implies, then, the immanence or indwelling of God in human, earthly reality. For our part, incarnation calls us to take seriously the world and times in which we live. It summons us to be present in the world, affected by it, responding to it, responsible for it, co-laborers in its transformation. It posits the world as the place where God is to be sought.

We seem to be rediscovering for our own time a genuinely sacramental spirituality. Instead of confining the experience of God to certain places or experiences designated "sacred," we are oriented toward viewing all reality as the locus of God. It is a sacramentality, a mentality that regards everything as holy, at least potentially. Its task is to expose the evil, the unjust, the UNholy, so that God's presence may be perceived and glorified. God is to be discovered, then, within ourselves and in the world around us—in the beauties and the groanings of creation, in the needs that evoke our energies and compassion, in the relationships that nourish and challenge us, as we experience them all. We know that we cannot look for a God "out there" to save us and take us to heaven "up there." We cannot seek God as an object separate from our world, outside our lived experience. Nevertheless, to say that God is to be sought and discovered as immanent does not exclude God's transcendence. More than ever, we recognize that God cannot be limited by names or by systems. God cannot be confined to the particular experience or perception of any individual or group.

To search out the immanent God demands that we reflect upon our experience, and that we make the effort to find words for what we know. It may be that if we were rigorously honest in examining our experience for what we really *know* of God, we would have much less to say than we might have assumed. We might discover that we have allowed theological language or ideas to *substitute* for the reality of experience. It may be that we received formulas like "the indwelling of the Trinity, Father, Son and Holy Spirit, in our souls"—formulas that no doubt originated in experience and were intended to help interpret the experience of life in and with God. But we were rarely if ever encouraged to examine our experience to see to what that formula referred. We risked living on two levels—a level of ideas, notions or language, and a level of experience—with no integral connection to one another. Now, however, we know that some of those formulas, particularly those that limit divinity to exclusively masculine formulations, are inadequate. We now have to confront the dichotomy between language and experience.

To encounter our experience honestly can be frightening. We are learning how to honor silence, even as we struggle to speak. Even so, we must take the risk of sharing, and honor the privilege of listening as others share, so that we can continue to build a community of faith. We may continue for a while to live out of the resources that nourished us in the past. But it is imperative for the future that we struggle to articulate, in old words and new ones, a spirituality that can help us as we try to respond to the new horizons that the world of our time opens before us.

As women, we find the present moment intensely challenging and, somehow congenial, for we are pointed toward our own experience and encouraged to join with others in validating it. We find ourselves receptive to and grateful for women theologians in the feminist movement who insist that this process is necessary as we move from a tradition that has provided us with exclusively masculine images of God, and come to claim our own names and images born of our own experience. While this new responsibility sounds appealing and exciting, it is no simple process that can be accomplished overnight. It is a long, slow process that takes a lifetime. As in childbirth, we have to adjust ourselves to its rhythm and surrender our desire to get it to happen when and as we want it. We co-operate, but we do not control. New insights into the nature of our relationship with God are born of individual experience, in the labor of articulating that experience, not only for ourselves but for others.

The effort to share our faith is part of a larger process of an emerging collective consciousness in which women's insights and experience will be integral. Our sharing and our being in solidarity as a community of believers are essential to the process. Perhaps what is most exciting is that we have claimed our *author-ity* and our *response-ability* for this development.

Some persons live close to their own experience and are able to name it fairly easily. Others will find it more difficult. Some may be gifted with helping others name their experience. As we listen and share, our own experience is clarified and we are able to own it more integrally. Differences of age, experience and temperament will necessitate different approaches to working with experience. We are learning to recognize that sharing is a process essential to building and maintaining community of faith. It is a task in which our different gifts and temperaments will come into play. "Having gifts that differ according to the grace given to us, let us use them." (Rom. 12:6)

Naming and imaging an immanent God is a difficult and even paradoxical process. The difficulty is not just that many of the old images do not work and that new ones are not yet articulated. It is not just that we are in a time of cultural transition with effects that are disconcerting to traditional ways of naming *all* reality. It is difficult because the experience of God is in itself hard to locate and to fit into names and categories.

The paradox comes with the sense that God disappears into life—something that is not inappropriate, one might say, for an incarnate God. For some, God is a clear presence and Jesus, a very available image through whom to relate to God. For many others, among whom I count myself, that is not the case. When we examine our experience, we do not ordinarily or often find God as a distinct Other. We may be able to work out a sense of who God is from our experiences of being sustained, or enabled, inspired, encouraged, forgiven, accepted, loved. We may name God the Source of these experiences. Still, we have not known God, but only certain effects, God's "traces." Like Moses, we see the back-side of God who, apparently, just passed by. Like Moses, we can name the ground holy, but we do not often see the bush burning. God is experienced not so much as a separate Being, but God is sensed as the deepest dimension of our own being. What we find is not God but *ourselves*. We are, as it were, given to ourselves enhanced, and often also purified, by what must have been the presence of God.

The process of self-knowledge is the process of knowing God. But knowing ourselves is ordinarily not a process of adding anything, but only of having the pretenses, the false assumptions, the unreal images both negative and positive, gradually stripped off. Like Eustace, the bad little boy in C. S. Lewis' *Voyage of the Dawn Treader*, who turned into a dragon, we have many layers of dragon scales and skins that have to be peeled off. Eustace tried to do it himself, but it was useless. Aslan, the Christ figure, had to tear it off: ". . . when he began pulling the skin off, it hurt worse than anything I've ever felt. The only thing that made me able to bear it was just the pleasure of feeling the stuff peel off."[2] Self-knowledge is often painful, but it "feels good" because we know it is true. God, through our life experience, reveals us to ourselves, and knowing the truth of ourselves is a step deeper into the knowledge of God. We are, after all, the image of God, and the closer we come to our own truth, the closer we are to the Reality reflected in the image.

God disappears as a separate entity and emerges as immersed in our lives, experienced as Power of my power, Heart of my own heart, Life of my life. Though we may sense God as close and intimate to our lives, God at the same time becomes also darker and more form-less, quite literally *Namenlos,* nameless, as Rahner liked to say. If our religious maturing has taken this direction, then to search for images will at some times be regressive, and experienced as an exercise in frustration. We will not necessarily experience ourselves as more comfortable with God for there is something un-securing about the development, since God is less definable than ever, less graspable or controllable, more difficult to "relate to" in the old ways. And yet there is Something true, Something trustworthy, Something that gives a very fundamental grounding and sense of integrity to our lives.

The God whom we thus know so obscurely can scarcely be separated from our own life, or from Life, hardly recognized as personally distinct. And yet, closer reflection indicates that there is distinction, because we experience unequivocally that all, including our own life, is Gift, and not our own. In a way, this Something is *more* intensely personal than our limiting notions of personality can comprehend. We trust that God is becoming more rather than less, that is to say, in our experience God is becoming *God,* and as such will always be beyond our comprehension or naming. Paradoxically, then, to speak of God as immanent is inevitably to speak of God as transcending human defining. Though we may yearn to be able to say more, and even feel that we know less about God than we ever did, our deepest instinct is simply to trust. We recognize the value of silence.

But once again we will reach for images. We recognize that we cannot accurately or adequately give expression to the presence of a God who is the very ground of our being. And yet we reach out with images, with metaphors that try to express our experience because it is only thus that we know ourselves united with others in our faith. The moment of silence and the moment of imaging are like inhaling and exhaling. Both are essential to life.

This God is the God of our own life, Life of our life, Source of all that is. To trust this God is to trust the process of our own lives. The "life-giving water springing up within us," promised by Jesus in the fourth chapter of John's Gospel, is an image whose reality we know as God dwelling at the center of our lives. God is the Source that binds my life to the lives of others, my gifts to the needs of others, and others' gifts to my needs, in an invisible design of reciprocity, giving and receiving. It is this Source that links every human destiny with every other, and with the destiny of the planet and the universe. It is this God that our diverse experiences reveal, shaped with the shape of our own lives.

As communities of apostolic women religious, we are situated in a complex world, encouraged to read the signs of the times, and open to act with a new sense of mission in the world. Because many communities now no longer rely on the isolated command of the superior to determine our individual ministries, we need to learn skills of discerning, both individually and communally. Our question becomes: what part of my energy is fueled by my own ego needs—my need to be needed, my need to look like a good Christian (even to myself!), my need to feel significant? What part is God's call working through these needs of mine, to sensitize me to the real needs of my neighbor and the world? We are trying to learn to distinguish and to monitor, in other words, the Heart and the heart, to learn how they are related. Many experience God as the restless stirring of a compassionate heart that feels continually prodded and drawn toward the needs of the poor, a heart that rises in protest and action in response to perceptions of injustice, a heart that is stirred to action by the threatening thought of the tragedy of nuclear annihilation. Is it God or is it my own heart that is summoning me? If it is the Heart of my heart, it is God.

We find ourselves experiencing a deepened commitment to disciplined reflection and prayer, both individually and communally, in order to remain aware of what is going on within us as we engage the world, precisely so that we can recognize the traces of God when we encounter them. We are learning—to ponder, to share, to trust. The traditional prayer forms may not be sufficient for this task, and so we find ourselves engaged in new ways of exploring and "ministering to" the needs of our inner lives, as well as the needs of the outer world. The popularity of journaling and of methods of meditation and centering prayer, some influenced by Eastern traditions, is evidence of the exploration. Groups often begin a meeting with simple silence, and the Quaker-like instruction to "center down," as if to recognize that we do not know now what words to use to gather one another into the Presence. Or perhaps it is recognition that the Center lies deeper than words can reach.

Karl Rahner suggested that we stand at a critical juncture in church history, as the Roman, Western Church begins for the first time to be a universal church.[3] Our situation both necessitates and affords opportunity for real dialogue with the tradition as it has been taught to us. Now we are searching the tradition for what lies buried or forgotten or suppressed and waiting to be brought once again to light. Moreover, we now have access to the riches of traditions other than our own—not just the Jewish and other Christian traditions, but the many other traditions in which, according to Vatican II, there is "a sort of secret presence of God," "hidden seeds of the Word."[4] What can we learn from them that can enhance our ability to recognize and to name the incarnate God?

In this process, we have always to be careful and attentive to our tradition and its wisdom, but critically so. Sometimes we have simply to wait, and to hold a formulation until we have more insight or maturity. Sometimes, if the language is too limiting, we have to work until we can find words that do fit. Always we have to be honest.

As the outer ambiance becomes larger, as our consciousness broadens to include the globe (and perhaps the universe), we rely more and more deeply upon the Center within, which we know to be a source of life-giving energy. Sometimes we feel shaken by the absence of a steady frame. But if the old frame has cracked, it is letting in new light, setting us in new relationship with the whole earth and all its people, and releasing new energy. There is a simultaneous darkening and deepening of faith—a sign of growth and of life, though not in the way we might have expected or desired. Faith is being stripped of its accretions and honed to a fine point. It seems clear that not inertia, but sharpened and broadened vision, and new creative energy, have resulted. Spirit has been released.

The image that endures is the image of Jesus that keeps on pointing us to humanity, that of others as well as our own, as the dwelling place of God. And humanity points us to our earth with which we are intimately bonded in a relationship of dependence, gratitude and responsibility. We are challenged to search out all that impedes human beings from becoming all that they can be, to hear the cry of the poor and oppressed, to hear the cry of the earth itself ravaged by greed. We are called to use the resources of the earth and our own personal gifts with reverence and care so that life may develop to greatest abundance.

The one God is the Source of all that is. We are learning to trust that if our eyes and ears and hearts are open, we will be called, each in her own way, to share who we are and what we have. We will enter into that design of giving and receiving that is God's own Law for the universe. We will lose ourselves and find the God who holds it all together and continually makes all things new. This God, who is immanent to the world and interior to our experience, will be discovered as infinitely transcendent, for the kingdom of God will always exceed our grasp. The One who nudges us into action and draws the world forward through and with our acting is Destiny as well as Source. We only catch glimpses.

Insights on the Immanence of God from Jungian Psychology

As I have read and pondered the work of the Swiss psychologist Carl Jung, I have found that some of his ways of conceptualizing and naming have been helpful in my own attempt to interpret some of my own experience and that of others. As he outlines the process of individuation, there is a development that I believe relates to the immanence or interiorizing of God that I have been describing. It also helps to explain some of the difficulties that women religious are encountering at this time in our history. In this section, I want to apply some facets of Jung's theory to our religious life as communities of apostolic women religious.

My experience leads me to believe that as a religious person of any sex or tradition matures, there is a kind of dislocation. God seems to move from the outside in. This development corresponds to what takes place in the second half of life as Jung described it.

According to Jung, in the first part of life, we humans are engaged in ego development and take our cues predominantly from the outer world of family, society and culture, with their expectations, their authorities, their demands of performance and adaptation. We must learn, in other words, how to "make it" in the outer world, and we do this by gradually developing our own ego, our sense of who we are as distinguished from everyone else. God, at this period, is an Other who, under various titles, supports us as we grow.

At some point, called "mid-life," we may find ourselves catapulted into an enormous upheaval equal to a "paradigm shift." New inner resources become available to us, and old patterns of thinking, behaving and being have to be re-arranged, sometimes in drastic ways.

Jung spoke of an ego-Self axis. The ego is the ordinary conscious center of the personality, the part that thinks it knows what it means when it says "I." The Self, on the other hand, is the deeper Center of the total personality, an all-inclusive wisdom that transcends our conscious viewpoint. The Self is the source of those impulses or instincts within us that prod us to deeper, fuller life. The Self in us can represent the larger picture of Life and guide us to find our role in it. Jung spoke of the Self as the image of God, or the God within. It lies, apparently, on the other side of the conscious personality and is not therefore directly accessible to the ego.

The relation of the ego to the Self is delightfully illustrated in an incident that I saw described at an exhibit in Nashville, Tennessee. Alongside the beautiful carvings of an uneducated black man, William Edmonton, were stories, some in conversational form, of how the carvings had come to birth. One went something like this: "God put a piece of stone in front of me and said, 'William, carve that stone.' I said, 'I don't think I can.' God said, 'Yes, you can so too.' " And William did. The exhibit was testimony to the truth of that conversation. William Edmonton's story is like conversations of Moses or Jeremiah at the beginning of their prophetic vocations. It is also like conversations many of us had with God at the beginning of our "vocation," and at various other points along the way. It provides an example of the relationship between ego and Self as Jung saw it. The Self, spelled by Jung with a capital S, is that in us which summons us to transcend our present self-image, a product of the ego, and move on to fuller life. The ego is intended to serve the Self, to be in a listening-obeying relationship with the Self. When Jung uses the term "the Self" in this way, it is very congenial of translation to our experience of the God within, or the Holy Spirit.

At mid-life, if a person is disposed to being attentive and responsive, the ego-Self axis shifts. For persons with a deep religious commitment, what can be a rather total psychological upheaval seems to be accompanied by a very thorough-going dark night, with its attendant loss of the sense of God's presence, and absence of the familiar landmarks or footholds on the spiritual path. What was previously satisfying to desire is no longer so. It is a time of affective purification as desires are being liberated from the ego's agendas. Formerly the ego held itself in the position of command. Now it moves from its posture of maintaining dominance and control. It is able to function in a freer, more detached manner, listening to and discriminating among the many promptings that come from within and without.

As a result of this shift, a person is now increasingly willing to place herself in the service of transpersonal values, values that affect the future of humankind and the planet. She becomes less interested or invested in succeeding *vis a vis* the outer world of prestige and privilege, and more intent on responding to the signals that come from the deeper dimensions of her being. She begins to live from the inside out, rather than the reverse. Her sense of meaning, value and purpose lie within and she has shifted from outer to inner authority. She owns her own life in a new way, is able to accept her limitations and to take pleasure in her gifts. She finds herself operating with wider awareness but, paradoxically, with a new, free kind of un-self-consciousness.

While energy was invested in accomplishments to benefit the ego, it was limited in its content and scope to what would serve the individual with her needs and desires for acquisition and aggrandizement. While they were held at the service of the ego, one's desires were aimed at self-gratification and self-fulfillment. Now that energy can be released into a broader vision in new and creative and life-giving ways for the world. Now that energy can flow into non-possessive, free and compassionate love for other human beings and for all of creation.[5]

The foregoing, as I understand it, is a description of a mature religious person. As such it is idealized. It is not as though one now emerges a once-and-for-all perfected human being. One will always need to monitor the role of the ego, so that it does not reclaim its dominance. One will always need to discriminate the personal from merely collectively held values. The shift that we are considering is simply one critical juncture in a process that continues throughout life.

The opportunity for this shift, the opportunity to undergo the purging dark night, is, I believe, offered to everyone. Not everyone will choose to respond. Those who do respond can do so on positive grounds but more often because the crisis presents itself with a kind of inescapability. Certainly, it is not an appealing process. The ego will fight for all it is worth to stay in command, because the alternative is a kind of death. It should be understood that the ego does not die. The ego is necessary to keep a person related to the world in making choices and in acting. The ego is asked only to renounce its position of control and to hold itself ready to serve the Self, to listen for its promptings, to follow its leadings freely, with neither compulsion nor constraint. But for the ego to lose its position of commander is experienced as a painfully difficult kind of death. It is an internal enactment of a design that exists antecedent to our choice. One must lose oneself in order to find oneself. The result, renewed energy for loving and healing the world, is the truly marvelous evidence that the Creator has instilled in our being a law of Life. It is the enactment of the mystery of death and resurrection within us.

An important facet of this shift in the ego-Self axis, and an area of particular significance for women religious, is the transfer of authority from the outside in. As I have stated, Jung thought that we spend the first part of our lives learning to live in the world by doing what others tell us is good to do, thinking as others teach us to think about the meaning and value of life, trying to be acceptable in the eyes of others by fulfilling their expectations. At the point when the shift occurs, one finds oneself oriented and directed from within. One is not now dictated to by any collective—society, community, church. One places much less reliance on external figures, rules, authority. The new orientation requires continual discrimination between those elements of the collective expectations that are meaningful and valuable, and those that are not. One begins to live according to her own meanings and values and to assume personal authority. The change is difficult. One suffers guilt feelings when she doesn't measure up to what she has learned is expected, or when she takes a divergent path. There is a certain loneliness involved, as one owns one's individual self.

This is not to say that now one completely divorces herself from society and culture and goes her own way. Indeed, many of the most important contributions to society and culture can now be made, because a person has no longer the same kind of ego-investment in what she does. She can approach her work in the world with a new kind of freedom. She knows her gifts, has enough experience to know what she can best contribute, and can leave aside the rest. One can and must find appropriate ways to "pay her dues" to the society and culture that have nurtured and continue to nurture her. She does it with a new kind of integrity that comes from acting in congruence with her own inner authority. She does it also with new energy.

In religious language, the shift means that God moves from the outside in. Images of God as Other that previously inspired may now become dysfunctional. One knows, and knows that she can trust, the within-ness of God, the indwelling Holy Spirit, for guidance and insight. Here feminist theology, with its emphasis upon attending to our own experience, is very congenial and helpful.

For me, this psychological language is enlightening, and has clear implications for women religious. For example, it is well known that the median age of many communities is upwards of sixty years. I can speculate, then, that we as a group of women would be ready to make the shift in the ego-Self axis, or have already made it. The opening provided by Vatican II and the changes in our community structures now permit us to live out of this new post mid-life posture of inner authority. We are able to view the world more broadly and are willing to place our energies at the disposal of the many-faceted needs we find there, but now in ministries diversified according to our gifts. We are able to live and work more individually and autonomously and indeed, we need to do so. We have sufficient life experience to trust our own wisdom, insights and sense of ourselves. One might have anticipated, then, a shift in our posture *vis a vis* both political and Church authorities, especially where they touch upon self-definition. We know and appreciate who we are and who we are becoming, and it becomes difficult for us to accept a heteronomous structure that would define us from outside ourselves.

Given that we understand the continual need to monitor the role of the ego in service of the deeper guidance of the Spirit within, it is appropriate and necessary that our community structures and procedures be such that they respect our individual ability to live out of our own inner authority. Community processes should not only allow, but require, that we be responsive from within, that we act not from a sense of what is expected, but listen for what is needed. These are very different postures. The implicit transfer of authority is difficult both for individuals and for communities. It is always easier, and sometimes necessary, to go with the crowd, to do what everyone else does, or what we have always done the way we have always done it. There is an uncomfortable element of unpredictability when we place our trust in the working of the Spirit in each one. The urge is always to control and manage from outside, by mandate from a superior, for example. Certainly management from outside, or from above, appears more efficient, but one has to question whether or not it is the appropriate mode for groups claiming to be religious.

Still, we do not live in an ideal world with perfect people. There will be ego-centered actions and behavior. The community's loving challenge, our own prayer and reflection are essential. We are in process of developing horizontal processes of "discerning" which, while they trust and respect the free decision of the individual, afford the opportunity for "input" or "feedback" from significant others in decisions that affect one's life and ministry. In my view, this shift in the locus of authority is one of the most exciting, and the most critical, developments in United States communities of women religious.

Like any other group, religious communities readily form new collective patterns and ideas, new bandwagons. That women religious are "about justice and peace," for instance, might be only a new collective notion that we as groups take on with no change in individuals' outlooks or life-styles. Each one needs to watch for the slogans, the "in" words and phrases, discriminate whether or not to appropriate them personally, or to challenge their truth. Dialogue among discerning and discriminating individuals is the fundamental process by which a community will be able to articulate the values it wishes to promote, and still be open to change and to new points of view.

These observations about the post-midlife experience of inner authority raise questions, touchy questions, about the relationship of an individual to the Church, specifically to the hierarchical aspect of the Church. We have been taught always to be "dutiful daughters," the role expected of women religious by the official Church. Structurally, there is no provision for us to grow from daughters to mothers, or even to adult stature. In fact, only a few males in the Church can ever grow beyond children, and they grow not into adults, but into "Fathers." Psychologically, we grow to maturity and make our own decisions, but in the official Church we must always remain as children, never making the shift from outer to inner authority. I do not believe that Jesus intended such stultification for the members of the Church.

I believe that mature persons, individually and corporately, must own their own authority in the religious sphere, the sphere of life in the Church, just as they do in all the other areas of life. Many religious communities are at a particularly critical juncture in this regard as we continue work on our constitutions. It is difficult for us to deal with a Church structure that would define us *a priori*, apart from our own participation, or that would put closure upon our development. That this is and will be a source of tension is clear. We are as committed as ever, and intend to be attentive to and respectful of authority in the Church. But we are also newly committed to work together and to find ways to insist upon being viewed and treated with the respect due to mature and faithful adult persons in the Church.

Of course, in this area as in others, both individuals and communities must always monitor the ego's investment in being right, in "doing it our way," in becoming intractably fixed on certain ideas. The ego is just as active on the collective or community level as it is on the personal, individual level. Like individuals, groups have a tendency toward narcissistic self-justification. The problem can be more difficult to detect because of the power and diffuseness of a collectivity. Genuine truth needs both humility and courage as companions.

The Vows. Channeling Life Energies

I have spoken several times of a release of energy that comes when the ego is not blocking the way and usurping energy for its own purposes by keeping in control, imposing its agendas, maintaining a certain image of oneself. All of that takes our life's energy away from attentiveness to cues from the Self that are the source of the summons to genuine service of the world. To translate back into religious language, our service of God and our service of the world are integral components of a unified whole. In this final section, I want to examine the vows in the perspective of the shift from ego to Self that I have been describing.

Fundamentally, our life-energy is not our own. It is the energy of the universe, and we are its channels. To speak another way, we *are* only by the continuing gift and sustenance of God. We hold the gift of our lives only as stewards whose role is to be careful and caring channels of energy. With respect to our life-energy, we are *con-servers* who serve with and by means of that energy. Such service will involve some discipline so that we do not impede the flow of our life-energy by our own selfishly designed and contrived agendas.

In many religious traditions there are disciplines that are intended to harmonize energy and to facilitate that gradual loosening of the ego's hold over the particular energy that manifests itself as "me." The Western Christian tradition has known little besides external, structurally enforced disciplines, and discipline of the will. Fasting, for instance, while it affects the body, has been most commonly experienced and interpreted in the West as a question of "will *power.*" One undertook bodily disciplines as a sort of spiritual muscle-flexing. Disciplines can be that, to be sure, but there are other approaches, some known to native Americans, and some, like the yogas, known to Eastern traditions. These would seek to work with energy in a more internal and integral way aimed at educating a human being to function within a harmonious whole, aligned with and sensitive to the rest of the universe. There is a potential source of great enrichment for Western tradition if we can learn from native Americans and from the East the wisdom they have cultivated over many centuries. Religious orders of women and men may have a particular contribution to make in this facet of the Church's movement to become genuinely universal.

One form used notably in religious orders in the Western Church has been to try to give direction to life energies by focusing on three areas that are recognized almost universally as areas where energy gets constellated or gathered. Humans seem particularly prone to constellate energy for use in pursuit of wealth and possessions of various kinds, and to use these as means of feeling powerful and secure. We gather our sexual energy and use it to make a claim on another person, to win that person for our own, or to enhance our own sense of power. We gather energy to assert our own plans—for the ordering of a day's activity or for the ordering of the world, and thereby try to secure a feeling of power *vis a vis* what happens in our life or in the world around us.

It is not without wisdom that these three areas became the focus of vows that embody a commitment to pay attention to energy as it gathers around these three areas of particular human vulnerability where ego is most prone to erect its strongholds. Before proceeding, however, we need to raise the question of whether or not the traditional vowed commitment, arising as it did in a male ambiance, might be related to specifically masculine energies and designed to address areas of concern experienced specifically by males. Would the experience of a community of women lead them to design something similar? Are the vows really compatible with feminine consciousness?[6]

I do not know the answer. Perhaps research has been done, or will be done, that can present evidence one way or the other. Perhaps women's religious communities have never heretofore been sufficiently conscious of their own identity as unique entities distinct from the male "super-vision" to have had the freedom to create their own forms and disciplines. It would in any case be a creative project for women religious to imagine starting from scratch. What energies feel most likely to be diverted into selfish pursuits? What are those that feel most in need of direction, and how? It is interesting to notice that, when the Sisters for Christian Community began, they did adopt the vows, but modified their interpretation to fit their own vision. Still, most of their members had come from other communities, so their kind of adaptation might have been expected. More evidence probably needs to be gathered.

The vows have undergone some evolution and suffered some distortion in the course of centuries. Although they were intended simply to give direction to energy, to free it from the ego's domination and to put it to service of the world around us, the vows sometimes became reified and made into ends in themselves. History shows too that they could be used as instruments of a different form of domination.

Poverty sometimes became a means of control and efficiency in maintaining community resources. Chastity became a means of controlling relationships and ensuring a dependent membership. Obedience was an easy way of maintaining institutions and work forces. A whole system of canon law, intended under the best optic to protect freedom, could become a means of preventing any change or divergence and consequently served as a means of control. None of this was ever conscious or intentional, of course, and precisely for this reason there is the problem. It is surely instructive for us to reflect on the potential of even very deep spiritual resources to be co-opted by institutions or collectives and turned into their very opposite.

As close as I can come in examining my own experience, it appears that the vows have served me well—not as objects of devotion or particular piety, but as a subtle backdrop that simply gave direction to certain of my energies. That they apply in the areas they do seems to me to have been appropriate and helpful. I am not precisely grateful for the forms used to express the vows—"permissions," for instance, or "assignments" without consultation, or the prohibition of "particular friendships." Admittedly, usage had hardened into meaningless or even hurtful forms. Nevertheless, the vows still provided me with the viable means for spiritual deepening.

I am glad, for instance, that the community context has helped me to be conscious of my own instinct to possess. I can chart an evolution in that area that seems to be in the direction of greater inner and outer freedom. I am glad that the Roman Catholic Church offered me and other women the option of life in a celibate community. That too has fit my own personal development and the discipline of maintaining that commitment has felt congruent and gradually freeing. To have had a community context in which to learn to listen deeply to the inner voice of the Spirit, the challenges of the community and friends, and the needs of the world has been invaluable. For me the vows *worked* in helpful ways. But I am perhaps already too deeply shaped by them to be completely objective.

This is not the place to analyze in detail each of these areas, nor to present a full-blown theology of the vows. My purpose here is to focus only on a consideration of the vows from the standpoint of giving direction to energy. Lived in terms of the Gospel, the vows are a means of transforming energy to make it available in service to the Body of Christ in the world. My reflection here is simply one way of imagining how it works. That it will be limited and inadequate must therefore be accepted from the start.

The task presented by the vows, at least in the first part of life, generally seems like something to be done. One must become poor, or generous, or unpossessively loving, or open and docile. The longer one lives the more one sees that one cannot *make oneself* poor, chaste, obedient. One must try, of course. Ordinarily one spends many years doing just that. One tries, only to come to a reverse view of the task. With what we have called the mid-life shift, one sees that the task is simply to get out of the way with one's agendas, even very virtuous agendas, and let life live itself through us as unself-consciously as possible.

On the way there are some pitfalls. Poverty can get tied up with a certain image of myself that is acceptable in a community where collective value is placed on simplicity, on not needing much, on being frugal. Then once again energy is diverted by the ego to accomplish its own purpose, projecting an image of myself as righteously and piously poor. Chastity can get tied up with an image of myself as Bride of Christ invulnerable to human loves, and energy is diverted into the ego's trap of a kind of self-sufficiency, specialness, secure isolation. Obedience can divert energy into maintaining an image of myself as one who does it right and keeps all the rules and laws and thereby wins God's favor—not unlike the posture attributed to the Pharisees in the Gospels. For a time, these self-images may serve the purpose of forming identity. But then they will need to be left behind.

Little by little, life will modify whatever noble and high images we had of ourselves and strip us of pretense. If we are open and alert to what is around us, God, in the guise of life, will offer to detach us from those things, those identities, we cling to as securities. Life will bring diminishments that must be accepted. Life itself will give us opportunity to realize that we are essentially poor. We have nothing, except for the Treasure, the true Self/self, that is always elusive, something we can never grasp or own, but that dwells hidden in the depth of these earthen vessels. And the energy that is released as ego-centric investment is loosened, becomes, without any false heroics, a simple, compassionate identification and solidarity with all who are poor, and a willingness to work for whatever liberates us all together into fuller humanity.

Ordinarily, we experience our sexual energy as bound up with "I want you," or "I want you to love me"—both connected to ego's attempt to use a person to prop itself up or to secure itself by way of progeny. If we are open and alert to the movement of instinctive sexual energy within us, life will offer us the opportunity to *suffer* this energy, that is, to carry it from beneath, *sub-fero,* and to hold it until it can be separated from its bonding to ego-desires. This will at times mean a very conscious containment of powerful energy that can be difficult and even painful. A celibate commitment must also include conscious effort to become aware of both feminine and masculine parts of ourselves and to develop them both. Eventually we may experience the uniting of those masculine and feminine energies within ourselves. The process is one of gradually becoming *virgin* in the early sense of *one in herself.* The virgin in this understanding is one who is not conditioned by needs and expectations from outside. She acts from her own deepest center where God's love flows freely together with her own. This virgin embodies the description of Wisdom, "While remaining in herself she renews all things." (Ws. 7:27) Transformed and released from attachment to personal ends, from demand for satisfaction and fruition, the virgin's life-energy can flow freely in the service of all life as compassionate love ready to embrace the whole of creation.

If we are truly alert and listening, we will little by little become aware of the marvel of the gift of life, of all that is, and experience a profound respect for the laws of each and all creatures' own being. We will begin more and more to operate in harmony with the fundamental patterns of things—our own bodies, our environment. We will hear and feel as our own the pain caused by all that is inharmonious—the wars, the unequal distribution of goods, the violations of human dignity, the violations of natural beauty and resources. The Spirit within will lead us to place ourselves where our own gift matches the need. We will hear the challenges of the community, of our friends and our enemies, and be open to change our ideas or behaviors. Our energy will, in other words, flow freely in response to the world about us.

Of course, these too are idealized descriptions. Still, I believe that, lived with conscious attentiveness and openness, the vows can function to give this kind of direction to energies most vulnerable to being caught in traps set by the ego. In other words, they put us on a path that leads to transformation of energies and help us to be attentive to what might impede the free flow of energy, and what might facilitate it. It is the path to freedom of Spirit/spirit. The vows represent a commitment to "husband"[7] our share of energy so that it contributes to the harmonizing of the universe. They have functioned for us as a fundamental symbol system and have also given a certain structure to our lives. As interpretations of the vows have changed, we have been creating new structures within our communities so that new insights can be translated into life. We will continue to examine whether and how they are means to deepening and renewal. Because they touch universal dimensions of human experience, I believe the vows can be avenues to profound depths of both inner and outer reality, and finally to the awareness that inner and outer are one.

Conclusion.

I have attempted in this article to reflect on the life of apostolic religious communities of women "from the inside." Limited as they are, my reflections cannot begin to scratch the surface of the variety and richness that are manifested in the lives of individuals, each with her own particular gift for the Body of Christ, each with her own experience, each with her own approach to articulating the experience. Further, each individual is joined in community with other individuals, and each community manifests its own unique configuration of the life of the Spirit. Having come through the traumas of identity crisis, we are in a position to bring energy and creativity to the particular poise of the Church at this moment of our history. The tasks seem formidable. But we have experienced the Spirit in our midst, turning crisis into opportunity.

ENDNOTES

1. *Pastoral Constitution on the Church in the Modern World, #1.*

2. C. S. Lewis, *Voyage of the Dawn Treader* (New York: Collier Books, 1970) 90.

3. "Towards a Fundamental Theological Interpretation of Vatican II," *Theological Studies* 40 (1979) 716–27.

4. *Decree on the Missionary Activity of the Church #9*, 11.

5. For an excellent discussion of this process, see Eugene Bianchi, *Aging as a Spiritual Journey* (New York: Crossroad, 1985).

6. It may be relevant here, and for the preceding discussion as well, to note Sheila Murphy's observation: "Responding to questions about adult developmental life tasks, women religious revealed experiences more androgynous than those of either women or men in general. Although not confronted with growing children and returning to the marketplace, sisters are similar to *women* in general in approximate onset of the midlife transition, emotional experiences of the transition, intimacy/sexuality concerns, and identity issues. Although not confronted in the same way with professional advancement and financial responsibilities, sisters are similar to *men* in general in vocational development, career adjustment, and mentoring experiences." See *Midlife Wanderer* (Whitinsville, MA.: Affirmation Books, 1983) 11. We are reminded once again that the socially defined concept of "masculine" is not limited to men, nor is "feminine" limited to women.

7. If "husband" is considered in its root meaning of one who is bound to a house (and therefore is responsible for the careful tending of its resources), it is an apt metaphor for our role in relation to planet earth.

REFLECTION QUESTIONS

1. What is your experience of incarnational spirituality? What names and images for God are rising out of your experience at this point in time?

2. The process of maturing is one of living out of our own inner authority, a living true to the God within. How can members of religious communities of women help each other and others in this process? How can congregational government structures help or hinder this process?

3. Do you see the vows as integral to your spirituality as a woman religious? Do you experience that the vows enable you to channel your womanly life energies creatively?

RECOMMENDED READING

Bianchi, Eugene C. *Aging as a Spiritual Journey.* New York: The Crossroad Publishing Company, 1985.

Murphy, Sheila M. *Midlife Wanderer.* Whitinsville, MA: Affirmation Books, 1983.

Outward Orientation in Declining Organizations
Reflections on the LCWR Documents

Patricia Wittberg, SC

At the fourth time, rhythm was established. Ebbing and flowing, contracting and expanding, pain and joy, sun and moon, beginning and ending. The labour of love progressed.
And it was very good.

A study of the ways in which the women in United States religious congregations identify themselves and articulate their mission or purpose reveals patterns that appear highly unusual to sociologists who have studied other organizations. Business, government, philanthropic and religious organizations typically display a "life cycle" pattern of youth, maturity and decline, with identifiable behaviors and attitudes evident among the members at each stage. The documents analyzed in this study, however, show that religious communities of women in the United States do not conform to the usual pattern. In this paper, I hope first to delineate what is atypical about the documents of religious congregations when they are analyzed from an organizational perspective, then to explore some possible explanations for this difference, and finally, to suggest implications and strategies for religious congregations in the future.

Organizational Life Cycles and Religious Congregations

It is generally accepted that most religious communities of men and of women in the United States and in Europe are declining organizations. Whereas between 1950 and 1966, the number of women religious in the United States rose over 23 per cent (from 147,000 to 181,421), the subsequent two decades have seen a decrease of over 30 per cent (from 181,421 to under 126,000). The median age of members in most congregations has risen dramatically, as fewer and fewer young women enter to counterbalance the many aged and retired (Kolmer, 1984:16,41; Neal, 1984:18–19). This pattern is not unique to U.S. women's religious institutes. European congregations began shrinking in 1950 (Kolmer, 1984), and both male religious orders and the diocesan clergy are also undergoing a "demographic transition" to a smaller and older population (Schoenherr and Young, 1986). Women's congregations are well aware of this trend. According to a content analysis of their administrative reports and chapter documents (Munley, 1987), they have "a realistic grasp of the problems and challenges . . . This is evidenced by statistics about declining numbers, rising median ages and ministry shifts, and by information about fiscal and retirement needs and projections." While it may indeed be that a new cycle of birth and growth will follow the current one of decline, this does not exempt communities from the joys and pains of living through their present situation (Cada *et al.*, 1979:75).

Several sociological studies have investigated the behaviors of the members of declining organizations (See, for example, Lipset, 1960; Downs, 1967; and Reed, 1978). As Barry Stein comments, "Organizations rarely die gracefully. There is too much invested in their immortality for people to let go without conflict or tension, or for leaders to be perfectly honest about the possibility of system death." (Kanter and Stein, 1979:373). Typically, members of such groups display an unwillingness to risk and a concentration on their own personal interests. There may be intra-organizational "turf" battles ("Nobody's going to reduce/close *my* department!") as the total "pie" shrinks. A pervasive atmosphere of despair and cynical self-interest may develop. As one personnel director in a large industrial corporation commented, "Going about our job is like re-arranging the deck chairs on the Titanic." (Kanter and Stein, 1979:398). Alternatively, the organization may attempt to manipulate its environment in order to ensure its survival. The major U.S. pharmaceutical companies, for example, in order to secure their monopoly of the market, regularly fought legislation that would have allowed generic drugs. (Perrow, 1986:189–90). Finally, some organizations may change completely their primary goal rather than disband. David Sills' (1957) analysis of The Foundation for Infantile Paralysis, the organization that invented the March of Dimes to combat polio, showed how the group adopted a new goal of reducing birth defects once its original objective had been achieved.

Although women's religious congregations are also declining organizations according to most sociological criteria, the documents and other evidence analyzed for this paper show no evidence either of the attitudes or of the behaviors that such organizations and their members typically exhibit. Not one of the summary statements at the end of the content analysis of community documents (Munley, 1987) in any way reflects unwillingness to risk, internal division, or fear for organizational survival. The LCWR paper prepared by the Task Force on Religious Life for the Fifth Inter-American Conference similarly reveals none of these attitudes. While the authors do acknowledge "dispossession of security, of status, of clear and safe answers" as a reality for religious congregations, this acknowledgement is celebrated as a liberation rather than lamented as a source of divisiveness. Indeed, all the sources of conflict, division, tension, etc., mentioned in the document are located outside the congregations in the society at large.

> Our society has . . . a history which divides peoples from each other and the earth: native Americans, people of color, and immigrants; the homeless, battered, and imprisoned; the unemployed, unemployable and retired; Third World peoples; women, children, elderly, sick; victims of violence—military, domestic, sexual, structural.
>
> (Q.2, Section A.3.b, Appendix, p. 177)

By comparison, the reflection statement of the Conference of Major Superiors of Men prepared for the same Fifth Inter-American Conference, while listing the same societal trends as the LCWR paper, acknowledges in at least eight separate statements the existence of internal difficulties and tensions, and states in its prologue that the gap between the emerging vision and present attitudes has led, not only to growth, but also "to dysfunctional behavior, and excessive preoccupation with security and survival."[1]

Not only do the reflections and self-definitions of women in religious congregations not correspond to the predicted behavior of declining organizations, many of the statements imply the exact opposite. Far from an unwillingness to risk and despite an insecurity about the future, the content analysis of congregational documents indicates "a sense of life and movement," as well as a willingness to adopt new ministries. Elizabeth Kolmer, in her recent review of literature about U.S. women religious, found that, even with fewer members, religious communities have moved gradually into a diversity of new apostolic works (1984:58). This movement hardly indicates a fear of taking risks. A major theme in the documents of women's congregations was simplicity of life-style and sharing material resources with the poor—again, an opposite finding from the careful husbanding of resources that would have been predicted after research on other declining organizations.

Earlier studies of other religious organizations have emphasized that the establishment of clearly defined boundaries between members and non-members is necessary for the group's survival (Kanter, 1972:84–85; Zablocki, 1971:172). Prior to Vatican Council II, religious communities typically emphasized their special "quasi-clerical" character (Colgan, 1975) and their "state of life" as one of special "perfection." After the Council, the women religious began to understand themselves as sharing spiritual life and ministry with the rest of the laity. Congregations in the 1980s, however, go beyond a simple refusal to set up boundaries, and instead express an active identification with the poor, the oppressed and the marginalized. Of the documents analyzed for this paper, seventy-five per cent contain a statement that identifies the members with the poor; thirty-four percent articulate similar sentiments about women as an oppressed group (Munley, 1987). The LCWR paper for the Fifth Inter-American Conference has thirteen separate statements of identity with the poor and the oppressed in its answer to the second reflection question alone, even though that question was about *awareness* of the poor, not necessarily about *bonding* with them. It is noteworthy that the documents from the other participants in the Inter-American Conference did not interpret the question in this way, but rather spoke of the necessity to support, learn from, and find Christ in the marginalized of society, while continuing to consider these groups as distinct from the members of religious congregations themselves. The blurring of boundaries and the outward focus of U.S. women religious is, therefore, highly unusual, even unique.

There are many statements in the documents concerning the need for religious to work for systemic change. Themes of justice and peace and the use of the congregation's resources to take a corporate stance are mentioned frequently. In contrast to other declining organizations, however, these attempts at influencing the larger society are not made in order to ensure the survival of the congregation, but rather to empower the poor and oppressed. Nevertheless, the congregations do not seem to be defining the empowerment of the poor as the new *raison d'etre* for their existence, in a manner comparable to that of the March of Dimes when it directed its efforts to birth defects once polio had been controlled. The self-definitions in the documents still list community life, incarnational witness, and spiritual renewal as the chief reasons for the continuance of religious life. Again, it is highly unusual, from a sociological standpoint, for an organization, especially a declining one, to commit its resources toward a societal change that does not directly benefit its own survival.

The documents of the religious congregations of women in the United States that provided the data for the content analysis (Munley, 1987), therefore, reveal behaviors and attitudes that are quite different from what would have been predicted from the sociological study of similar declining organizations. Far from evincing an unwillingness to risk, an inward-looking focus on turf battles and boundary maintenance, and an attempt to alter the environment to one more favorable to their organizational existence, women's religious communities are doing the opposite—celebrating risk-taking, blurring the boundaries of their orders in solidarity with the poor, and committing their resources toward systemic change, not for their own survival, but for the empowerment of the most oppressed. They show a striking deviation from expected behavior. It could be argued that these published articulations do not reflect the real lived experience of the congregations, and that the members are merely expressing high ideals to which their actions do not conform. Such a suspicion is not borne out in fact, however. Data on the allocation of resources and personnel that accompanied the documents indicate true organizational commitments.

It should be emphasized here that an extroverted focus and a willingness to risk may actually be dysfunctional for organizational survival. During the same period that congregations have been moving toward risk-taking and solidarity with the poor, there has also been, as Kolmer points out (1984:77), a corresponding de-emphasis on internal concerns such as membership recruitment or maintaining a distinct group identity. Several previous studies (Sarther, 1983; Wemhoff, 1981; Greeley, 1972) have indicated that a major reason for the decline of vocations to the priesthood and religious life is that priests and women religious no longer actively try to recruit young people. Although the outreach from congregational vocation offices does attract some new members, it does not substitute for personal contact and encouragement. In addition to the negative effects of de-emphasizing membership recruitment, the blurring of organizational boundaries and solidarity with out-groups make the advantages of belonging less obvious to potential members. According to Kanter, not one of the communal religious groups in her study that began to ignore membership recruitment and boundary maintenance survived beyond a generation (Kanter, 1972).

Organization-based Explanations

What possible factors might account for the atypical responses of congregations of women religious, especially given that these behaviors may actually be detrimental to their survival? Several circumstances, both within and outside the organizations, could offer a partial explanation. Patricia Jean Manion refers to the shocks to the belief systems and self-identification of communities that arose from their participation in the civil rights and antiwar movements, and from their missionaries' first-hand experience of the poor and oppressed in Latin America. The Sister Formation Movement, in educating the young women in formation throughout the 1950s and 1960s, also encouraged them to apply their theological studies to challenge unjust and oppressive situations (Schneider, 1986).

It should not be assumed, however, that the increased receptivity of women religious to calls for risk-taking and solidarity with the oppressed was an inevitable result of either congregational or societal events. Religious congregations need not have interpreted either the Vatican II mandate or their founding charism in this way. Kolmer (1984:26) points out that Pius XII's 1950 call to renewal in religious orders did not have much effect on the life of the average member. Superiors often were unwilling or unsure of how to respond. Similarly, other Vatican II documents and other aspects of congregational history could have been emphasized to give a different, more institutionally inward-looking focus. Immediately after the Council, as Kolmer points out (1984:50), there was little emphasis on solidarity with the poor or on risk-taking. Only one of the 1960s books she reviewed dealt directly with these topics. The bulk of the literature published immediately after Vatican II dealt more with questions of internal renewal, a focus that continued through the mid-1970s (Kolmer, 1984:49–55).

Why, then, do the current documents of religious congregations exhibit such a profound shift? One possible reason is that, during the past decade, there have been structural changes, both in the Church and in society at large, that have directly affected religious communities. Many women religious have moved from positions in congregational institutions to jobs as single individuals in parishes, dioceses, or secular organizations (Neal, 1984:28–29). In these new situations, they often experienced personally for the first time gender discrimination that blocked upward mobility (Heslin, 1983:6). The women so disadvantaged were able to compare their experiences with the opportunities for upward mobility that traditionally had been available in their own congregational institutions, as well as with the increased alternatives at least theoretically open to women in the larger U.S. society. Since many had formerly had administrative responsibility in schools or hospitals, they were less apt to blame personal failings for their difficulties, and more likely to be aware of system-generated causes. Women religious are also members of an extended network—one of the oldest "good old girl" networks in the country (Thompson, 1986:288). They thus had access to a large number of acquaintances with whom they could share their experiences. This increasing identification with the oppression of others as a result of changes in one's own occupational environment corresponds to a recently advanced sociological model for the rise and spread of gender consciousness (Chafetz and Dworkin, 1986).

Interviews which I have conducted with women religious in a wide variety of ministries support this hypothesis. Religious working as pastoral associates or directors of religious education expressed a greater dissatisfaction with their jobs. They were the only respondents who spontaneously mentioned plans to leave their employment because of this dissatisfaction. The pastoral ministers and those in diocesan chancery positions were also the only ones to volunteer the information that their goals and expectations as new employees had not been met. In contrast, the respondents who had continued to work in congregational institutions—whether as subordinates or as supervisors—expressed far less dissatisfaction.

The women religious occupying positions outside their congregations were less protected by written contracts or by evaluation and grievance procedures. Indeed, many served at the whim of their employers. Their occupational situation was similar to powerless occupations in the "secondary labor market" often held by poor and marginalized groups in the larger society (Doeringer and Piore, 1971). The experience may have led to the feelings of solidarity with the poor expressed in the LCWR documents. Thus, while participation in the various justice and peace movements of the 1960s and 1970s may have alerted them to the oppression of the poor and minority groups, and while their commitment to the Vatican II documents and papal encyclicals on justice and peace may have legitimated their concern, it was often their personal experiences of discrimination while working in overseas and non-traditional ministries that fostered their actual identification with these groups.

The Role of Ideology

While purely organizational explanations for the extroverted focus of religious congregations of women in the United States might cite the explanations given in the preceding section, these cannot be considered sufficient. The powerful forces of self-preservation that are dominant in declining organizations are not neutralized by the members' individual experiences of powerlessness and injustice. Indeed, a more organizationally rational response to discrimination would be to pull the members back into internal occupations. Rather than squander valuable, and increasingly scarce, human resources in outside positions, the organization could enhance its power, including its power to serve the poor, by utilizing the efforts of all its members to strengthen its own institutions. Recent attempts by other disadvantaged groups to patronize black-owned businesses, or to establish women's banks, illustrate this tactic. Organizational theory, therefore, can perhaps explain why religious communities began to have an extroverted focus in the late 1970s, but not why they neglected their own survival needs in the process. In de-emphasizing organizational imperatives, congregations appear to be motivated by a profound ideological stance that has shaped their priorities. Other researchers have studied the role of ideology in communal religious groups, and their findings may be helpful in uncovering further bases for the beliefs and values articulated in the congregational documents.

Religious congregations typically arose as small groups of individuals profoundly committed to the goals and ideals of a charismatic founder. Since the founder usually was trying to establish a utopian community whose basic values were in some way countercultural, the commitment of the members was constantly in danger of being eroded by the values of the surrounding secular society. Their emotional and psychological fervor was sustained by "communion"—which Kanter defines as "a feeling of unity and brotherhood [sic] necessary to maintain commitment"—and by devotion to the charismatic founder. Communion is notoriously ephemeral. As Veysey comments, "Unless there is strong unhesitating leadership . . . American individualist antinomianism soon begins to tear things asunder" (1973:273). During the founder's life, such leadership was available. Afterward, however, congregation members were faced with the crisis of "routinizing" their charismatically based communion (Weber, 1978:235–50). According to Zablocki (1980:289), routinization occurred in two ways. The first entailed the adoption of commitment techniques that have traditionally typified Roman Catholic monastic communities: enforced homogeneity of members, communal sharing and renunciation of private property, communal work, and regularized group contact allowing little time to be either alone or with outsiders. The experience of persecution, if it occurred, was also helpful, serving as a "vaccination" against the corrupting values of the larger society (Kanter, 1972:99–100).

There were profound costs attached to the adoption of these "community survival techniques," however. Researchers have agreed unanimously that they were potentially dangerous to the members' mental health. Veysey stated that "all monastic communities, no matter how enduring, pay a severe price in psychological terms for their success (1973:273)." Zablocki, too, noted that the tension involved in self-abnegation for the sake of group goals could lead to immaturity at best and to outright pathology at worst (Zablocki, 1980:326). The members of most of the congregations whose documents were analyzed for the LCWR Task Force on Religious Life have repudiated the psychologically destructive, rigid commitment systems of their past and adopted Zablocki's second alternative: becoming an apostolic association (Zablocki, 1980:289; see also Futrell, 1986:16 and Wittberg, 1985:167). In an association, "members retain virtually full personal autonomy and the commune becomes a co-operative venture in support of its members' individual self-interests. Many of these associations last for two or three decades, *but rarely are they able to produce a second generation*" (Zablocki, 1980:289. Italics mine).

In an *apostolic* association, members do not work for their individual self-interests, but rather for the mission of the group. Thus, there is still a need for them to be willing, at times, to subordinate their personal goals to congregational ones. A fundamental discrepancy, therefore, exists between the autonomy that is characteristic of the associational form and the commitment mechanisms that continue to be necessary for the congregation's apostolic goals. To the extent that a congregation's stated ministry remains countercultural—and a preferential option for the poor is indeed countercultural—a shared world of subjective meaning is assumed. These shared beliefs and values continue to be in danger of erosion unless some of the very practices that conflict with members' autonomy are used to strengthen them. Many congregations have resisted the idea of imposing ministerial or geographic uniformity upon their members, or even planning in advance for future staffing needs, because such actions are seen as contrary to respect for the individual. As women religious increasingly move out into individualized occupations and living arrangements, a certain attenuation of their ties to the congregation often occurs, with professional and secular values, commitments and beliefs assuming a more salient role. The congregation thus becomes less able to require of its members those actions or behaviors which are needed to maintain its own existence or that of its particular ministries.

Consciously or unconsciously, religious communities have chosen the prospect of decline and extinction rather than risk a return to the psychologically destructive group survival mechanisms of the past. It could be argued that this preference is the reason for their neglect of organizational needs in favor of individual autonomy, despite the danger to organizational survival (Kanter, 1972), and despite the increasing evidence of congregational decline. Within the next decade, many communities will have fewer than ten per cent of their members under the age of fifty.[2] Even those orders that can be confident of having the funds to care for a membership almost totally composed of aging and retired women must still ask whether they might not pass some threshold point in their median age beyond which young people will no longer enter. Many congregations may have reached this point already. The prospect of the demise of a life-style in which they have invested so much creates in the members a state of profound "cognitive dissonance" (Festinger, 1956). Rather than endure the tension involved in facing the prospect of extinction, religious congregations may avoid the topic altogether and focus on "outside" issues. In addition, the blurring of boundaries evidenced in solidarity with other groups and in working for the empowerment of the oppressed may give women religious a sense of belonging and offer more permanent goals. Looked at in this light, the extroverted focus of religious communities may be a result, not only of historical and social circumstances impinging on the congregations from the outside, but also of an internal reluctance to face the seeming incompatibility between the actions necessary for the organization's survival and the perceived needs of the members for personal autonomy and psychological health.

To point out that the profoundly held beliefs and values articulated in the communities' documents may have arisen in part from such mundane roots as the members' individual experiences of discrimination in the labor market, or from their feeling of helplessness when confronting the prospect of their congregation's extinction, is not to denigrate these beliefs or to diminish their beauty or authenticity. Berger speaks of "a Kantian sort of Protestant Ethic" entailed in the ascetic notion that only those moral beliefs that arise without any environmental support or personal self-interest are worthy ones (1981:184). "False consciousness, in this context, then, is the result of an inability or a reluctance or a failure to risk the credibility of one's beliefs . . . by passing them through the fire of sociological analysis, which constitutes a critique of their contextual sources and consequences" (Berger, 1981:178). As long as religious communities are unwilling or unable to examine these "contextual sources and consequences," they will not have truly chosen them. Whether their ultimate choice is to accept their gradual decline or actively to seek new growth, congregations will have to adopt specific strategies and avoid specific dangers.

Strategies for Growth and Survival

Some communities may choose strategies to arrest and reverse their decline. To survive any organization must normally provide some resource that is needed in its environment. Religious congregations that wish to avoid extinction must first establish the fact of their value and usefulness, in order both to assure a continued supply of material and personnel resources from the larger society, and also to legitimate their own members' continued commitment and willingness to sacrifice personal needs for the good of the group. Historians of religious congregations have long documented the contributions their members have made. In the past, however, this research was not made public. Almost no mention appears in the standard histories of the American Church concerning the contributions of women religious (Kolmer, 1981:127; Schneider, 1986), and women's studies research has been similarly lacking in attention to women's religious congregations (Thompson, 1986; Wallace, 1975). As a result, potentially supportive publics in the Church and among women are less aware than they might be of the value of religious communities. Thompson points out that

> . . . the exclusion of sisters from studies not focused directly on them, or on the Church, persists almost unabated. It would be hard to conceive of analyses of social welfare work, for instance, that did not devote considerable attention to Jane Addams and other women settlement workers. Yet even feminist accounts of this kind tend to ignore the fact that virtually all the efforts of Addams and her peers were preceded (often by several decades) by similar ones on the part of nuns. Few Americans realize, either, that sisters were the first in this country to provide training and education for the deaf or that, long before Prudence Crandall was pilloried for trying to open a school for Blacks in Connecticut, sisters were making similar efforts in places like Baltimore, Louisville, and Charleston   (Thompson, 1986:285).

Women religious have had experiences that other women have only recently begun to acquire—in centuries-old networks and mentoring systems, in ideals of sisterhood, in role modeling of leadership and responsibility, and, most recently, in attempts at collaborative, non-hierarchical government (Thompson, 1986:288–89; see also Ewens, 1981:107). Only when both the members of congregations and the surrounding society are convinced that religious congregations have unique and valuable contributions to make, is it likely that they will mobilize to ensure the necessary input of money and personnel. At the present time, however, many congregations are inadequately equipped to publicize their contributions. There is a lack of "marketing research" to discover exactly what the image of women religious is among various populations, what is inaccurate about this image, and what techniques can be used to change it. While individual congregations may have used non-random samples of the personnel or clients of a given institution to investigate some of these questions, the results of these studies have not been widely shared (Blasi and Cuneo, 1987). Communities are also relatively inexperienced in using the media to present to the society at large a coherent picture of who they are and what they do.

It is even more important that, other than a single chapter in a 1979 Knights of Columbus study (Fee *et al.*, 1981), there has been no national, scientific research published on the desires and needs of young, potential members. Only 12 per cent of Catholic women between the ages of 14 and 30 report that they have thought seriously about having a vocation to religious life, as compared to 22 percent of Catholic men (Wemhoff *et al.*, 1981:8). Little is known of the reasons for this lack of interest. Conducting a randomly sampled, scientific survey of young Catholic women would be expensive and time-consuming, but it may be essential if the communities that choose the alternative of striving for growth are to learn where and how to offer the option of religious life to potential members.

Finally, an investigation of congregations with growing membership is needed. In the past, it has often been asserted by conservative writers that less liberal religious communities are growing while the "radical" ones are, deservedly, declining (Hitchcock, 1984). While research by the Sister Formation Conference disproves this assertion, it contains few concrete prescriptions for growth other than that congregations establish formation committees (Wemhoff *et al.*, 1981:27). Congregations that choose a strategy of promoting growth will have to investigate whether or not there are additional tactics that can be adopted. Existing studies indicate, for example, that it is necessary to eliminate any unspoken norms that prevent women religious from personally inviting individuals to share their lives (Greeley, 1972). The institutional turmoil of the 1960s and 1970s often inhibited congregational members from encouraging women to join their congregations. Religious congregations may also have adopted the values of mainstream U.S. society, in which the only persons who actively promulgate their religious views are members of lower-class sects with whom middle-class Americans do not want to be identified (Brinkerhoff and Mackie, 1986:154). Given the importance of active personal contact and encouragement in the vocation decisions of potential members, a reluctance of members to become personally involved would be detrimental to any congregation that chooses actively to promote membership growth.

Congregations adopting the strategy of fostering their organizational growth would also have to avoid the pitfalls that this strategy entails. It must not be forgotten that some of the mechanisms for promoting group survival operate at the psychological expense of the members. Techniques have been suggested for how communities can support simultaneously both group and individual needs (Futrell, 1986; Wittberg, 1985). Since research shows that personal autonomy is a desirable characteristic in communities that wish to attract new members (Wemhoff *et al.*, 1981:27–28), care must be taken to ensure that the subordination of autonomy to the group does not destroy it altogether.

Redemptive "Letting Go"

An alternative choice for communities stems from the belief held by some religious that congregations cannot, and should not, return to the numbers and life-style of their most recent growth period in the 1950s. Cada *et al.* (1979) hold that religious life is currently undergoing one of its cyclic moments of death and subsequent resurrection in a new, and yet to be determined, form. Each past transition period was linked to profound changes in the economic and social organization of the surrounding society. The coming of the post-industrial era may mandate a similar transformation in religious life that cannot be stemmed by any one "old style" attempt at membership recruitment. Adherents of this perspective might argue that religious communities are facing not only death, but also resurrection. If the new form toward which a congregation is moving does not seem to conform to the accepted model of religious life, neither did any of the preceding models when they were new (Cada *et al.*, 1979:31). Holding on to outdated structures might actually hinder the growth toward which the Spirit is calling religious life.

Instead of attempting to perpetuate their present organizational existence, religious congregations choosing the second strategy might foster and even imitate the emerging forms. It would be helpful to locate and investigate these alternate religious groups to discover if aspects of their life-styles meet the needs of contemporary society. My own, decidedly unscientific, impression is that emerging forms of religious life display four characteristics: they serve the poor almost exclusively; they offer the option of temporary affiliation (often in connection with a core group that is permanently committed);

they are open both to married and to single men and women; and they demand an intense communal prayer life. Research is needed to determine whether this preliminary impression is in fact the case. Should these characteristics prove to be the identifying charism of the next model of religious life, existing congregations will have to decide whether or not to adopt them. Adopting the more intense life-style of many emerging groups is likely to prove unpalatable to older congregations which have become accustomed to a looser, less demanding form of associational membership. By definition, the newly-founded communities are still in their "communion" phase, perhaps still committed to a living charismatic leader. Charisma supercedes the authority of rules, of democracy, and especially of the followers' own autonomy. Thus charismatic leaders are likely to appear dictatorial to outsiders (Weber, 1978:227). Older, more associational congregations may well resist submitting to such perceived authoritarianism, even if the alternative is organizational decline and death. Chittister points out that over sixty-five per cent of the religious communities founded before the beginning of the current cycle of religious life have since ceased to exist (1983:30). There is no reason to assume that the mortality rate of present congregations will be any less, once the transition to a new model has occurred.

While the documents of U.S. religious congregations indicate an awareness of their situation as declining organizations, they do not deal explicitly with the possibility of their actual death. Yet, as Cada and Chittister point out, the past cycles of religious life indicate that, for many orders, extinction is a strong probability. And, of the minority that remain alive, most will continue only at a level of "minimal functioning" (Chittister, 1983:30). Such a future may be part of an inevitable and natural progression. As Cada states: "A central insight of the myth of original sin is that humankind is not capable of sustained development; breakdown and disintegration are ever-recurring manifestations of the human condition . . . These bleak realities should be embraced with humble acceptance . . . and faith-filled hope that the Lord will, in time, resurrect life-giving initiative from the death-dealing processes of breakdown" (Cada *et al.*, 1979:76). The demise of contemporary congregations and their institutions is occurring, however, at a time when American society is shaped by large bureaucratic organizations to an extent unimaginable at any of the prior transition periods. Since bureaucratic domination effectively stifles innovation (Perrow, 1986:188), the emerging religious groups may find themselves at a severe disadvantage *vis a vis* pressures by governmental, economic and ecclesial bureaucracies to preserve their status quo. These large-scale organizations are also male-dominated. Women religious may be moving away from maintaining their own institutionalized forms of power at precisely the time when other women are laboring to construct equivalent resources in order to counter organized male domination.

Conclusions

It is beyond the scope of this paper to suggest which of these two strategies—growth and survival, or letting go—religious congregations should adopt. Its purpose has been instead to use some of the existing research on declining organizations, especially that on declining communal religious groups, to investigate the situation facing communities of women religious today. Based on the findings of this research, certain conclusions can be drawn, both on the sources as well as on the probable consequences of current organizational behaviors in religious congregations. Their extroversion of focus has been explained as a result of particular events in societal and Church history, as well as of individual experiences of discrimination on the part of many women religious. Their reluctance to consider and plan for the survival of their congregations has been traced to the cognitive dissonance involved in the perceived incompatibility between such survival mechanisms and the psychological health and autonomy of the members. Together, these explanations may account for the atypical patterns of outward focus in a declining organization.

Communal religious life-styles will not disappear from the United States. American society historically has been a fertile ground for such groups, both in traditional denominations and in newly formed "cults." Catholic history also indicates that organized religious life has been an integral part of our own heritage. The specific form of this lifestyle, however, depends upon the steps taken today—both within and outside the Catholic Church, in present congregations, in emerging groups, and among isolated individuals. The study of the roots and results of these actions can help the actors to choose their futures with greater self-awareness. It is hoped that this paper will provide one of the steps in that direction.

ENDNOTES

1. Needless to say, I do not mean to imply that religious women do not experience these tensions while the men do, merely that the men's statements articulate this tension, while the women's do not.

2. This estimation is extrapolated from several sources: 1983-4 statistical information for the diocese of Cleveland, nationwide figures reported in the Cincinnati Post on June 25, 1986, and the membership projections of my own religious community.

BIBLIOGRAPHY

Berger, Bennett M. *The Survival of a Counterculture*. Berkeley: University of California Press, 1981.

Blasi, Anthony and Michael W. Cuneo. *Issues in the Sociology of Religion*. New York: Garland, 1987.

Brinkerhoff, Merlin B. and Marlene M. Mackie. "The Applicability of Social Distance for Religious Research: An Exploration," *Review of Religious Research*, 28 (1986) 151–167.

Cada, Lawrence, *et al*. *Shaping the Coming Age of Religious Life*. New York: Seabury Press, 1979.

Chafetz, Janet S. and Anthony G. Dworkin. *Female Revolt: Women's Movements in World and Historical Perspective*. Totowa, N.J.: Rowman and Allanheld, 1986.

Chittister, Joan. *Women, Ministry and the Church*. New York: Paulist Press, 1983.

Colgan, S. M. "Nuns and the Women's Movement," *Origins*, 4 (No. 38, 1975) 594–597.

Doeringer, Peter B. and Michael J. Piore. *Internal Labor Markets and Manpower Analysis*. Lexington, Mass: D.C. Heath, 1971.

Downs, Anthony. *Inside Bureaucracy*. Boston: Little and Brown, 1967.

Ewens, Mary. "The Leadership of Nuns in Immigrant Catholicism," in R. Ruether and R. S. Keller, eds. *Women and Religion in America*, Vol. I. New York: Harper and Row, 1981.

Fee, Joan, *et al*. *Young Catholics in the United States and Canada*. New York: Sadlier, 1981.

Festinger, Leon. *When Prophecy Fails*. Minneapolis: University of Minnesota Press, 1956.

Futrell, John C. "Evaluating Apostolic Religious Communities," *Human Development*, 7 (No. 2, 1986) 12–18.

Greeley, Andrew. *The Catholic Priest in the U.S.: Sociological Investigations*. National Opinion Research Center Study for the U.S. Catholic Conference, Washington, D.C., 1972.

Heslin, Julia A. *In Transition: A Study of Women Religious Administrators in Non-traditional Roles*. Ph.D. Dissertation, Fordham University, 1983.

Hitchcock, James. "Vocations Holding Up in Traditional Communities," *Catholic Universe Bulletin*, Cleveland (July 6, 1984) 10, 1984.

Kanter, Rosabeth M. *Commitment and Community: Communes and Utopias in Sociological Perspective*. Cambridge, Mass: Harvard University Press, 1972.

Kanter, Rosabeth M. and Barry Stein. *Life in Organizations: Workplaces as People Experience Them*. New York: Basic Books, 1979.

Kolmer, Elizabeth. "Catholic Women Religious and Women's History: A Survey of the Literature," in Rosemary Ruether and Rosemary S. Keller. *Women and Religion in America,* Vol. II. New York: Harper and Row, 1981.

Religious Women in the U.S. Wilmington, Del.: Michael Glazier, 1984.

Lipset, Seymour M. *Political Man: The Social Bases of Politics.* Garden City, N.J.: Doubleday, 1960.

Neal, Marie Augusta. *Catholic Sisters in Transition: From the 1960's to the 1980's.* Wilmington, Del.: Michael Glazier, 1984.

Perrow, Charles. *Complex Organizations: A Critical Essay.* 3rd ed. New York: Random House, 1986.

Reed, Theodore L. "Organizational Change in the American Foreign Service, 1925–1965: The Utility of Cohort Analysis," *American Sociological Review,* 30 (1978) 843–861.

Sarther, Catherine, *et al. Vocation Decisions.* Chicago: National Sisters Vocation Conference, 1983.

Schneider, M. "The Transformation of American Women Religious," Working Paper Series #17. paper #1. Cushwa Center for the Study of American Catholicism, University of Notre Dame, 1986.

Schoenherr, Richard A. and Lawrence Young. "The Demographic Transition in Religious Organizations: A Preliminary Reconnaissance." Paper presented at the 1986 Association for the Sociology of Religion meeting, New York, NY, 1986.

Sills, David. *The Volunteers: Means and Ends in a National Organization.* Glencoe, Ill: Free Press, 1957.

Thompson, Margaret. "Discovering Foremothers: Sisters, Society, and the American Catholic Experience," *U.S. Catholic Historian,* 5 (Nos. 3 and 4, 1986) 273–290.

Veysey, Laurence. *The Communal Experience.* Chicago: University of Chicago Press, 1973.

Wallace, Ruth A. "Bringing Women In: Marginality in the Churches," *Sociological Analysis,* 36 (1975) 291–303.

Weber, Max. *Max Weber: Selections in Translation.* W. G. Runciman, ed. Cambridge: Cambridge University Press, 1978.

Wemhoff, Gertrude, *et al. Women in Religious Communities.* Chicago: National Sisters Vocation Conference, 1981.

Wittberg, Patricia. "Transformations in Religious Commitment," *Review for Religious* (March-April, 1985) 161–70.

Zablocki, Benjamin. *The Joyful Community: An Account of the Bruderhof.* Baltimore: Penguin, 1971.

Alienation and Charisma: A Study of Contemporary American Communes. New York: Free Press, 1980.

REFLECTION QUESTIONS

1. Does a religious congregation as an organization differ from an industrial corporation, a pharmaceutical company, an organization established to raise funds for a humanitarian purpose, or an internally-focused commune? If so, how?

2. The crux of this analysis of organizational life cycles and religious congregations as well as a significant amount of research done by congregational leadership focuses on *quantitative and rational* indicators of organizational vitality, such as size, median age, entrance data and degree of financial security. In the years since Vatican II, have there been *qualitative* signs of vitality in your particular congregation? What are they and what do they suggest about the revitalization of religious life?

3. The paper suggests that the extroverted focus, willingness to risk, blurring of boundaries, and active identification with the poor, oppressed and marginalized on the part of U.S. women religious may be dysfunctional for organizational survival. Do you agree with this interpretation? If so, why? If not, why not?

RECOMMENDED READING

Blasi, Anthony and Michael W. Cuneo. *Issues in the Sociology of Religion. A Bibliography.* New York: Garland Publishing, Inc., 1987.

Thompson, Margaret Susan. *The Yoke of Grace: American Nuns and Social Change, 1808–1917.* New York: Oxford University Press, 1988.

Women of Presence, Women of Praise

Sheila Carney, RSM

At the fifth time, there was ceaseless activity. Fluttering like the wings of the dove, humming like the murmur of the dragonfly, swimming like the darting golden fish, wriggling like the lithe serpent, leaping like the flashing deer, surging like the mighty lion. And it was very good.

In the years following the Second Vatican Council, congregations of United States women religious have experienced significant change. One such change is manifested in the growing movement toward collaboration that can be seen in the relationships of congregational members with one another and with other persons and groups.

This paper reflects on Mary of Nazareth as a model for such collaboration. Beginning with a consideration of the implications of traditional Marian devotion and moving to reflection on the story of the Visitation, it suggests that we may find in the interaction of Mary with Elizabeth, a paradigm for collaborative activity.

Against this background, collaboration as experienced by members of religious congregations is regarded as an expression of the spirit of Mary and Elizabeth and their story is proposed as a new "emblem" for United States women religious.

Most religious communities of women have encouraged in their members a devotion to Mary of Nazareth. In pre-Vatican II days we all bore her name and her feast days were times of special celebration among us. She was presented to us as a model, par excellence—serene in all circumstances, secure in the possession and exercise of her preternatural gifts. Her pictures and her statues smiled on us benignly in classrooms, hospitals and convents. Her rosary clicked at our sides, signaling our approach to generations of students, gratefully forewarned.

But gradually our unquestioning devotion to this woman, who was sometimes more plaster goddess than friend, began to fade. During the years of renewal, when religious life has been fraught with questions and when congregations, as well as their individual members, face the none too serene experience of transition and change, Mary seems remote and unappealing—more a symbol of "the way we were" than of our present reality. In the midst of doubt, uncertainty, personal and institutional convulsion, it seems futile to invoke one who has been depicted as a stranger to uncertainty or conflict. She has nothing to say to us, nothing to offer. Or so we believed.

This experience of alienation has been further aggravated by a device commonly used in devotional literature: the comparison of Mary, Mother of God and Virgin of Virgins, with Eve, representative of all other women. Beginning with the writings of Tertullian and Origen and continuing through the centuries to our present day, the comparison of Mary with Eve has been a popular one, described by Marina Warner as a "specially graceful analogue, architectural in its harmoniousness, a great vault thrown over the history of Western attitudes toward women, the whole mighty span resting on Eve the temptress on one side, and Mary the paragon on the other."[1] The comparison is a negative one, slighting similarities between the two, emphasizing the pre-eminence of one over the other, and increasing for "real" women a sense of inferiority and hopeless yearning.

The writers who employed this device did so with a great deal of creativity. The central image of Mary and Eve remains the same through the centuries but the trappings are widely varied and imaginative. Sensory images are among the most common. Mary is characterized as the bright eye that illumined the world while Eve's eye is dim.[2] Satan crept into Eve's heart through her sense of hearing and it was through this same sense that Jesus entered the body of Mary.[3] Images of food are found as well. Mary gives us access to the heavenly banquet. Eve satisfies her craving for the apple and we are punished by an eternal fast.[4]

Another significant aspect of this comparison is emphasis on the fact that both women were virgins who conceived as a result of intercourse with a supernatural being. The offspring of Eve was disobedience and death, while Mary brought forth the savior of humankind.[5] Some sense of balance seems to be restored when a virgin's acquiescence to God's word repairs the damage inflicted by a virgin's disobedience.

This brief and incomplete sampler [6] of the comparison of Mary and Eve offers support to the assertion that Marian devotion has developed in ways that are denigrating to women.[7] The entire body of literature may be summarized by two quotations borrowed from Marina Warner's work on the myth and cult of Mary. A fifth century poet wrote of Eve:

> I am Eve, wife of noble Adam; it was I who violated Jesus in the past; it was I who robbed my children of heaven; it is I by right who should have been crucified. I had heaven at my command; evil the bad choice that shamed me; evil the punishment for my crime that has aged me; alas, my hand is not pure. It was I who plucked the apple; it went past the narrow of my gullet; as long as they live in daylight women will not cease from folly on account of that. There would be no ice in any place; there would be no bright windy winter; there would be no hell, there would be no grief, there would be no terror but for me.[8]

In the eyes of the writers who compared Mary and Eve, and many others like them, all women share in the identification of Eve as sinner, thief, seductress, terrorist. Mary, on the other hand

> had no peer
> Either in our first mother or in all women
> Who were to come. But alone of all her sex
> She pleased the Lord.[9]

Generations of women have been encouraged by the Church and enjoined by the customs of their religious congregations to model their lives on the example of Mary. Many of these women, however, have viewed this encouragement against the backdrop of the dichotomous attitude toward women described above. The Mary they find pictured here is not friend but goad, not inspiration but unattainable ideal, not companion but antithesis. Mary and Eve, Sarah and Hagar, Rachel and Leah, Mary and Martha— Scripture and tradition offer us repeated examples of women competing for attention, resenting one another's choices, vying for ascendancy. These images of woman against woman create a paradigm of alienation that must be redeemed if we are to reclaim Mary and the other women in our ancestry.

In her article, "Women's Center: Incarnational Spirituality," Catherine Osimo describes a shift in emphasis from descending to ascending christologies. A descending christology takes as its starting point the divinity of Jesus and interprets the life, mission, and significance of Jesus from that perspective. The historical Jesus provides a focus for ascending christologies, allowing us to reflect on our own human experience by contemplating Jesus who was human as we are and who came to teach us about God and the nature of God's Reign.[10] Perhaps a similar shift is occurring in mariology as women today seek to reappropriate Mary—not for purposes of traditional devotion, but in hopes of establishing a relationship of kinship, of sisterhood.

Marian teaching that emphasized Mary's sinlessness, freedom from temptation, superiority to all other women, unquestioning willingness to be the handmaid of the Lord, her mysterious ability to be both virgin and mother—all these bear the marks of a descending mariology. "Mother inviolate; Mother undefiled; Seat of Wisdom; Mirror of Justice; Vessel of Singular Devotion; Tower of David; House of Gold; Queen of angels, prophets, patriarchs and apostles; Queen assumed into heaven"—all these invocations from the Litany of Loretto describe a Mary who is most assuredly above us, who gazes down on us, who descends to our level. It is interesting to note, in this context, that the only exercise of papal infallibility since its definition in Vatican Council I has been in the proclamation of the doctrine of the Assumption.

As with christology, an ascending mariology is rooted in human experience.[11] It begins when women, as women, confront the biblical texts dealing with Mary's life and examine them from a feminist perspective—that is, from a perspective that "critically but lovingly rejects relationships and structures based on stereotyped roles of dominance and submission,"[12] that calls all persons to an awareness of their uniqueness,[13] and that sees men and women together as the norm for authentic humanity.[14] Viewing Mary through the prism of our own human experience and the experience and reflection of others opens the way for an appreciation of her as person rather than paragon.

Elisabeth Schüssler Fiorenza, in her book *Bread Not Stone*, suggests a fourfold hermeneutic to be employed in arriving at a feminist interpretation of Scripture and tradition.[15] This same process may be helpful in our quest for an ascending mariology.

A hermeneutic of suspicion reminds us that our Scriptures reflect a patriarchal culture and are androcentric in nature. As such, they are written and interpreted to serve patriarchal purposes. A hermeneutic of proclamation insists that texts which are oppressive in nature and which support patriarchal interests must not be preached in the assembly. In the same spirit, women are called to search the teaching and tradition that surround Mary, to discover how and when these teachings are used to denigrate women, and to repudiate the perpetuation of such teaching. The Mary/Eve dichotomy must be rejected as well as interpretations of biblical texts characterizing Mary as subservient, blindly obedient, superior, sexless.

A hermeneutic of remembrance calls us as women to reflect on a history that extends backward in time to the stories of women who lived at the center of the apostolic community, claiming a discipleship of equals and acting in the power of the Spirit.[16] The ability to remember actively flowers in the hermeneutic of creative actualization and encourages women to reimage and reconstruct biblical texts employing all the creative expressions at our disposal—drama, dance, music, ritual, art. Such recreation enables us to participate in the lives of the women remembered, to experience their power and their potential. These are transformative, liberating moments.

Remembrance and creative actualization invite us to reconnect with Mary, to strip away the accretions of centuries of male dominated teaching about her, to reenter her experience. In doing so we discover a woman whose life contains vestiges of our own questions, our own struggles and our own hopes. Mary, the woman of Nazareth, becomes available to us again.

If we abandon the punishing comparison of Mary and Eve and turn our creative imaginations to the Scriptures, we find in the Gospel of Luke the inviting story of the Visitation (Luke 1:39–56). Here we encounter two women in a warm and welcoming relationship, evocative rather than antagonistic, who discover in their shared experience a call not to competition but to collaboration.

This rich and gentle passage provides much food for reflection. For me, however, one question raised by Luke's story has become central. The journey from Nazareth to Ain Karim, as I have personally experienced it, is a trip arduous even by modern conveyance, as it traverses miles of forbidding territory. The question is simply this: Why did Mary do it? Why did she make such a difficult journey to visit Elizabeth?

In response to this question, traditional answers suggest that she fled Nazareth in order to conceal her pregnancy or that she traveled to Judea in order to assist with the birth and care of Elizabeth's expected child. Raymond Brown focuses on Luke's description of Mary going "with haste" (Luke 1:39) and concludes that the abruptness of her departure was to prevent her pregnancy from being discovered.[17] Other authors, Patricia Noone and Carroll Stuhlmueller among them, write that Mary hastened to Elizabeth in order to assist her older cousin.[18]

These answers fall short of adequacy. The text states that Mary stayed in Ain Karim about three months, and that she returned home, then, at the point when her own pregnancy would just have begun to "bloom." She does not seem to be present for the birth of John.

There is yet a third possible explanation for Mary's hasty journey. Perhaps she sought Elizabeth's support and confidence. In considering this proposition we might ask why Mary chose not to confide in Joseph or in family and friends in Nazareth. The answer lies, I believe, in the fact that Mary knew, from the words of the angel, that Elizabeth had been similarly favored by God with the promise of a long awaited, yet unexpected, child. Instinctively, she felt drawn to Elizabeth as one whose life experience matched her own, whose life had been suddenly and inexplicably touched by God. Elizabeth would *know,* would understand the overwhelming newness that suffused her life. So Mary reached out to her cousin knowing that she was similarly blessed. And Elizabeth responded.

My own appreciation of the story of Mary and Elizabeth has been greatly enhanced by reflecting on Ranier Maria Rilke's poem "The Visitation of the Virgin" alongside the biblical text. It is Rilke who has provided insight into a second question: What transpired between these two women at their meeting? What breathed between them?

> She still breathed easily at first,
> but climbing sometimes she was already
> aware of her wonderful body,
> and there she stood, breathing, upon the high
>
> hills of Judea. But not the land,
> her abundance was spread about her;

as she went she felt one could never exceed
the bigness she was feeling now.

And she craved to lay her hand
on the other body, that was further on.
And the women swayed toward one another
and touched each other's dress and hair.

Each, filled with her holy possession,
sought protection of her kinswoman.
Ah, the savior in her was still in flower,
though the Baptist in her cousin's womb
already leapt in transports of joy.[19]

What do we see in this portrait of Mary and Elizabeth reaching out to one another? It is a model, I think, for the kind of collaboration and bonding that we see among women today. Women who have been touched by life in similar ways, positive and negative, are finding and supporting and encouraging one another. It is the kind of mutual enrichment that Paul sought with the Church at Rome: "I long to see you . . . that through it we may be mutually encouraged by each other's faith, both yours and mine" (Romans 1:11–12). It is the sense of mutual awe that Rilke describes when he says that Mary "craved" the sight and feel of Elizabeth and that "each filled with her holy possession sought the protection of her kinswoman." The women pictured here know their own gifts and the gifts of the other. Each knows, and celebrates the unique, yet collaborative, roles they play in the unfolding of God's plan. Each knows that this shared experience marks the beginning of an entirely new order. For these women are pregnant with more than their sons and the words that they speak to one another are words of revolution: the rich and powerful will be frustrated; the poor and lowly will be raised up; the sons of the virgin and the barren one will initiate reversals of the world's standards.

Reflection on the self-aware and confident spirit evident in the Mary of the Visitation can provoke an interest in recent discussions concerning the use of the term "virgin." Moving away from a strictly physiological definition, Elizabeth A. Johnson describes the virgin as one whose personal power center wells up, who is autonomous, "one-in-herself," who is free from male domination or control.[20] Even more pertinent to this discussion is the realization that the angel announced to Zechariah the news of John's impending birth while the coming birth of Jesus is revealed directly to Mary. In bypassing Joachim and Joseph, both men who would have been expected to stand in a position of dominance over Mary, Luke is emphasizing the emergence of an entirely new order.[21]

In the story of the Visitation we find a Mary very different from the one who smiles benignly from the height of her pedestal. She is remarkably like ourselves with no models of her own to follow, no programs to help her deal with her situation, no groups or institutions to show her the way. There was only her cousin Elizabeth and the unshakable conviction that God was the source of the upheaval in her life. She was continually thrown back on her own resources, her own creativity, to find the support she needed to convince others of what she *knew* to be true.

We see in Mary, not a woman who is maddeningly prescient, but one who had a brief, but startlingly clear, revelation of who she was, in herself and before God. She immediately affirmed that revelation by setting out to visit Elizabeth. But then she lived year after year in darkness and apparent contradiction—pondering, trusting, waiting, struggling to understand. Elizabeth declared her blessed in her ability to believe in God's promises and she has been called the perfect disciple—the one who believed the word of God and acted upon it.[22] But this ability to trust God's word and keep it was balanced by her ability to believe first in herself, and then to make this trusting confidence the basis of her collaboration with others. This image of Mary as one who struggles with life as we do belongs to an ascending mariology. "Mary who lived with uncertainty, Disciple who struggled to communicate your beliefs, Friend who trusted the experience of others, Minister who knew yourself as a channel of God's life"—these are the names by which we might invoke her now. And our request is not "pray for us" but "walk with us."

The same "landscape" traversed by Mary from secure knowledge and appreciation for her personal uniqueness to the desire to collaborate, to the conviction that, through God's presence in this process, the world can be changed, is a paradigm for the territory traversed by U.S. women religious in the years since Vatican Council II. Our own experience and the documents upon which these papers are based give ample evidence of this fact. Part of the Council's mandate to religious congregations was the revivification of founding visions. Individual congregations began, with energy and enthusiasm, the process of rediscovering their uniqueness, their distinctive features, their personal characteristics. Archives were searched, histories scrutinized, primary sources revisited. We emerged from this process with a renewed appreciation for our founders' intent and a determination to make it operative in our day. We were invigorated and strengthened for mission. We felt a new confidence that manifested itself in a certainty about our place in the Church and in the "world."

The movement toward individuality among congregations was mirrored by a similar process among the members who were encouraged to identify and develop personal gifts. The document prepared by the LCWR Task Force on Religious Life for the Fifth Inter-American Conference on Religious Life names religious life as a "medium within which the individual woman is facilitated in personal growth toward freedom, an activity which in itself exemplifies the liberating activity of the Gospel" (Appendix, p. 179). The values of conformity and legislated commonality faded before a kaleidoscope of persons rich with interests, talents and creativity. Individuality found expression in dress, life-style and ministry. Similarly, the paper "An Exploratory Content Analysis of Major Themes Present in Selected Documents of United States Women Religious" reports that the congregational documents surveyed evidence a movement toward participatory government (p. 185) through collegial decision making and collaborative group process (p. 189). Also cited as values were diversity, unity and interdependence in local community life (p. 189). The LCWR paper for the Fifth Inter-American Conference names interdependence, collaboration, integration, bonding and cooperation as life-giving modes of relating (p. 175).

Individuality also marks our personal spirituality. The LCWR composite paper, "Regional Reflections on the Communitarian 'Face of God'," reveals a stunning variety in the ways U.S. women religious image and experience God, coupled with the assertion that we are beginning to trust that experience. No longer bound by common habit, common horarium, common recreation, we are seeking and naming deeper bonds of shared faith and shared vision.

The second part of the mandate to religious congregations required us to live in the spirit of the Gospels. In the years following the Council women religious delved into the Scriptures as never before. Congregations offered courses to their members; biblical studies became part of every formation program. If the first mandate underscored individuality, the second emphasized common sources, for the renewal of each congregation was deeply rooted in the Revelation to which all are heir.

The awareness of a common biblical heritage and of the shared struggle to deal with the changes introduced by the renewal process created a new sense of bonding among religious congregations. Competition and isolation gave way to a tremendous burgeoning of collaborative efforts at national and local levels.

On the local scene intercommunity formation programs were born and the competitive spirit that once existed among vocation directors gave way to programs for vocational discernment that are cooperatively sponsored. The emphasis shifted from an effort to recruit potential members for "my" community to identifying future ministers for the Church. Shared planning at the diocesan level resulted in joint staffing and intercongregational living. The religious congregations in the Dioceses of Pittsburgh, Greensburg and Altoona-Johnstown have recently established a personnel office that will serve members of all congregations in southwestern Pennsylvania. This development is just one example of the many results of post-conciliar collaboration. The content analysis of documents of LCWR member congregations reveals solidarity with the poor, responsible stewardship and the necessity of taking a corporate stance on peace and the arms race as significant themes (Appendix, p. 186). Many congregations have concretized these concerns by joining other church groups in organizations such as the Interfaith Center on Corporate Responsibility. Such a joint venture allows them to coalesce their individual investment power into a broader base from which to address, as stockholders, the policies of specific corporations. Still another form of collaboration can be seen in the number of programs for association or co-membership initiated by religious congregations. Vatican II asked religious women to reflect on their past. The result is a group of forward looking women who, having renewed themselves, are now forming bonds across congregational lines to become a force for renewal in the Church.

As we saw in the story of Mary and Elizabeth and its application to U.S. women religious, the phenomenon of collaboration among persons and groups who respect and nurture their own uniqueness has powerful consequences. The cousins of the biblical story blessed one another and rejoiced in God's favors to each. This attitude of blessing and calling forth, rather than defensiveness or competition, engendered the awareness that they were pregnant with the possibility for an entirely new world order.

The LCWR paper prepared for the Fifth Inter-American Conference on Religious Life is suffused with the spirit of Mary and Elizabeth. In this document, women religious claim the transformation of culture as integral to their mission (Appendix, p. 179). Named as feminist values with transforming potential are interdependence, bonding, collaboration, hospitality, enablement of persons (p. 175). Also seen as part of their role in the contemporary world are identification with the poor, countering societal values, shaping new visions and new values, critiquing social structures, institutions and systems (p. 176).

"An Exploratory Content Analysis of Major Themes Present in Selected Documents of United States Women Religious" lists seventeen elements apostolic women religious name as part of their self-identification. Of those seventeen, more than half reecho Mary's joyful outpouring of praise sung in response to God's great gifts to her and to her cousin. When women religious name themselves as persons called to justice and peace, standing in solidarity with the poor, seeking to live simple, responsible lives, desiring a global vision and consciousness, valuing collaboration as a means of creating a civilization of love—then they are espousing "Magnificat values."

In the story of Mary and Elizabeth we come to know two women who understood themselves to be singularly gifted, who felt new life stirring within, and who realized that these stirrings would eventually break forth into something brand new. We meet women who respected themselves and one another, who appreciated their uniqueness and who, therefore, felt no threat before the giftedness of the other. Gerard Manley Hopkins, in "The Wreck of the Deutschland," wrote "For I greet him the days I meet him and bless when I understand."[23] Mary and Elizabeth teach us the deeper wisdom that understanding need not be a condition of blessing. Comprehension and assent, while they are welcome dimensions of any relationship, cannot be prerequisites for affirming another. Rather, the ability to affirm and to bless issues from trust in the integrity of another's struggle to listen and to be responsive to the unique forces moving within. Collaboration then becomes possible when our individual struggles reveal a common energy and a common goal. Collaboration among women religious is rooted in the energy that emanates from the conviction of God's personal love coupled with the desire to see that love become the basis for all human interactions. With Mary and Elizabeth we have come to know the transforming power of this effort.

For centuries the story of the Exodus has been emblematic for individuals and groups bearing the burden of oppression and has supplied hope and courage for the journey toward freedom. Elisabeth Schüssler Fiorenza has called upon women to find in the Exodus saga incentives for moving out from the traditional structures of home and church, insofar as they are suffused with patriarchy, into an *ecclesia* of women—a gathering of women into a free, decision-making assembly of God's people, into a discipleship of equals.[24] Perhaps for United States women religious the journey from Egypt to *ecclesia* is through the energizing, heartening experience of the Visitation. Its spirit and its message may become focal points in the labor of birthing a new creation. Hints of that new creation have been described in this paper in the examples of collaborative efforts within and between congregations and with other persons and groups.

Integral to the Exodus story was the expectation that freedom from oppression, once achieved, was to be shared with others still in the condition of bondage. If it is true that something new is aborning among us, then the expectation of sharing this new life is incumbent upon us now as well. Strengthened by our own experience, we are called to make collaboration characteristic of our interactions with all persons and groups—even, or especially, those groups that bear a decidedly hierarchical stamp.

From the perspective of traditional devotion, Mary on her pedestal, unruffled and unruffling, was easy to love. Mary, secure enough in herself to be unthreatened by the gifts of another, daring in her conviction of her role in God's plan, conscious that she is called to be a disturber of the peace and to topple comfortable standards, is not quite so appealing. Just so with "the sisters." Self-effacing, serene and silently obedient, we were easy to admire. Convinced of the dignity and uniqueness of all persons, ready to expend our education and skills in the creation of a new reality, anxious to meet others in collaborative circles, we are, to many, confusing if not dismaying. And yet this is the call we hear.

Mary's conviction did not save her from times of uncertainty and darkness. Nor will ours. But, like Mary and Elizabeth, we hope that our ability to hold steadfastly to our convictions and to bless ourselves and others will carry us along. In identifying with the Visitation story, in claiming the spirit of Mary and Elizabeth, United States women religious may stand in our world as "women of prayer, women of presence, messengers of joy, and prophets of hope" (LCWR Document, Appendix, p. 175).

ENDNOTES

1. Marina Warner, *Alone of All Her Sex* (New York: Alfred A. Knoff, 1976) 60.

2. *Ibid.* 60

3. Hilda Graef, *Mary, A History of Doctrine and Devotion, Vol. 1* (New York: Sheed and Ward, 1963) 56.

4. *Ibid.* 207.

5. Warner 60.

6. For further reading on this theme see Warner and Graef cited above as well as Rosemary Radford Ruether, "Misogynism and Virginal Feminism in the Fathers of the Church," *Religion and Sexism: Images of Women in the Jewish and Christian Traditions* (New York: Simon and Schuster, 1974) 150–83.

7. Elizabeth A. Johnson, CSJ, "The Marian Tradition and the Reality of Women," *Horizons* (December, 1985) 121.

8. Warner 50.

9. *Ibid.* xvii.

10. Catherine Osimo, "Women's Center: Incarnational Spirituality." See page 9 of this volume.

11. *Ibid.*

12. "Defining Feminism," Sisters of Loretto, Nerinx, Kentucky.

13. Mary Giles, ed. *The Feminist Mystic and Other Essays on Women and Spirituality* (New York: The Crossroads Publishing Company, 1982) 36.

14. Johnson 116–135.

15. Elisabeth Schüssler Fiorenza, *Bread Not Stone, The Challenge of Feminist Biblical Interpretation* (Boston: Beacon Press, 1984) 15–22.

16. *Ibid.* 20.

17. Raymond E. Brown. *The Birth of the Messiah* (Garden City: Doubleday and Co., Inc., 1977) 331.

18. Patricia Noone, *Mary for Today* (Chicago: Thomas More Press, 1977) 54.
    Carroll Stuhlmueller. *The Gospel of Luke* (Collegeville: The Liturgical Press, 1964) 24.

19. M. D. Herter Norton, *Translations from the Poetry of Ranier Maria Rilke* (New York: W. W. Norton and Company, 1938) 203.

20. Johnson 133.

21. Susan Dunfee, Newsletter of Pittsburgh Theological Seminary, December, 1984.

22. Paul VI, *Marialus Cultus*, #35.

23. Gerard Manley Hopkins, "The Wreck of the Deutschland," *The Poems of Gerard Manley Hopkins*, ed. W. H. Gardner and N. H. Mackenzie (London: Oxford University Press, 1967), stanza 5, line 8.

24. Elisabeth Schüssler Fiorenza. *In Memory of Her: A Feminist Theological Reconstruction of Christian Origins* (New York: The Crossroad Publishing Company, 1983) 348–49.

REFLECTION QUESTIONS

1. The article suggests that there is a connection between our experiences of collaboration and bonding with women and reinterpreting scriptural and traditional images of Mary, a connection between our lived experience and our spirituality. Has this connection been borne out for you? What images of women inspire your spirituality?

2. What has the image of Mary of Nazareth meant to you, in content and importance, at different times in your life? How do you understand the continuities and changes you experience with this image?

RECOMMENDED READING

Jegen, Carol Frances, ed. *Mary According to Women*. Kansas City: Leaven Press, 1985.

Warner, Marina. *Alone of All Her Sex*. New York: Alfred A. Knoff, 1976.

A World Church and Christian Feminism

Margaret Gannon, IHM
in Collaboration with Mary Elsbernd, OSF

At the sixth time, there was a momentary, endless hesitation. Then a child was born. And the child looked just like the one who had given it life. The child too was born with power to create and to make decisions, and to love.
The labourer looked at all that had been accomplished, and rejoiced, for it was very good.

Introduction

There are two world significant movements developing in these last years of the twentieth century that promise to have important impacts upon contemporary religious life. They are the initial appearance of an authentic World Church and the assertion of Christian feminism. In many ways these movements have the same purpose: they seek to advance in all its fullness the proclamation of the message of Jesus. In pursuing that purpose, each movement calls for acceptance of a wide diversity of expressions of the message, that the richness of the Good News might better be experienced. Each presses toward equal participation of all members in the shaping of the Church's presence and action in the world. Each focuses on the role of personal human experience in the discernment of God's presence and will, and demands reverence for all persons' gifts and full opportunity to use those gifts for the advancement of Jesus' mission of love. They are similar in another crucial way: they are both in process—in some ways already in place, but in large part still to be achieved. Especially as they await acceptance and incorporation by the institutional Church, these movements are still very much in the "not yet."

The purpose of this article is to explore the meaning and characteristics of the two movements, to see how they may interface, and to examine how women religious may be both affected by the movements and helpful in shaping their development. A nineteenth century instance of the Church's response to the developing aspirations of its people will be examined as a way of offering a bit of encouragement from history.

World Church

In the last years of his life, Karl Rahner described the prospect of the World Church, tracing its initiation to the work of the Second Vatican Council. Through the Council's deliberations the Church began to evidence awareness of its truly universal nature. It began also to acknowledge its responsibility for welcoming diversity in the expressions of its essential mission and message, "a pluralism of proclamations." In an authentic World Church Christianity would never again be a European export to be transmitted unchanged into other societies, unmindful of the cultural discordance involved. Rahner suggests that this is only the second historical and theological break in the history of Christianity. Paul's first-century declaration of Gentile freedom from Judaic traditions was the first such departure from the perception that the Christian message is definitively engaged in certain culturally articulated images and practices and cannot be separated from them.

While Vatican Council II validated the emergence of the World Church, the challenging and sensitive task of promoting its development lies before us. There will be new ways of imaging the message of Jesus, and new expressions of discipleship in harmony with local cultures. Rahner envisions an open approach to the body of Revelation in which some peoples will focus on certain truths that speak most vividly to their experience, while persons of other cultures, acknowledging the truth of these elements of faith, will choose to concentrate on other truths that are for them most revelatory of the Christian message. The result will be varying emphases from a rich tradition of faith and they are apt to be unexpected and threatening to the more nearly monolithic traditional understandings of Western Catholics. We are called to the delicate task of discerning the work of the Spirit and facilitating its acceptance by open and generous cooperation.

Like so many features of religious existence, the World Church combines elements of present and future reality, the "already here" and the "not yet." The Church is already a World Church in terms of membership since the majority of the Church's population lives in the non-Western world. All over the planet culturally accommodated emphases and practice have been developing in the local churches. These churches are incorporating the beauty and wisdom of distinctive cultures in responding to the aspirations of local populations.

The full, rich and liberating expression of the World Church, however, is far from being achieved. Nothing is a clearer sign of the "not yet" than the present dominance of the institutional Church by a Western-oriented perspective. Its official theological interpretations, its structures, policies and practices remain far from the appreciative diversity which the notion of World Church connotes. But if the Church is to fulfill its mandate of continuing the mission of Jesus—announcing the universal and particular love of the Creator—it must be at the service of that love both as community and as institution.

What will the authentic World Church look like? Four characteristics can be identified: it will be enculturating, dynamic, communal and collaborative.

The Authentic World Church Will Be Enculturating

The simple, basic message of salvation has evolved into a broad, multi-faceted body of faith expressions. In different settings, certain tenets of faith strike with particular power and appear more central to a people's grasp of the message. In the same way, the images people create to express their religious understanding vary from one culture to another. Religious practices will therefore be of varying effectiveness for different cultures, and ethical interpretations will be conditioned by the concrete experiences of people's lives. There is doubtless a basic body of beliefs and ethical standards, but the emphases and expressions of a particular culture spring from the experiences of the people. The focus on these emphases will produce in one place a spirituality and ecclesiastical practice that may look very different from that of another location.

It is a delicate undertaking to respect the diversity of these religious expressions while assuring their authenticity as faithful embodiments of the message of Jesus. It is clear, however, that a faithful World Church cannot be merely a Roman transplant in Third World areas. It cannot be promoted by demands for conformity to images, emphases and practices that may have served a Western society, but do not meet the religious needs of non-Westerners. Rahner comments that, "None of us can say how exactly, with what terminology, under what new aspects, the ancient message of Christianity must be proclaimed in the future . . . in order to make this message really present everywhere in the world. The other peoples and cultures must slowly find this out for themselves . . ."[1]

The Authentic World Church Will Be Dynamic

The traditional societies of the Third World are themselves undergoing rapid transformations. The forces of tradition, modernization and reaction are all at work, creating new cultures that combine the effects of these forces in dynamic interplay. In many areas, particularly in parts of Asia, rapid industrialization is destabilizing personal and societal life, while in the Third World urbanization is having the same effect. The pervasive presence of Western media challenges the power of traditional values and creates new sets of expectations and aspirations. Shifts are occurring in such basic traditional understandings as humankind's relation to nature, the role of the family and its members, and the significance of time, labor, leisure and territory. While some members of the societies welcome the innovations eagerly, others are afflicted with a sense of alienation both from their traditional societies and from the new experiences. Out of the mix of these competing orientations new societies are taking shape. The Church functioning within these societies is similarly affected by these shifting cultural trends and must see the task of reflection and reformulation in presenting the message of Christ as a continuing process.

The Authentic World Church Will Be Communal

Many members of the World Church are persons who have recently freed themselves from positions of domination and humiliation. They prize the equal dignity they share with each member of society. Others are still struggling to free themselves from governmental structures that deny their equal human dignity and from economic and social systems that exploit them and refuse them equal opportunities for human development. All such persons are drawn by the model of the Church as a gathering of believers, patterned on the community of equals Jesus created during his lifetime. Structures that set some members above the others in status or personal privilege and neglect the radical equality of all persons have no place in Christianity. They are particularly inappropriate in a World Church, many of whose members have been profoundly affected by a new experience of liberation.

In a World Church that is truly communal, each person will be regarded with equal respect in light of her/his position as one loved by God. Distinctions of ministry and service will not become the bases for privilege, much less of domination over other members of the Church. The human temptation to build institutions that stratify persons and ensure status and power for a few will be firmly resisted. Instead, the thrust will be always to foster a community of peers gathered in love for Jesus and for one another.

The Authentic World Church Will Be Collaborative

The essential dignity of the human being entitles each one to participate in the formation and direction of the institutions within which s/he lives. In religious concerns, that participation is especially crucial. Since each culture, like each person, captures so little of the reality of God and is so limited in expressing the little that is known, it is essential that all members of the World Church participate in the process of discerning God's presence and call. The unique experiences of individuals are means by which the whole Church learns the ways of the Spirit. In a Church celebrating the experiences of diverse cultures it is especially vital that concrete and particular experiences be formative of the local Church and ultimately of the World Church. Acknowledgment of personal lived experience as a vehicle of the Spirit's enlightenment of the Church requires that the decision-making processes honor the insights of all and provide for their incorporation in the directing of the Church.

Religious Congregations Reflect World Church Characteristics

It is interesting to notice that the characteristics attributed to the World Church can also be detected in the post-Vatican II development of U.S. congregations of women religious. This correlation is very clear in the LCWR paper prepared for the Fifth Inter-American Conference on Religious Life. U.S. congregations have undertaken the task of enculturation in a variety of ways. Attention to the needs of the particular society in which the ministry takes place has led to a pluralism of life-styles and apostolic directions. Women religious commit themselves to be intensely present to the people in the local community and to share their hopes, anxieties and labors. As expressed in the LCWR paper, "American religious are keenly aware that the call to apostolic religious life includes sharing in the movement of God in concrete circumstances of society, history and culture" (Appendix, p. 174). Even the interest in the distinctive charisms of congregations, with its search for the particular wisdom of the founding and sustaining spirit, has similarities to the enculturating thrust.

The experience of women religious since Vatican Council II mirrors the dynamic element of World Church. They recognize that their response to societal realities requires profound, extensive and ongoing changes in their lives. Their openness to change is expressed in continuing flexibility in the face of new challenges and in willingness to explore new approaches to ministry.

Perhaps one of the most significant changes in religious congregations after Vatican II is the renewed appreciation of the inherent dignity of the individual and the radical equality of all individuals. Traditions of status and rank no longer operate within religious life as they did in pre-Vatican II days. Furthermore, the communal direction is evident in the rejection of distinctions that attempted to set women religious apart from and above other lay persons. They find themselves "like Jesus . . . invited to learn with and from the poor and marginalized, to become poor and marginalized [themselves]" (Appendix, p. 175).

Contemporary religious life also demonstrates a distinctly collaborative mode. Respect for each member's gifts and insights has led to the creation of a variety of participatory and consultative processes. The restoration of personal responsibility in determining prayer, living and working circumstances also reflects appreciation for the individual and for the work of the Spirit in her life. The collaborative thrust of contemporary religious life is reflected in the variety of techniques that have been devised for sharing authority. Positions of leadership are truly seen as opportunities for serving the members. Over time many individuals are asked to take a share in the service of leadership.

Christian Feminism

Simultaneous with the emergence of the World Church is another event of major significance: the contemporary assertion of Christian feminism. Just as one must return to apostolic times to trace a precedent for the shift to World Church, so one must look to the early years of the Church to find women regarded as equals within the Christian community. A return of the Church to this way of living would mark a dramatic change in the treatment of its members.

Elisabeth Schüssler Fiorenza, in *In Memory of Her, A Feminist Theological Reconstruction of Christian Origins,* analyzes the position of women in the Palestine community gathered around Jesus, as well as in the early apostolic communities. She demonstrates that radical equality among the members was the hallmark of these communities. Persons regarded by the general society as insignificant or unworthy of participation were treated with acceptance and dignity in the communities inspired by Jesus. The equal treatment of women and men was a source of discomfort to the surrounding society where it contributed to the unpopularity of Jesus with the traditional leaders. Similarly, women in the early apostolic communities provided initiative and leadership equal to that of men. The adaptation of the Church to the customs of imperial Rome, in both domestic and public arenas, gradually produced the suppression of women's leadership as well as the elimination of equal treatment for women within the community.

The current movement of Christian feminism seeks to recover, in and for the Church, the commitment of Jesus to equality for all human beings, a commitment based on the announcement of God's unconditional and total love for each person.

Perhaps the simplest definition of Christian feminism as it is used here is that it is an effort to assure that women are regarded and treated as Jesus regarded and treated them. This means that their full humanity is acknowledged and their rights as humans are respected. It means that their potential in every area of development is able to flourish unhindered and that their gifts are esteemed and employed in the building of God's world. It requires especially that women participate on a basis of freedom and equality in the decisions that shape the direction of the Church.

Christian feminism unites women in the pursuit of justice. It draws attention to the fact that the oppression of women is bound up with the whole panoply of oppressions—economic, political and religious. When Christian feminists focus on eliminating the sinful structures of sexism, they do so in solidarity with all who struggle against oppression and marginalization.

The exclusion of women from the decision-making processes of the society and of the Church has greatly impoverished both. Christian feminists understand that official discounting of their experiences and insights causes continuing harm, not only for themselves but for the entire human enterprise.

In the Western world the exclusion of women has been intensified in the last several centuries by dichotomizing society into public and private spheres. The public sphere—where work is done, where rationality rules, where important things happen, where civilization thrives—belongs to men. Women are assigned to the private sphere—where the family is cared for, where emotion is dominant, where a refuge from the stress of doing important and civilizing things is provided. The private sphere has been put at the service of the public and women have been put at the service of men. The evil of such limitation upon women is obvious.

Another serious damage resulting from the splitting of spheres is the denial to both men and women of the full scope of human experience. Each has tended to cultivate those characteristics of thought and action most effective in the assigned sphere. However, "women's modes" of thought and action—not inherent female traits, but characteristics developed because of the circumstances in which women have found themselves—have generally been regarded as less mature, less significant for the progress of society.

It is now becoming obvious that these so-called women's characteristics are vital for the very continuance of society, and for the transformation of the Church into the authentic World Church. These characteristics must be increasingly operative if such a transformation is to occur. The Christian feminist commitment to this transformation, as well as to concern for women's basic right of participation, is the basis of the call for involvement of women.

Four of these characteristic modes will be examined here as particularly necessary for the success of the World Church. It must be clearly understood that no claim is made that these are "inherent" qualities of women or that they are universally identifiable in women. They seem to be gifts many women have developed because of the roles they have played in a number of societies. They do not constitute in themselves a "women's culture"; they have been developed as various cultures have had an impact on women. They are very powerful gifts and their effective operation will foster the development of the authentic World Church.

The first of these characteristics is a concern for persons as opposed to concern for institutions and structures. Gilligan's demonstration of women's ethical priority for persons over abstract principles can probably be verified in one's personal experience. Such an approach, which refuses to absolutize structures at the expense of personal well-being, could greatly facilitate the accommodation of institutions to persons and their well-being in World Church development.

Secondly, women are often adept at collaboration. They can develop power-sharing techniques that promote participation and joint ownership of projects. Women have developed facility for sharing the power involved in leadership and decision-making.

Related to collaborative action is a flexible and open approach to learning that women develop, particularly because of their continual adjustments to the changing needs of growing children. The dynamic of family life presents women with a series of challenges and adjustment throughout their lives; thus the capacity to relearn, reshape and reimage ideas has grown with practice.

Finally, women have developed a sense of the importance of the concrete, the particular, the experiential. Abstract theory cannot stray too far from concrete experience if it is effectively to demonstrate wisdom and truth. Women have particularly developed an awareness of vulnerability in the concrete experience of human suffering and fragility, probably because many roles traditionally assigned women put them in the daily presence of tears and pain and helplessness.

Since it is women who have maintained these modes of thinking and acting, they must be the agents for inserting them into the decision-making processes of the Church and society. The ideal is the provision of opportunities for both women and men to exercise these modes, thereby overcoming the damage of the historic dichotomy of public and private spheres. But this will not happen until women first share in the shaping and eventual integration of both spheres.

Women religious in the United States have been powerfully affected by Christian feminism. There is a certain historical ambivalence in their position compared with that of other women. To some limited extent they have experienced greater opportunities for initiative and leadership than other women have. They have founded and operated colleges, hospitals and other large-scale institutions in years when other women lacked access to such opportunities. Yet these very achievements helped to highlight for women religious the fact of their exclusion from other opportunities on the basis of their sex. Because of the canonical and patriarchal structures of the institutional Church in regulating their institutes, they have also experienced a unique kind of control over their lives. The inadequate participation afforded women religious in forming the policies that directly affect their lives is the kind of abuse that Christian feminism confronts.

Women religious recognize the pervasiveness of the injustices committed against women and acknowledge their responsibility to stand with them against those injustices. The LCWR report at the Inter-American Conference openly expresses commitment to oppressed women. "A spirit of kinship with all women prompts special concern for women who are abused, deprived of opportunities to achieve their potential as victims of the 'feminization of poverty' phenomenon in American society" (Appendix, p. 174).

Although the life experiences of women religious have been somewhat different from those of other lay women, they demonstrate some of the same characteristic modes of thinking and acting. Concern for persons rather than for institutions is one of the hallmarks of post-Vatican II renewal in congregations of women religious, a characteristic contrasting with the formalisms and uniformities of the past. At the same time women religious indicate a growing appreciation of collaboration in promoting effective service. The report of LCWR at the Fifth Inter-American states: "Life-giving modes of relating emerge from willingness to use gifts for the sake of the human community and from valuing interdependences, integration, cooperation, collaboration, [and] bonding" (p. 175).

A long and rich heritage of teaching involves women religious intensely in the process of learning. In their efforts to provide effective education for persons in all kinds of diverse circumstances, they have developed their capabilities for flexibility and creativity.

The experiences of women religious have also made them aware of the great fragility and vulnerability of human beings. Work in health care, social services, advocacy, and education have put them in close contact with suffering and distressed persons, and their concrete experiences in these areas have shaped their responses to the causes of the oppressions. The Fifth Inter-American paper states, "a heightened sense of mission and awareness of unmet survival needs of suffering brothers and sisters is leading American religious to critique social structures, institutions and systems from a Gospel perspective" (p. 174).

The Interface of World Church and Christian Feminism

Effective involvement of Christian feminists is vital for the success of an authentic World Church for at least three reasons: first, the values of Christian feminism will foster World Church development; second, women's experience of domination equips them to identify with the peoples of the World Church; and third, a focus on women within the

World Church, particularly in the developing nations, will be a responsibility of that Church.

There is an obvious match between the perceived characteristics of an authentic World Church and the values of Christian feminism. The effective involvement of women in the direction of the Church will therefore facilitate the transformation to World Church. The World Church thrust toward enculturation would benefit greatly from women's appreciation of the importance of the particular and the experiential. Since the enhancement of persons and relationships is for women a higher priority than the maintenance of institutions, women are freer to welcome new and diverse institutional expressions of faith.

The flexibility of learning that women have cultivated enables them to learn from all, and to respond with openness and creativity to the unfamiliar circumstances in which the World Church is developing. As noted at the outset, the equality of all in the Christian community is a highly prized principle for proponents of both World Church and Christian feminism, and women's adeptness at collaboration can further its realization in an authentic World Church. Since Christian feminists recognize that the oppression of women is part of the web of injustice trapping the powerless globally, their sensitivity to the vulnerable and distressed is galvanized into active solidarity with them. The work of U.S. women religious in the worldwide missionary sphere demonstrates the present effectiveness of this solidarity and offers a promise of how the increased participation of women can prepare the institutional Church to respond to the challenge of becoming an authentic World Church.

There is another reason why the involvement of Christian feminism is important for the success of the World Church. It is because, among members of the Western Church, women constitute the largest group who have had experience similar to the peoples of the developing world—the experience of colonization.

It is striking to notice how closely women's experience parallels the classic features of colonization. Like all colonized persons, women have been treated like children, judged unable to manage their own lives. They have been led to believe that the purpose of their existence is to serve the dominator's interests. Their choices in the areas of work, ownership, education and political and social decision-making have been limited by the roles their dominators have needed them to fulfill. Like the colonized they have been taught the superiority of the dominator and the greater significance of his achievements. They have been manipulated by threats and bribes to accept the dominator's control.

Women, like other oppressed groups, even demonstrate a favorite hypothesis of colonialism advanced by scholars—the collaborator theory. This theory holds that there are always certain members of the colonized who cooperate with the dominator and who benefit their own interests in the process. Such collaboration seems to be absolutely essential for the success of the domination for without it the dominator could not make vital inroads into the community and achieve the controlling power he desires. It is probably fair to suggest that women have sometimes taken this collaborator role—one vastly different from the collaboration of equals described previously. The comfort of an assured though subservient place in the society and the praise of the dominator, even if condescendingly bestowed, seem to be the benefits of their colonial collaboration. Some women have also demonstrated the other familiar psychological effect of colonialism, indeed of all forms of oppression—acceptance of the dominator's definition of the dominated, with all its pejorative and constraining implications. In overcoming these aspects of psychological colonialism, Christian feminism shares with the peoples of the World Church the continuing task of personal and systemic liberation.

The third reason that Christian feminism is vital for the World Church is that women in the developing nations have their own agendas that the World Church must take into account. As a Church that recognizes action on behalf of justice as an essential component of its mission, the World Church must attend to the range of distresses that plague women in these nations. Participation of women in the Church's response will help to make its action appropriate and beneficial.

There are three areas of distress afflicting women in the developing countries: poverty, traditional limitations upon their lives and the effects of misdirected development policies. It is clear that for many poor women in these nations, their children's survival and their own are daily concerns. Liberation from hunger, illness and illiteracy is the focus of their life activities. In many societies, women's needs are the last to be addressed in the family. Usually working outside the paid labor force, Third World women struggle to provide for the basic human needs of their families.

In the social organization of many developing nations the average woman is still bound by traditional limitations and expectations. Her activities are confined to the household and her role within the household is a subservient one. She is constantly subject to the actions of males, including at times, arranged marriages, physical abuse and deprivation of independent income or property. She has little influence in determining the lives and futures of her children, nor has she much recourse in the event of her husband's desertion. She is apt still to be excluded, either by law or by continuing practice, from participating in political life. Even movements for economic and political liberation are apt to be as male-dominated and deprecating of women as are the established regimes.

Development policies and practices have often worsened women's situation in the developing nations. Western development planners have regularly transferred to the developing countries a bias toward male-centered development programs. Planning and education for development have been directed toward men. Women's major contributions to work, particularly in agriculture, have been overlooked; technological training, subsidies and credit opportunities have been offered only to men.

Another development strategy that has been detrimental for women is the expansion of the cash economy. Cash crop production reduces the food available to women for feeding their families. Women are often required to add work on these crops to their prior tasks of subsistence farming and household maintenance. If the woman is drawn into the cash economy of the urban areas, as is happening so frequently to young women in the newly industrializing countries, she faces all the harrowing effects of exploitation usually experienced by an unorganized, unprotected labor force. In any case, contemporary development strategies are apt to lay new burdens on women in the Third World, without relieving those they have traditionally borne.

Women in the Third World will therefore present a triple challenge to which an authentic World Church must respond. They have been reared in distinctive local cultures; they are apt to be poor; and they seek liberation from the burdens imposed on them as women. The Church will need to respond on all these bases.

Women in the World Church will also present a challenge to Western expressions of Christian feminism. It will be vitally important for Christian feminists to comprehend the Third World woman's appraisal of her own experience, her agenda, her sense of what constitutes liberation and salvation and her aspirations and her anxieties. Clearly this will be quite a different perspective from that of women in the Western Church. Although there will probably be some aspects of spirituality shared among women through the World Church, cultural influences are producing a multiplicity of "women's spiritualities." The World Church's "plurality of proclamations" will embrace a variety of women's ways of imaging God and relating to God and to others. To supply appreciation and support for women in the World Church, Western women will have to employ all their experience-honoring, collaborative, person-centered resources. The movement will have to stretch itself to become adequate to the depth and range of Third World women's experiences.

The effort calls upon Christian feminists to continue creating a spirituality of learning. Such a spirituality is born of reverence for God as Life and Truth. It recognizes a human responsibility for continued efforts to expand and deepen understanding of all life's truth. Christian feminists must exercise the disciplines and pursue the experiences they need to continue the process of learning. Humble openness to new information and courage to experiment with new approaches are the hallmarks of such a spirituality. By the cultivation of such a spirituality of learning, Christian feminists equip themselves for the urgent and sensitive task of promoting women's participation in the World Church, as well as of facilitating the communication of Third World women's understandings and concerns to the rest of the Church. Since for so many women in the Third World liberation is expressed in the simple terms of physical survival, the Christian feminist's focus will often be on issues of economic and political justice, and her role in the Church will be the prophetic calling of the Church to action in these arenas.

Alienation and the Pursuit of a Just Community

As indicated at the beginning of this article both Christian feminism and World Church look to the same transformations in the institutional Church—respect and acceptance of diverse gifts and experiences and equal participation in shaping the direction of the Church. Both movements are in the process of emerging from the present monolithic domination of white, Western males. They seek to change the attitudes, structures and policies that fail to meet the needs of the persons who constitute the World Church and of women everywhere. The institutional Church has been slow in acknowledging and even active in opposing these claims of self-determination and participation. The result, most notable among women in the West, has been a deepening alienation from the Church.

The alienation of women in the Western Church is manifested in a whole range of actions. Some women are publicly renouncing their membership in the institution in protest of Church policies and pronouncements. Others are more quietly withdrawing their support for Church enterprises and directing their energies and resources to other undertakings they hope to find more spiritually affirming and enriching. Still others remain within the institutional Church, struggling to effect change and seeking ways to bond with other women in fashioning an effective Christian feminist presence within the Church. The LCWR paper for the Fifth Inter-American Conference speaks to these aspirations:

> We seek new patterns of relating to Church hierarchy. We seek . . . ways of collaborating with other women . . . We expect dialogue as peers to replace parent-child relationships. We work for patterns of mutual accountability with structures for responsible dissent (Appendix, p. 178).

Wholesale alienation of women from the Church would be tragic. The loss of their contribution to the advancement of the World Church would make their withdrawal all the more damaging. The Church simply cannot afford to neglect the intensifying alienation of women. But can it respond?

In the case of the Church in the United States it is possible to propose a bit of historical encouragement. The Church faced a similar crisis of alienation in the nineteenth century, namely, the alienation of the working class. Since the Church in the United States was able to respond effectively in that instance, it may be helpful to examine it and attempt to draw some insights from it.

The Church faced the danger that a significant portion of the membership, failing to find support for their needs and aspirations, would withdraw their active affiliation. The Church, both in the United States and in Europe, confronted this concern but with contrasting method and result. It can be asserted that a large portion of the working class was indeed lost to the Church in Europe. In the United States, however, working persons recognized the Church as a champion of their rights and they consequently became the most vigorous supporters of the American Church. The particular circumstances of the latter development will be examined as especially relevant to our question.

The European Church's response to the problems of workers was complicated by a number of factors. During the most distressing period of European industrialization, the period from 1820 to 1890, the Church was distracted by other serious concerns. Its traditional position in the European states was under attack, the arguments over its temporal power were unresolved, and its former role in cultural and educational affairs was being contested. To some extent, the social question was neglected in the midst of these other struggles. Moreover, the Church was regularly identified in workers' eyes with the social and economic elites who were profiting from the workers' distresses.

Even those Catholic reformers who were interested in improving the workers' lot had little confidence in the workers' capacities to lead their own movement. Instead, the proposed reforms demonstrated a paternalistic insistence of an official or elite control of the movement. Furthermore, the Church feared the workers' association with socialist movements lest contacts with atheists jeopardize the faith. The secret character of some labor organizations with their oaths and clandestine ceremonies also seemed a threat to religion, since they required the workers to give higher priority to their identity as workers than as members of the Church.

For all these reasons, the European Church did not respond effectively to the workers in the nineteenth century. The publication of *Rerum Novarum* in 1891, while blazing a path for the Church's social influence in the twentieth century, came too late to secure for the Church the loyalty of the European working class.

The response of the U.S. Church to the needs of the workers was very different. Initially, the hierarchy in this country held the same suspicion as had their European colleagues. Their distrust of organized labor sprang from the same two concerns—the secrecy and quasi-religious traditions involved in the organizations and the suspected socialist orientation of the movement.

These suspicions of the U.S. bishops came into critical focus with the threat of Vatican condemnation directed toward the first general labor organization in North America, the Knights of Labor. In 1885 Cardinal Taschereau of Quebec succeeded in eliciting from the Holy See an opinion that the Knights fell within the ban on secret societies the bishops were required to uphold. The reaction of the U.S. hierarchy was crucial for the Knights' future, particularly in their perception that, since so many workers were Catholic, a condemnation would have dire effects upon the Church. A particular group of U.S. clergy, those of Northeastern Pennsylvania, played a decisive role in the crisis.

It happened that the Grand Master of the Knights, Terence Powderly, was a native of Carbondale, a coal industry center in Northeastern Pennsylvania. He had both supportive friends and ferocious opponents among the clergy. In an effort to gain clergy support he strove to eliminate the elements of secrecy and cult from the Knights and to present the organization as a saving alternative to the radicalization of the workers. His most effective strategy was suggested by his pastor, Reverend Francis Carew. Powderly wrote a letter to Carew, expressing his loyalty to the Church and his willingness to revise the Knights' practices in order to remove any remaining objections of the hierarchy. He argued that a condemnation of the Knights would benefit only the "anarchist, infidel element" of the labor movement and would "do a great deal of injury to the struggling Catholics who have to compete in the labor market." Historian Henry J. Browne calls this letter "the most important [document] for the settlement of the Church's vexation over the Knights," because Carew forwarded the letter to Cardinal Gibbons, who used it as the basis of a personal defense of the Knights in Rome in 1887.[2]

It was a thoroughly successful mission. The Holy See withdrew its earlier sanctions and the Knights were acknowledged as an acceptable organization. This marked a turning point in Church-labor relations in the U.S. From that point the clergy became more and more supportive of the labor movement. By the time of the first major union victory in U.S. history—the successful resolution of the Anthracite Coal Strike of 1902—the clergy were distinctly in the vanguard supporting workers' claims against the organized strength of monopolistic business.

This response of the clergy to the laborers' needs truly fostered loyalty to the Church in the working class. What might have been a history of alienation became instead the development of a Church whose most distinguishing social feature is its working-class character. That character is reflected in U.S. religious congregations, both in their membership and in their emphasis on the education of working class children as a major ministry focus.

In a very real sense the action of the U.S. Church had global effects, for it constituted an experiential prelude to the publication of *Rerum Novarum*. Focusing its attention on the social question, the Church produced its rich body of social justice teaching. That teaching continues to expand, embracing the rights and concerns of persons throughout the world.

Key to the resolution of the nineteenth century crisis was the insight born largely of personal experience. Many of the clergy supporting the workers' movement were sons of laborers. Some of them had themselves been employed in and around the mines from the age of six and they understood first hand the exhaustion and terror of this burdensome work as well as the injustice and callousness to which workers were subjected. They could comprehend the workers' case and represent it to others because of their own personal experience.

Is it possible for the U.S. Church once again to avert the alienation of a major portion of its membership—its women? Can it in the process once again provide clarification and enlightenment for the Church in Rome? The situations have similarities. Both the nineteenth century workers' movement and the twentieth century women's movement pursue the guaranteeing and the facilitation of the human rights of the persons involved. In both instances the symptoms of alienation range from open hostility to an abandonment of involvement resulting from a sense of the Church's irrelevance to the group's needs and goals. Furthermore, the assertiveness of the group's position seems to take the institution by surprise, creating a good deal of confusion among those in power. Both groups had been and are expected to know and keep their places in the society.

There are, of course, differences to be taken into account. In the nineteenth century the Church was being asked to support the claims of justice in an area external to itself; in the twentieth century the arena is the Church itself as well as the general society. In a very real sense, the goal of the Church's support of the worker in the nineteenth century was the saving of membership; today the goal is salvation itself, which has justice as its constitutive element and expression in the world. Finally, in the nineteenth century, the response of the Church essentially involved the active sponsorship of the labor movement by the clergy. In our time, the work of affirming the dignity and right to equal participation of women belongs to the entire Church; the role of the clergy is to help remove the obstacles to the participation of women.

The key to resolving the present crisis would seem to be the same as that of the nineteenth century—the impact of personal experience. But how can the experiences of women be made accessible to those in power? How can those in power be brought to attend to those experiences and appreciate them? It may be feared that the chasm between male and female in the Church, between the powerful and the powerless, is too broad to be crossed. But for the sake of women and for the sake of the Church, a faith-filled persistent effort must be made to share an understanding of women's experiences, for experience, more powerfully than any other force, can supply the insights that lead persons to change. Experience must bring us to a turning point in the Church's understanding of women. From such understanding will spring the accommodations that will accord women acceptance and dignity in the Church.

Concluding Reflections for U.S. Women Religious

What roles can be proposed for U.S. women religious in the two great contemporary movements of World Church and Christian feminism? First, U.S. women religious can facilitate the welcoming of the World Church. Second, they can, by honoring and communicating their own experience as women, promote the full dignity and participation of women in the Church.

In order to facilitate the coming of World Church, U.S. women religious must be present in a variety of ways to the people who constitute World Church, present to their aspirations as well as to their needs and distresses. They must be especially concerned about the women of the World Church, sensitive to the particular oppression afflicting them and committed to promoting their participation in society and in the Church itself.

The work of women religious in mission areas demonstrates this promotion of World Church. Their openness to the experiences of the persons with whom they live is an indicator of World Church already in place. The many women religious engaged in education in the United States have the opportunity to foster an understanding of World Church realities. Congregations, as well as individuals, can be involved in advocacy for the peoples of the World Church, promoting those economic, political and ecclesiastical policies that can enhance their lives. Having appreciated the promise of a World Church for the future, U.S. women religious can educate the Western Church to welcome its arrival.

One effective way that U.S. women religious can promote Christian feminism is to communicate their own experience to other members of the Church, particularly to members of the clergy. Making their experience comprehensible to the clergy will require the exploration of language that clarifies the issues and sensitizes the listeners. A basis of common values must be identified in order to motivate the clergy to openness. The truth must be spoken with power and peace, whether or not it finds an immediate welcome.

Another challenge for U.S. women religious is the conversion of their own members to Christian feminism. It must be acknowledged that sometimes women, religious included, construct major obstacles to the progress of other women. Congregations face internal problems of conversion and re-socialization; the principle of solidarity with other women needs to be reenforced and implemented in the lives of those for whom it is not yet an operating value.

U.S. women religious can promote Christian feminism by consciously developing collaborative and participative modes of organization and action. As religious become involved in diverse expanding ministries with new colleagues from a whole range of backgrounds and concerns, they have numerous opportunities for experience with these modes. The creation of strong networks of committed creative persons is vitally important, particularly in efforts to confront unjust systems and structures.

Finally, U.S. women religious can further the progress of Christian feminism by rejoicing in the fact that as religious they share the status of laity and by resisting the "clericalization" of their position. This involves the rejection of distinctions and privileged treatment that distance them from other women who are not accorded special deference or "clergy" discounts.

Christian feminism and World Church are realities already in place and yet to be achieved. Those who promote them face misunderstanding and frustration as well as the experience of participating in historic pursuits of justice and the promotion of the Reign of God. One is tempted to pessimism about the possibility of change, especially on the part of those who hold power in the present Church. Perhaps the words of the U.S. bishops themselves, in an entirely different but similarly challenging context, can provide a heartening insight:

> To believe we are condemned in the future only to what has been the past . . . is to underestimate both our human potential . . . and God's action in our midst which can open the way to changes we could barely imagine. We do not intend to foster illusory ideas that the road ahead . . . will be devoid of tension or that peace will be easily achieved. But we do warn against that "hardness of heart" which can close us or others to the changes needed to make the future different from the past.[3]

ENDNOTES

1. *Concern for the Church,* trans. Edward Quinn (New York: The Crossroad Publishing Company, 1981) 87.

2. *The Catholic Church and the Knights of Labor* (Washington, D.C.: The Catholic University of America Press, 1949) 190.

3. National Conference of Catholic Bishops. *The Challenge of Peace: God's Promise and Our Response* (Washington, D.C.: United States Catholic Conference, 1983) #258.

REFLECTION QUESTIONS

1. Does Elisabeth Schüssler Fiorenza's analysis of the early Christian community as fundamentally a community of equals match your own perception of the group gathered around Jesus? Why, or why not?

   Have you ever experienced yourself as a member of a "community of equals," or of unequals? If so what biases did you have to overcome in order to remain a member? What privileges and/or oppressions did you have to discard?

2. Have you, or do you, experience yourself among "the colonized"? What concrete steps have you taken, or do you take, to liberate yourself? What learnings from these steps would you offer to other women and men?

   What supports do women need to "de-colonize" themselves and their relationships with others?

RECOMMENDED READING

Brown, Henry J. *The Catholic Church and the Knights of Labor.* Washington, D.C.: The Catholic University of America Press, 1949.

Buhlmann, Walbert. *The Coming of the Third Church: An Analysis of the Present and Future of the Church.* Maryknoll, N.Y.: Orbis Books, 1977.

Fifth Inter-American Conference on Religious Life. *Apostolic Religious Life in a Changing World and Church.* LCWR/CMSM, 1986.

Fiorenza, Elisabeth Schüssler. *In Memory of Her: A Feminist Theological Reconstruction of Christian Origins.* New York: The Crossroad Publishing Company, 1984.

Gilligan, Carol. *In a Different Voice: Psychological Theory and Women's Development.* Cambridge, MA: Harvard University Press, 1982.

Gray, Elizabeth Dodgson. *Patriarchy as a Conceptual Trap*. Wellesley, MA: Roundtable Press, 1982.

Parney, Constance. "Re-membering: A Global Perspective on Women," *Christian Feminism: Visions of a New Humanity*, ed. Judith L. Weidman. San Francisco: Harper & Row, Publishers, 1984.

Rahner, Karl. *Concern for the Church. Theological Investigations*. trans. Edward Quinn. New York: The Crossroad Publishing Company, 1981.

Schneiders, Sandra. "The Effects of Women's Experience on Their Spirituality," *Spirituality Today* 35 (Summer, 1983) 100–116.

Soelle, Dorothee. *The Strength of the Weak. Toward a Christian Feminist Identity*. trans. Robert and Rita Kimber. Philadelphia: The Washington Press, 1984.

Weaver, Mary Jo. *New American Women: A Contemporary Challenge to Traditional Religious Authority*. San Francisco: Harper & Row, 1985.

What's at Stake: Women Religious Naming Ourselves Women Exploring Implications

Mary Elsbernd, OSF and Marilyn Thie, SC*

At the seventh time, the labour was finished. The task was complete.
And the labourer rested, for she was very, very tired.

What's at stake? We women religious are naming ourselves women. We women religious are changing the ways we speak about God. Indeed we are doing our own naming of God. We women religious are relating in new ways within ecclesial structures and seeking new patterns of collaboration with those in the institutional hierarchy. These phenomena emerge as central notions in data collected from women religious, members of the Leadership Conference of Women Religious (LCWR).

The evidence suggests that a fundamental change in our lives and relationships as women religious is taking place, a change comparable to the Copernican Revolution both in significance as well as in the gradual realization of its effects. Our understanding of ourselves as women is interrelated with how we speak of God and how we relate within church; they are not separate phenomena occurring coincidentally. The renewal of U.S. apostolic religious life in the years after Vatican Council II is shifting the center of our lives from external authorities to a personal and communal inner authority: the Spirit of God dwelling within us, working in and through the world and its peoples. Speaking of God in new ways, naming ourselves *Church* and so claiming greater personal and communal authority for defining ourselves and our mission—these trends disclose that women religious are revitalizing apostolic religious life by responding in profound faithfulness to the Gospel's call to be attentive to the Spirit in us and around us. Naming ourselves *women* epitomizes the magnitude of the shift and suggests the fundamental political nature of these activities.

What is at stake when women religious do our own naming of God and claim a determinative voice in our relationship within Church, a reality we understand broadly as the people of God but at the same time as an institution governed by a male clerical

*The authors extend special thanks to those who read and critiqued this paper, especially to Anne Clifford, SSJ, Shawn Copeland, OP, Margaret Gannon, IHM, Janet Roesener, CSJ, and Mary Daniel Turner, SNDdeN.

hierarchy? What is at stake when women religious call ourselves *women* and assume our responsibilities as ecclesial women? What will be our response when we understand better that these activities are political and carry profound implications within a still largely patriarchal Church and society?

The following pages explore these questions further. Some of what is at stake in identifying ourselves as women can be seen in two fundamental changes we are making: first, a move away from using traditional theological language about God to speaking of God in fresh words born from our personal and collective experience; and second, a shift from a role as women *of* the Church—language suggesting that we are possessions—to claiming ourselves to be *Church*, thereby entering as collaborators with others who name themselves Church, including the Church hierarchy. What is at stake with these changes, however, becomes clearer by examining the implications that arise when we women religious name ourselves *women*. The concluding pages frame crucial questions now challenging women religious who are attempting to assume responsibilities toward Church and society by touching into their own personal and collective resources.

Naming God

In her recent book, *Women and the Word*, Sandra M. Schneiders holds that the real problem with language about God rests "not in the area of systematic theology but in the area of religious experience or spirituality." She continues, "Unless educated and aware women can find a creative and liberating understanding of God and of Jesus, one which does not glorify masculinity at the expense of femininity and does not justify the oppression of women by men, they have no future in institutional Christianity."[1] In an effort to assess their experience of God, the women who gathered for the fifteen LCWR spring regional meetings in 1986 participated in a collaborative reflective process that elicited both their images of God and the experiences that gave rise to those images. A careful reading of the summary responses furnished from thirteen regional meetings (Appendix, p. 193) reveals some patterns in how U.S. women religious speak about God. These patterns suggest that educated and aware women are actively involved in creating a liberating understanding of God, born of their cumulative religious experience.

A first significant pattern appears in the use of cosmic images to describe God. Eleven of the summary responses specifically attribute the name 'energy' to God. In a similar vein, expressions suggesting a dynamic source of life, of freedom, of mission and of unity emerge, such as "transforming life, spirit, energizing power," "breath of life," or "ever present freshness." Other articulations focus less on the "whatness" of this "energy" and more on its dynamism through expressions like "process toward wholeness and growth," "ongoing creation integrating all life," "life force toward goodness," "vision of future life," "eternal growth and discovery." Although this vital energy is termed a "wellspring within," women religious more often understand themselves as participating or immersed in an "encompassing totality," or "cosmic energy."

This clustering of images, evident in all thirteen summaries, suggests an understanding of God both as a vibrant core out of which we live, and an energizing life in which we live and move and have our becoming. Our God is both all-encompassing reality and particular experience. From another perspective, "energy" requires an embodiment in the human situation if God is to be experienced. These images may suggest that we are the continuing incarnation of the divine in the historical situations in which we live. Such an understanding encourages and witnesses the variety of ways in which the divine life-energy *is* among the people of God, that is, in ways accessible to women.

A second pattern describes God from the perspective of apparent opposites, of paradox. This sense appears in eleven of the thirteen summaries, although the seeming opposites vary. Within this variety, the masculine/feminine dimensions are most frequently affirmed (six times). Two summaries specifically suggest that these two ways of being are transcended into non-sexual "one-ing-ness" or "life-giver." Over half of the summaries address the paradoxical dimension of God from the perspective of sexuality. The paradox is resolved either by affirming a bisexual image for God, or by moving beyond the opposites into a nonsexual and nonanthropomorphic image.[2] None of the other paired opposites are transcended into a unity. Rather the tension is affirmed as revelatory. God is imaged both as unchanging and changing, concrete and abstract, presence and absence (three times), with and other than, awesome and intimate, within and without, connection and connector. This pattern suggests an understanding of God as inclusive. The God known by U.S. women religious is not a God of either/or but of both/and. There is room for apparent opposites with such an understanding of God, as well as for tension and ambiguity with a God who is paradox.

There is not room, however, for exclusively masculine images of God. The supposed intrinsic connection between God and maleness that promoted the superiority of males and the subordination of females is giving way. This pattern is also reflected in the variety of human values and qualities that were attributed to God: hope, unconditional love, abiding peace, joy, promise, delight, strength, justice, risk, wonder, freedom, surprise and mystery. These qualities are those that women *experience* in their relationships with God. They are not uniquely male in women's consciousness and in that respect they diminish for women the presumed connection between maleness and the divine.

Another pattern in the responses given by the LCWR members describes God in personal terms, as a *someone*. These responses can be subdivided into action-words and personal relationship words. Again two-thirds of the summaries image God as doing, as active in personal or communal life. Many of the descriptions typify the human services: liberator from exploitation, listener, healer, provider, protector. Other words pertain to divine activity as experienced: one who tends life, (co)creator, life-giver, nurturer, nourisher, sustainer of life, gardener. Divine action in human living is also likened to a "player/coach," who is actively involved in shaping the unfolding course of events. Another image is of one who "calls us to integrated and integral development" and who is "response-elicitor." These action-words envision a God who is concerned about human persons in the fullness of their living.

With one exception, every group makes reference to an image that reflects personal relationship. Yet again, eleven of the summaries specifically mention the image "presence," although they sometimes added qualifiers like "enduring comfortable presence," "energizing presence," "intimate presence within," "constant presence," "active, nurturing, personal presence" or "loving presence." Derived from the Latin adjective *praesens*, presence connotes more than material location "in front of." It carries with it the sense of "personally" and, in some instances, "favorable, aiding or propitious." To enter into someone's presence suggests personal encounter or a "being-for" the one encountered. From their experience, U.S. women religious name God as one who has our well-being at heart, one who is personally there for us. Such an image suggests a close, even intimate, relationship with someone who desires what is best for our human becoming.

Besides the frequent use of "presence," other relational words are suggested. Four or five times each, "friend, lover," or "companion" (one with whom bread is eaten) are used. "Partner, spouse," and "an intimate" appear less frequently. All of these images taken together reveal a close, personal relationship of mutuality. Inclusive terminology is preferred to images describing relationships or activities exclusive to the experience of women. The God experienced by U.S. women religious is immanent rather than transcendent and an intimate rather than a patriarchal figure.

A final pattern that emerges is a sometimes conscious departure from classical neo-scholastic God-language. This shift is apparent when the answer to *The Baltimore Catechism* question "Who is God?" is compared with the foregoing images of God. U.S. women religious are not speaking of God as "Supreme Being, self-existing" or "infinitely perfect Spirit." "Trinitarian" occurred a single time, although "indwelling Spirit" and "incarnate in Jesus" were each cited twice.

This departure is reinforced through comparing the "attributes of God" in Chapter Two of *The Baltimore Catechism* with the characteristics of God in the LCWR regional summaries. The former lists and explains the following attributes of God: "eternal, all-good, omniscient, omnipresent, almighty, all-wise, all-holy, all-merciful" and "all-just."

The characteristics given by the LCWR members reiterate the patterns described earlier. Connected to the image of "energy" are the characteristics "dynamic, in-process, ever-changing, in transition, birthing." Related to the inclusivity of opposites are the expressions "masculine/feminine, hidden/present, waiting/active, immanent/unknown" or "incomprehensible." In striking contrast to the attributes posed by *The Baltimore Catechism* are a host of desirable human qualities: "nurturing, personal, creative, loving, caring, accepting, compassionate, leading toward integration, faithful," and "peace-loving." It is worth noting, of course, that *The Baltimore Catechism* presents characteristics of God flowing from a theological framework informed by the rational categories of Greek philosophy. The attributes of God described by the women in this survey flow from experience. They are more compatible in that respect to the descriptions of God that are found in the mystical writers.

In the discussion of the experiences that gave rise to images of God, the classical loci are also noticeably absent. A single mention of the Eucharist is the only sacrament to which reference is made. Three groups note the Scriptures as a place in which they have experienced God. One reference is made to the spiritual reading specifically of "women mystics." "Shared communal prayer," that might be a broad reference to the Liturgy of the Hours, receives a single mention. In place of these classical loci, frequent mention is made of ordinary, daily realities, "the stuff of life"; human interaction particularly with those in need or in suffering; personal religious experience and prayer; the works of creation; and the process of growth.

At no time are the "attributes of God" or the classical loci of religious experience decried. This absence of classical language does not appear, therefore, one of open rejection of past traditions. Rather, the vocabulary is noticeably absent from our active speech about the experience of God. There is a distancing from classical language and loci that do not fit the contemporary experience of U.S. women religious and an emphasis upon God as present in the encounters with people that are loci for apostolic ministry.

The religious experience and theological reflection that gave rise to neo-scholastic language about God is no longer ours. That experience and reflection belong to another age and the images with which we have been left no longer fit. We can delay the full emergence of this reality with an attempt to cling to words of the past. We can become impatient with the halting efforts to articulate new images, with the refusal of the past images to leave us, or with our own inability to change the situation. We can elect to use new images in personal prayer in hope that the pain of alienation in public prayer will go away. We can become depressed and overwhelmed by the suffering that the whole process entails.

We grieve over what is passing beyond our grasp in part because there is not yet an articulated consensus about images for God emerging from our personal and collective experience. It is true that two images, "energy" and "presence," show a certain prominence in the LCWR summaries, but the words may still feel new and elusive to a larger Christian community. In addition, certain characteristics, without clear names, frequently surface. Our God is the dynamism in human living, an inclusivity of opposites; our God engages in mutual and intimate relationships; our God is actively involved in human living. We are now in the transitional position of trying to find words capable of communicating the sense of who God is. This absence of a clear consensus of names for God can paralyze us in the grief process *or* it can entice us into the process of birthing a new God-language out of our personal and collective experiences. We suggest that the latter is what we are about and that it is of great significance.

Reflections on Naming God from our Experience

The analysis of the LCWR regional reports illustrates that U.S. women religious have been freed to experience God outside of the framework that had been handed on to us. Instead we are adding to our tradition the names and experiences emerging from ourselves. Like the friends of the Samaritan woman, we can say, "At first we believed because of what we heard from you about Jesus, but now we believe from our own experience" (Jn 4:42). We consciously acknowledge that the ability to make such an assertion marks a change for us.[3] In the process of transition U.S. women religious are acting on the conviction that the primary place of God's action is in the personal and communal life experience of the "folk," the people of God. This belief challenges a system that holds that knowledge about God comes exclusively from Revelation and through a static tradition interpreted by certain appointed persons in virtue of hierarchical positions.

If the personal and collective experiences of the people of God are contact points with God, then the process of coming to name God is of necessity collaborative. Together as an inclusive community we share our personal, as well as our collective, experiences and together seek to find words adequate to express the plurality of those experiences. Such collaboration requires a high trust level in one another and in the process itself. Naming God emerges from an interior authority flowing from the cumulative experience of all God's people. The process is probably inefficient, at least time-consuming, and runs the risk of ambiguity or misunderstanding. On the other hand the same process emphasizes personal involvement and facilitates renewal of heart. When only an elect few can claim a direct entree to God, then the framework for a hierarchical and exclusive ecclesial organization is put in place. The head, or patriarch, is the ultimate interpreter of God language. The head determines what information, power or truth is passed on, when and to whom. Individuals transmit what they have received supposedly without private interpretation or meaning. The potential for interior conversion of heart is minimized. This approach relies rather on external transmission from the top, and, by its structure, includes only those in the chain of command. In theory, though hardly in practice, this approach is efficient, free from error and ambiguity. It requires obedience to the superior and trust in the system.

It follows that any group employing the kind of collaborative process that produced this paper could rightly be charged with subverting the tradition. Naming God from our experience as U.S. women religious presents an alternative to the usual, that is, the dominant, way of doing or of thinking about things.[4] As an alternative approach to the dominant way of structuring life, a collaborative, inclusive, participative process of naming God threatens the way things are. U.S. women religious are deliberately, with an increasing awareness of the implications, choosing to participate and to encourage participation in describing our relationship to God. This decision is reflected in the organizational structures of our communal living. It is a choice that affects the way we experience and speak about God in public prayer and other public forums. It would be naive to view the collaborative process as less than a radical embodiment of an alternative worldview. The struggle over worldview within the Roman Catholic Church stretches back at least to the successful rejection of the divine right of kings during the French Revolution.

Hierarchical, patriarchal structures are not, however, the exclusive domain of the institutional Church. Wherever action or ideas must originate at the top to be imposed by enlightened superiors on supposedly less informed inferiors, there is hierarchy. Whenever one requires unthinking submission instead of responsibility from the masses, then patriarchy is operative. The hierarchical and patriarchal way are structural and attitudinal approaches toward life that may appear in any institution, even in congregations of U.S. women religious.

Explicit Questions

The process in which U.S. women religious are engaged, namely, that of bringing the experience of God to birth in language, can be facilitated by the conscious awareness of the strengths and weaknesses of what we are doing.

The LCWR summary reports testify that U.S. women religious are proactive. Our naming of God is *not* done by the negation of what we have received from classical language, that is, in reaction to an oppressive past. Rather our efforts to name God come from a position of trust in our cumulative experience and in our internal authority. This stance is not an arrogant claim to have the only valid insight about God, for we are self-possessed enough to acknowledge the need of ongoing conversion, to recognize the necessity of continuing dialogue with all women as well as men, and to embrace the ambiguity in our attempts. Such a proactive approach is a strength of what we are doing.

The conviction that language about God emerges from the collective life experience keeps the collaborative process firmly rooted in the historical situation. The result has the distinct advantage of avoiding the separatism and elitism of millenial communities. Separation from the "folk," or the claim of special insight, would undermine and destroy the alternative that we treasure. Fidelity to the participatory alternative requires that we identify ourselves as part of the "folk" in these times.

In our participatory approach to eliciting images of God, we recall the constitutive nature of language. Language emerges from our experience of God but also enables that same experience. Images for God take on a formative life of their own. The process of eliciting images needs to be sensitive to language that is capable of describing God faithfully and of facilitating the experience of God. The sense of God that has emerged from the LCWR reports is of a cosmic energy, an intimate relational presence active in human living and inclusive of apparent opposites. Is this description complete enough for our experience as U.S. women religious? We suggest three points for further reflection.

The image of God that evolved from the LCWR summaries was fundamentally that of a "nice" God. Even though the experience from which the images derived included pain, suffering, poverty, and conflict, the image itself was "pleasant." Is there room for a God who is angry at injustices, especially those perpetuated in the divine name? Is there a place for suffering in our understanding of God's way with us? Is there a place for a God who desires that patriarchal structures be shaken so that inclusive love may be experienced? Where is the God of the Exodus, the God of the Exile, the God of Jesus who called for the revision of the dominant worldview? It would seem essential that U.S. women religious must come to experience and embrace this God if we are to continue living an alternative to unjust, patriarchal structures. We wonder if the preponderance of "nice God" images might reflect a projection of our own desire to be the perfect exemplar of religious life, a woman who never gets angry or who never challenges structures. Is this absence a faithful description of God? Will it facilitate the experience of God in our struggle to embody an alternative structure of life-meaning?

The images of God in the LCWR report were noticeably devoid of images for God born from our unique experience as women. God was named "mother/father" in one summary and the adjective "birthing" was used once. There was, as has been seen, a tendency to transcend masculine/feminine or to keep them in tension. If our images of God emerge from our personal and collective experiences, what does the minimal reference to images specifically from woman's experience suggest about our experience of ourselves as women? Perhaps we do experience ourselves as women, but our religious imagination has been so shaped by the dominance of masculine language that we are not free to image a God from our womanly experience.[5] Or does the absence reflect the increased awareness that images for God derived from woman's experience are counter to the dominant worldview, or even threaten it? We are not able to image ourselves in a countercultural position. If we cannot experience or affirm personally and publicly that God can be described in images from women's experience, then how can we as women find reason to affirm that we are created in God's image; or that the Spirit of Jesus dwells in and among us? If God cannot be described in images from our own experience as women, where do we find the vision to claim an alternative worldview?

Finally, it is not clear at this point that we have come to grips with our Christian and biblical linguistic heritage. There is little explicit connection between the above images of God and the language of the Bible. There were two references to Jesus. Has the patriarchal language in the Bible rendered it useless for late twentieth century women? Does the fact that Jesus was a male destroy his significance for women?[6] These questions cannot be answered by dismissing the Scriptures or Jesus. Faithfulness to the structural alternative we espouse requires that we enter into dialogue with the Bible and Jesus. The cumulative community consensus is not just a present reality inclusive of the contemporary United States or even of the World Church. It must include the community of all ages. We cannot ignore the communities of the past. If we do not integrate the past, especially that which is most painful, the buried hurt will sap the energy we need to live out the inclusive alternative to which we are committed.

What is at stake when women religious are doing our own naming of God? We maintain that the collaborative, inclusive, participative way of structuring and experiencing meaning in the whole of living is at stake.

Ecclesial Women

One effect of naming God from our Gospel-directed experience as women is that our self-understanding as ecclesial women changes. As we name God differently, we bring different expectations to Church. Materials gathered from LCWR members by the Religious Life Task Force from 1984–1986 give clear indications that significant numbers of women religious are moving from understanding ourselves as women of the Church to claiming ourselves, along with other women, ecclesial women.[7]

The LCWR Synthesis prepared for the Fifth Inter-American Conference describes how many women religious understand Church and our relations within it. Some of the changes in our expectations of Church seem subtle at first. Women religious use language for imaging Church which is familiar since Vatican II: the Church as the people of God, a community, and pilgrim people (Appendix, p. 180). This document makes clear, however, that for women religious "there are new awarenesses of qualities which are inherent in the traditional images but which we have not emphasized in the past, . . . [and there are] new images, some of these reflecting a distinctively feminine mode of perception."[8]

Women religious expect the Church to embody the same images that it, through Vatican Council II, called us to incarnate in our lives and ministries. It is not surprising, then, that we look to other groups within the institutional Church also to embody the values these images invite: to be just, caring, inclusive, participatory, collaborative, mutually accountable, and attentive to those currently marginalized (Appendix, p. 181). These include those marginated socially, such as people living in poverty, women, people of color, Third World peoples; but also those disenfranchised by official church teachings, such as divorced people, homosexuals, those practicing birth control or terminating pregnancy, and laicized clergy.[9] Women religious, then, look to the Church to be prophetic in two senses: first, to model relations of mutuality, justice, and caring; and second, from this experience, to call for the transformation of all attitudes and structures that exclude and oppress, including its own (*Ibid.*). In calling the Church, including ourselves, to conversion, we perform a role appropriate to insiders who *are* Church.

What may first appear to be only nuances in how women religious understand and so relate within Church turn out to be important ways through which we are helping to shape Church. Taking seriously the incarnational basis of Christianity assures us of God's presence among us, within the world, enabling us to trust the revelatory dimensions of human experience (pp. 173–4). This conviction, when accompanied by the recognition that the whole institutional Church, including ourselves, is called to become what it is not yet, invites us to bring into Church the God disclosed in the midst of our living.

Nourished by a strong incarnational theology, women religious understand ourselves to have a responsibility both to transform unjust and uncaring structures, attitudes, and policies wherever we find them, as well as to give public witness to Gospel values.[10] For years following the Second Vatican Council, we engaged whole-heartedly in a process of renewal at the Council's behest. Ironically, obedience to these mandates led to discovering and embracing our own moral and religious authority, that is, the responsibility we have, personally and communally, for authoring the specific ways we embody Gospel visions.

The results are evident in how we describe ourselves and our mission: we "share the character of being agents of change and cultural transformation in the world . . . with all others . . . in the church . . ." (p. 179). The Fifth Inter-American LCWR paper speaks of our awareness of a "social responsibility that flows out of a social spirituality." This "means we are called to risk, to give public witness, to develop a mature conscience, to shape a new vision, develop new values, to speak and act for peace and justice" (pp. 176-7). The LCWR *Content Analysis* of congregational documents underscores our strong commitment to "justice and peacemaking" in a variety of modes (cited in 78% of the documents studied), as well as the "action dimension" of these commitments as "forms of public witness" (p. 187-8). These commitments lead many to a special concern with women in Church and society. Our commitment to those living in poverty—most of whom are women and those dependent on them (p. 176)—and to the "empowerment of the politically oppressed" (p. 186) positions us in new alliances with women and other disempowered people within Church and society.

What happens when women religious live out Gospel-inspired commitments to witness publicly against the "ecclesiastical, social, economic, and political structures that perpetuate the oppression and dehumanization of world peoples . . ."? (p. 180). The Fifth Inter-American LCWR paper succinctly summarizes the answer: "we seek new patterns of relating to Church hierarchy" (p. 178). The relational roles of women religious and Church hierarchy alter, much the way the roles through which children and parents relate change once the children are themselves responsible adults.[11] Earlier, women religious looked to the Church hierarchy to challenge us, at least through the Council documents, into Gospel-directed growth. Now we, like other peoples empowered toward liberation through Gospel-living, seek more collaborative ecclesial roles and structures, those that more faithfully will reflect and further encourage the responsible Christian living to which the Church calls us.[12] We see the effects in a number of ways: for example, in decisions to broaden ministries beyond ecclesial or congregational institutions and in working for "patterns of mutual accountability with structures for responsible dissent" within our congregations, ministries, Church, and society (p. 178). We find, however, that our efforts are not always welcomed by those in positions of authority.

In the last few years the U.S. press has reported a number of incidents in which the Roman Catholic hierarchy challenged ministry-related public actions by women religious.[13] Other recent experiences—the revision of canon law, Vatican promulgations about religious life, such as *Essential Elements*, and the role of women in seminary education as well as responses by the Congregation for Religious and for Secular Institutes (CRIS) to the constitutions of U.S. women's religious congregations—suggest that the Church hierarchy at times show more willingness to maintain their institutional power base than to attend to the groaning Spirit within our lives. Taken together, these experiences intimate that much is at stake when women religious begin to alter our place within Church.

At the same time, there is little evidence in congregational documents that women religious are experiencing tensions with Church hierarchy or inequities as women within Church. Although justice-related issues recur repeatedly in documents studied, the LCWR *Content Analysis* of selected congregational documents states that "the theme of conflict within the Church as a justice and peace issue" is mentioned in only 14% of the materials in one sample (Appendix, p. 186). This may be explained in a number of ways. Lack of reference to this conflict in congregational documents may mean that this is an unimportant issue. But there could be other explanations. This omission may reflect a prudent decision not to confront Church hierarchy in such documents, or it may represent a decision to live from our own authority rather than give primacy to external regulation. In contrast, this omission could indicate an inability or unwillingness on our part to assume full responsibility as ecclesial women.

Reflections on Becoming Ecclesial Women

Increasingly and with lessening hesitation, women religious are naming ourselves *women*. This is clear when we examine congregational documents or listen to our conversations—with God, ourselves, others within Church or in our ministries. And this is a new thing. Reviewing similar documents and conversations from just ten years ago will reveal the difference. Naming ourselves *women* strikes at the root of patriarchal delineations of women, perhaps especially of women religious who have been characterized as "nuns" and "sisters." Given the typical negative connotations that both Church and society attach to women, we affirm something positive about ourselves when we call ourselves *women*. As we women religious name ourselves *women* we symbolize something good.[14] But it is not clear that we understand fully the implications of this naming. Whether or not women religious fully understand what is at stake and whether or not we will pull back when the cost is high, we cannot presume. For us to continue in the direction we are already journeying, however, we must become clear about what is at stake, for us and for the rest of the Church.

Naming ourselves *women* aligns us, and, through us, the Church with the liberating movements of our time. Calling ourselves *women* is political, for it connects us with all those excluded by hierarchical institutional structures and commits us to using our resources and privileges towards liberation. More specifically, calling ourselves *women* says we participate in the global women's liberation movements shaped by and in turn shaping U.S. women's efforts. Even more to the point, consciously adopting the designation *women* in a Church that largely encourages traditional supportive roles for women commits us and other members of the Church to liberating the Church, as well as society, from sexism.

Our growing consciousness of ourselves as ecclesial women doubly compounds our relations within Church. We see ourselves "*as* Church, rather than being in relation *to* Church," and we bring a "consciousness of women, of ourselves, as responsible mature persons" (Appendix, p. 178). Two sorts of reflections on the implications of living as ecclesial women follow, one exploring the political dimensions and the other, the feminist.

Women religious are acting politically when we name God from within our experience as Christian women, when we seek more appropriate roles as ecclesial women, and when we call ourselves *women*. Implicit in these reciprocally related actions are our Gospel-inspired commitments to transform the world—structures as well as attitudes, institutions as well as hearts. Examining the many ways these activities are political illuminates the tensions many U.S. women religious experience within Church and, at the same time, recovers the usefulness of the controversial term *political* for understanding this experience.

Women religious are often wary about having our religiously motivated actions or reflections termed *political*. In part, this reluctance is due to the fact that in contemporary U.S. society, the term *political* carries many negative connotations: uncritical partisan allegiances, self-serving aggrandizement, accumulating personal control over others, sophisticated processes for camouflaging lies or manipulating truth, and monied interests representing the masses in elected office. These, however, are not the only or most important meanings of the term *political*.

Living humanly means living politically because human living is social and historical. We live embodied, with particular characteristics, such as race, nationality, sex, age and sexual preference. We live historically conditioned by factors such as geographical and cultural placement, technological level of advancement, economic position, national and global interrelationships, sometimes conflictual. And we live socially, among specific people, connected within a variety of social groups, such as family, friends, church, communities, associates in the workplace and interest groups. Admitting that human existence is political allows us to see that present configurations of power, money, influence, authority, food, work, whether in society or Church, are as political as attempts to change the established order. The civil or ecclesiastical *status quo* is itself one arrangement among other possibilities; it is not established by nature or Revelation. Understanding that human living is inescapably political demystifies the meaning of *political* by broadening it.[15]

Several more specific meanings of *political* are relevant for understanding where women religious now place ourselves within Church. Its derivation from the Greek *polis*, in spite of being limited to free male citizens by the Athenians, emphasizes participation in a community with shared responsibility for shaping something in the perceived best interests of the community. Consequently, being political involves social activity. When we act in communion with others or affect others by our acts, we engage in political action. By application, communal action, or an individual's action as part of a community—for instance, as women and men of the Church—is by its very nature political action.

The root definition of *political* also means that all public acts—those that affect the whole or the part, those performed openly or in secret—are political, whether they coincide with or challenge established views. The word *political*, then, is not in its root meaning pejorative but rather it describes actions that are social and public. In practice, it usually acquires negative connotations when the actions described challenge prevailing structures and attitudes.

This distinction helps us understand that women religious publicly claiming ourselves ecclesial women is political in multiple ways. If we were naming ourselves ecclesial women in secret societies or whispering our names for God only in our hearts or affinity prayer groups, then the political significance of these acts would be less than what is claimed here. What once was said in private or only to spiritual directors, however, is frequently discussed in governing assemblies, printed for congregational prayer gatherings, and published in congregational communications. Increasingly, we come together expecting that our common prayer will use gender free language and that God will be described without patriarchal or hierarchical designations. Naming ourselves *women* and generating names for God from our experience as women, and uniquely as women religious, have become social, public and, thereby, political acts.

Identifying *political* with *public* is not without its problems for many women religious. This fact becomes apparent in disagreements over using secular vehicles—newspapers, television, radio, interest groups, women's meetings—to raise Church-related issues. What is clear, however, is that a narrow definition of what *political* means buys into the traditional dualistic separations of private and public, sacred and secular, without lessening the political nature of the acts.

Additional meanings of *political* emerge when the hope of effecting changes within Church encourages women religious to persist with certain actions in the face of disapproval from Church hierarchy. When congregations question some of the Church-prescribed requirements for their constitutions, for example, they do so for many different reasons: Gospel-based commitments to justice starting from those currently marginalized, obedience to broader Church mandates to be leaven in the world, respect for the responsibility and authority of their congregations to interpret their history and mission, or faithfulness to the prophetic charism of their congregations. Their concern to remain faithful in reading their own tradition invites Church officials to understand the congregation's practices as Gospel-inspired. The action of these congregations is political, then, in a double sense: it is action chosen deliberately, and it is chosen to influence the attitudes and practices of others. In addition, this approach of some congregations illustrates that ecclesial women sometimes embark on a course of action within Church in order to raise awareness about a value-laden issue even when we recognize that difficult consequences may result.

These meanings, then, expand conventional understandings of political activity to include actions that are communal, public, self-consciously chosen, intended to affect beliefs and practices and so to transform structures, attitudes, or relations. A further, and more common, meaning of *political* involves power and relationships.

Within our world, so largely shaped by hierarchical values, power is associated with control over others. Efforts to liberate ourselves and our world from the patriarchal worldview toward inclusive and collaborative Gospel values involve revisioning and restructuring what power means. Instead of presuming that all relations involve struggles for control of one person or group over another, feminists and other liberationists argue that relations among persons and things can be empowering. Cultivating "power-to" rather than "power-over" means first acknowledging and then enabling the potential energies in others. Doing this makes it possible to identify shared purposes around which to rechannel our energies cooperatively and constructively.[16]

The center of power has shifted for many women religious as we experience and affirm our own strengths. We nurture our spiritual energies, personally and communally, author our Gospel witness and ministries, fuel Gospel commitments with embodied powers, name ourselves and God from our Gospel-lived experience, create conditions and structures within our communities and ministries that enable others to claim their voice and power, and bond with others seeking liberation of persons, institutions, societies, and the earth. Actions that empower us will, of course, reduce the power others have over us. The shift from external authorities to internal personal and communal authority that women religious are experiencing alters, and therefore may threaten, authoritarian patterns where they still exist within Church and society.

As long as many women religious and Church hierarchy live within two different worldviews, the political activities of women religious to empower ourselves and others will appear within the patriarchal framework as direct challenges to those who see themselves in authority over us. If, however, we deny that our actions are political, in the many senses just described, then we forego the power to name accurately our lived experience. Moreover, persisting in actions without acknowledging them as political will not make these actions, or us, less threatening to patriarchal power structures.

Should we fail to take responsibility for the political nature of our actions, we would deprive ourselves of a rich term to talk about our realities with one another and to relate our efforts to other liberation struggles. As a result, the transformations toward which we strive would not be realized. Changing hearts and structures depends on our seeing and naming as accurately as possible both problems and alternatives.

Naming God from our experience, claiming ourselves ecclesial women, and seeking a liberating ecclesiology are indeed political acts. What *political* means, however, changes considerably depending on one's standpoint. When we look at it from the perspective of women theologizing from our experience as women, these acts are political in the root meaning of social, public activity deliberately chosen by full members of the community out of our Gospel responsibility for helping shape the world and, thereby, the Church. Looking at these same activities through a patriarchal lens, however, discloses the subversive dimensions of these acts for they challenge institutionalized patterns of patriarchy.

Subversive, from the Latin *subvertere*, literally means "to turn" from "down or under," suggesting efforts comparable to spading gardens in the spring, bringing richer soil to the top from underneath. The actions we have been describing are subversive in two senses: they seek to transform things from a rich foundation, and the starting point is the experience of those now kept under. Insofar as the Church is patriarchal, to claim ourselves ecclesial women and to take seriously our experience as women is subversive and hence political in this additional sense.

How we understand and name our women-centered actions is itself both important and political. The term *feminism*, and its corresponding adjective *feminist*, describe a specific kind of political action that, when properly understood, offers a description that is consonant with the purposes and values women religious pursue. Unfortunately, many seem to resist the term as impolitic, inappropriate, or controversial. Yet if we are committed to transforming the hierarchical, elitist structures and attitudes of patriarchy, then it behooves us to reexamine the feminist dimensions of our commitments toward just, participatory, and inclusive models.

The lure of the *feminine* as preferable to *feminist* holds many in its thrall, as is evident in the materials collected by the LCWR Task Force on Religious Life. *Feminine* is consistently used to ascribe to God characteristics traditionally associated with women's social roles,[17] a specific kind of spirituality and values,[18] and a distinctive mode of perception.[19] While "woman's consciousness" and "women-centered ways" of seeing the world describe how many women religious "live in the world," (Appendix, p. 176–8) and while we frequently describe ourselves as women, the term *feminist*, by contrast, seems to be carefully, perhaps deliberately, avoided.[20]

Appearing less political and more natural than *feminist*, *feminine* disguises the particular political ideology it carries. Since its nineteenth century invention, the meaning of *feminine* changes to mirror what is missing from the prevailing ideology of *masculine*. *Feminine* is always relational; *feminine* denotes characteristics that are defined in relation to the masculine, which is generally perceived as primary and normative. To be *feminine* is not then, as many would like to believe, to embody womanliness but rather to complement, and thereby complete, a masculine ideology. To be feminine is not being oneself but rather embodying the opposite of what men are supposed to be at a given historical moment. The word *feminist*, by contrast, speaks of exposing the political nature of personal feminine ideals.

Throughout its long and complex history, feminism has involved a commitment to political, economic, social, religious, sexual and educational equality of the sexes. To understand the feminism emerging globally in our time, it is helpful to contrast it with patriarchy. Both describe a worldview and consciousness, values and patterns of relating, attitudes and practices that are not confined to either sex. Just as many women can and do internalize and then act from patriarchal values, so it is possible for men to acquire a feminist consciousness. Feminism is an embodied stance in the world that criticizes the elitist, hierarchical, privileged, authoritarian modes of patriarchy and, at the same time, creates alternatives that are collaborative, mutual, inclusive, and empowering. Attention to the specific forms patriarchy has acquired historically within the web of international capitalism, racism, militarism, and imperialism structuring our world leads many feminists to work against sexism not in isolation but as it is interconnected with other oppressions. As a result, many feminists, including many women religious, increasingly understand that growing militarization is connected to escalating global poverty, especially among women of color, and that peacemaking requires changes within ourselves and our relations, as well as in governmental and economic priorities. Today the purposes, methods, and values of feminism overlap in many areas with those voiced by women religious described earlier. As a consequence, it should not be surprising that a growing identification of women religious as feminists exists alongside a corresponding effort to discourage feminism by those more comfortable within patriarchal modes, including some in our congregations and Church.

The choice to use the term *feminist* or *feminine* is political in either case. The *feminine* choice rejects the power of naming the personal as political conveyed by the word *feminist*, and consequently perpetuates patriarchal dualisms by separating what is integrally connected—the private from the public and the personal from the political. *Feminism* insists on exposing the connections among the personal and the political at all levels and seeks transformation of unjust oppressive attitudes and structures. It connects private, ideological, and psychological oppressions with global economic exploitation and military oppression of the earth and peoples whose cultures or social roles do not represent dominant patriarchal values. Choosing to use the term *feminist* is itself a political act, one that places women religious among those women and men committed to transforming interconnected oppressions by using the experience of oppressed women as both the starting point and the criterion for evaluating success.

We need to find terms other than the word *feminine* for speaking positively about values and qualities traditionally associated with women. *Womanly* and *women-centered* appear to be possible alternatives, although they are less inclusive and less political. Alice Walker's term *womanist* offers one option welcomed by several black feminist theologians.[21] While it may take time for satisfactory language to emerge from women's experience, it behooves women religious not to replace *feminist* with *feminine*, for the latter waters down an insistence on transforming patriarchy and instead perpetuates it. It is important, then, in calling ourselves *women* to discard all of the understandings that play into and reinforce patriarchal practices.

Explicit Questions: What is at stake in women religious calling ourselves women?

The materials amassed from LCWR members show that women religious refer to ourselves more frequently and self-consciously as *women* and we do this with a heightened consciousness of bonding with other women. Yet reflecting on how few emerging images for God come from women's concrete experience and how little attention congregational documents pay to ecclesiastical injustice to women leads to the conclusion that, on the whole, we have not internalized the implications of naming ourselves women. This is evident in several ways in the LCWR Task Force materials.

For many women religious, naming God from our experience does not seem to entail a critique of sexism in the Church or of naming the Church patriarchal. While these materials do not show that women religious draw a direct connection between traditional theological names for God and ecclesiastical patriarchy, the seeds for making this connection are already planted when women surface alternative names for God from our experience. Since our understanding of God affects our expectations of Church and its mission, as we generate names for God that are more attentive to our experience as women, we may discover more discrepancies between our God and our Church, at least in its present hierarchical forms.

Moreover, there is a lack of identifying ourselves as women in descriptions of women religious bonding with other women. Many, it seems, do not sufficiently understand that calling ourselves *women* implies bonding with women *as* women. We speak generally, expressing a "concern for women in the Church and society," a "commitment to collaborate with other women," and a "willingness to offer leadership in working with women and in enabling them and calling them to leadership . . ." (Appendix,

p. 187). Usually, we do not explicitly identify ourselves among the women we describe. Our language seems to reinforce the notion that women religious stand apart from those we seek to help.[22] Although we explicitly include women among those for whom we have concern, we do not identify ourselves strongly with them or name ourselves among the women marginalized and oppressed. This hesitation may indicate that we recognize our privileged positions as First World, middle class women in society, at least through our education, membership in a congregation, and status as women religious in the Church. Still, as long as we remain apart, in a position of helping others, we fail to bond with women *as* women, sharing comparable or even common experiences. What is at stake for women religious who own what it means to be women and cast our lot with women, bonded as women, is to risk losing our ambiguous, but still privileged, position within Church.

Women religious are in a complex place within Church. We have credibility, privileges, and status inside the institutional Church that are not accorded our other "lay" sisters. At the same time, as women within a Church that is still very patriarchal, we are marginal to teaching, sacramental, and administrative functions. In calling ourselves ecclesial women we confront this complex position that gives us both multiple responsibilities and possibilities.

Acknowledging this complex position, many of us conclude that we have a responsibility to address those teachings, sacramental practices, language, policies, and administrative decisions that now only partially express Gospel values. Naming ourselves ecclesial women acknowledges the particular perspective we bring and directs us to specific issues that have not yet been adequately addressed. As a result, many women religious insist that women need to help shape Church teaching and practice.

Crucial questions confront women religious once we recognize ourselves as ecclesial women with responsibilities as well as personal and congregational resources. Are we persuaded that naming the patriarchal similarities among ecclesiastical, governmental, and economic systems is a Gospel responsibility? Does it make a difference that we call ourselves *women* within a largely patriarchal Church and thereby place ourselves existentially among, rather than just alongside, the powerless? Do we accept that as ecclesial women, with more experience of powerlessness and less to lose than Church men, we have more "response-ability" to address ecclesiastical oppressions? What is our role within Church, especially when Vatican officials place great emphasis on the public witness of women religious but often use this to limit the scope of our responsibilities? Do we follow the example of many male Latin American liberation theologians and limit our critique of unjust structures to governmental and economic systems? Do we too withhold the light of our liberating critique from shining on ecclesiastical structures in order to maintain hierarchical approval to speak as Church people? Does our position as women religious entice us to make accommodations in our speaking and acting that may buy us official credibility at the expense of silencing parts of our truth?

Conclusion

Exploring the significance of these two related phenomena—emerging ways in which many women religious speak about God and identify ourselves as ecclesial women—clarifies what is at stake should we continue the journey these begin. We discover that what is at stake in naming God from our experience as women is more than a language change, just as what is at stake in seeking collaborative relations within the Church involves more than changing procedures. Once we generate names for God from women's experience, how do we pray with the Church in liturgies and theological concepts belonging to another worldview and consciousness? Once committed as ecclesial women to a Gospel-centered Church that is inclusive, justice-seeking, caring, collaborative, prophetic, and enabling of persons, how do we relate within a tradition and with Church hierarchy who embody patriarchal values?

Women religious now face an opportunity that comes at rare moments in history: to participate in transforming the institutional Church by continuing the transformation of ourselves and apostolic religious life that we have already begun. After encouraging others to reflect on God and the meaning of the Gospel as these are disclosed through their experience, many of us begin to heed our own advice. Once we recognize ourselves as sharing powerlessness, we come to seek self-determination for ourselves and for all marginalized peoples through the transformation of oppressive structures. The fact that many women religious may not yet see these connections, namely that calling ourselves *women* is central to how we name God and relate within Church, does not make the connections less real. It does mean, however, that women religious have only begun to experience and understand what is at stake in calling ourselves *women*.

ENDNOTES

1. Schneiders, *Women and the Word* (Mahwah, NJ: Paulist Press 1986) 6–7.

2. This pattern is consistent with the findings in Mary Farrell Bednarowski, "Outside the Mainstream: Women's Religion and Women Religious Leaders in Nineteenth-Century America,"

in *Journal of the American Academy of Religion* 48 (No. 2, 1980) 207–231, especially 208–209. Having studied Ann Lee who founded the Shakers, the Fox sisters who were closely associated with Spiritualism, Ellen G. White of the Adventists, Mary Baker Eddy of Christian Science and Helena P. Blavarsky of the Theosophical movement, Bednarowski concludes that women achieved leadership positions and equal status when the religious movement embodied the following assumptions: 1. a perception of the divine that deemphasized the masculine either by means of a bisexual divinity or an impersonal, nonanthropomorphic divine principle; 2. a tempering or denial of the doctrine of the Fall; 3. a denial of the need for a traditional ordained clergy; 4. a view of marriage that did not stress the married state and motherhood as the proper sphere for woman and her only means of fulfillment.

3. The following quotations from the LCWR summaries note this change: "We trust the revelation of God through all of life's experiences." We have "moved from what was taught about God to what had been experienced of God." "No longer having 'proscriptions' about our God-images, we are free to know God uniquely." We have come to "the conviction that our personal and communal experiences are the loci of God's revelation." It is now a matter of "trusting one's inner authority."

4. W. Brueggemann, *The Prophetic Imagination* (Philadelphia: Fortress Press, 1978) describes the prophet as one engaging in living out an alternative to the dominant worldview.

5. Cf. Schneiders, *op. cit.* 10: "To image God or speak to God as feminine does not change the God image for these people; it destroys it."

6. Schneiders (*Ibid.* 58–62) effectively makes the case that Jesus had to be male in order to reveal the true nature of God and of humanity. Her argument is anything but the stereotypical approach.

7. Most of these materials are included as Appendices in this volume. This section draws primarily on two sources: the LCWR paper prepared for the Fifth Inter-American Conference held in November 1985, and "An Exploratory Content Analysis of Major Themes in Selected Documents of United States Women Religious" prepared by Anne Munley, IHM. The selected documents, described more fully in the Methodology section of the "Content Analysis," include recent chapter documents, administrative reports of general and provincial government, mission statements, goal or priority statements, vow and vow renewal formulae but not constitutions or directories.

8. Appendix, p. 181. The implications of women religious using the term *feminine* are discussed more fully below.

9. The Fifth Inter-American LCWR paper states: "The church . . . is imaged [by women religious] in particular relationship with the religious and social outcasts of our times, the poor, the marginalized, and the oppressed" (Appendix, p. 181).

10. Several passages in the LCWR paper for the Fifth Inter-American state this strongly, as

these examples illustrate. "A heightened sense of mission and awareness of unmet survival needs of suffering brothers and sisters are leading American religious to critique social structures, institutions and systems from a Gospel perspective" (Appendix, p. 174). "Like Christ, we recognize that religious commitment is embodied in the world, thereby involving us with the specific social, political, economic, and intellectual realities shaping people's lives" (p. 176). See also the "Content Analysis" (p. 188) for reference to the prevalence of incarnational theology and related issues in congregational documents, as well as Catherine Osimo's article, "Women's Center: Incarnational Spirituality," in this volume.

11.   "We expect dialogue as peers to replace parent-child relationships" (Appendix, p. 178).

12.   Brief passages from the LCWR paper illustrate this point: "Increasingly women religious see ourselves less as women running church institutions and more as church women," and "We see ourselves moving from maintaining existing structures to creating alternatives" (Appendix, p. 178).

13.   The situations of Agnes Mary Mansour in Michigan, Elizabeth Morancy in Rhode Island, and Arlene Violet in Rhode Island are probably the best known incidents in which Church hierarchy criticized specific ministries of women religious holding public office, making it necessary for the women to choose between their ministries and membership in their congregations. *Authority, Community and Conflict,* edited by Madonna Kolbenschlag, presents a case study of the experience of Sisters of Mercy of the Union in public office with insightful commentaries and theological reflections (Kansas City, Mo.: Sheed & Ward, 1986).

Also well known are the events surrounding a *New York Times* statement (October 2, 1984), which affirmed that a diversity of opinion on abortion exists among committed Catholics and called for education about and discussion of reproductive issues. In this case Vatican agencies called upon religious superiors to begin canonical procedures for dismissal of the twenty-five women religious, who were among other Catholics signing the statement, if they were unwilling to retract the statement publicly.

14.   This conclusion was confirmed by Anne Munley, IHM, during a telephone conversation about the congregational materials used in the "Content Analysis."

15.   Latin American liberation theologians emphasize a broad notion of the word *political.* Gustavo Gutierrez announces, for example, that "Human reason has become political reason." *A Theology of Liberation: History, Politics and Salvation.* trans. Caridad Inda and John Eagleson (Maryknoll, New York: Orbis Books, 1973) 47. See also Juan Luis Segundo, SJ, *The Liberation of Theology,* trans. John Drury (Maryknoll, New York: Orbis Books, 1976), esp. Ch. III, 69–95.

16.   Several authors approach this in different ways. Especially insightful are Starhawk, *Dreaming the Dark: Magic, Sex & Politics* (Boston: Beacon Press, 1982); Paulo Friere, *Pedagogy of the Oppressed,* trans. Myra Bergman Ramos (New York: Seabury Press, 1970); Thomas H. Groome, *Christian Religious Education: Sharing Our Story and Vision* (San Francisco: Harper & Row, 1980).

17.   See "Images of God" from Regions 7 and 13 in Appendix, pp. 195, 198.

18. See LCWR "Content Analysis," Appendix, p. 183, and LCWR paper for the Fifth Inter-American, Appendix, p. 173.

19. See Appendix, p. 181.

20. In contrast to other materials collected by the LCWR Task Force on Religious Life, reports from table discussions at the 1984 LCWR National Conference explicitly use the term *feminist* with great frequency. Perhaps this fact reflects the influence of at least one major paper at the conference addressing feminist spirituality. These discussions suggest that at that time there was a greater prevalence among LCWR members to speak of *feminist* than is found in the other materials gathered by the Task Force.

21. Alice Walker, *In Search of Our Mothers' Gardens: Womanist Prose* (New York: Harcourt Brace Jovanovich, 1983) xi–xii. See also Katie Geneva Cannon, "The Emergence of Black Feminist Consciousness," *Feminist Interpretation of the Bible*, ed. Letty M. Russell (Philadelphia: Westminster Press, 1985) esp. 39–40; and Delores Williams, "Womanist Theology: Black Women's Voices," *Christianity and Crisis* (March 21, 1987) 55–70.

22. There are some exceptions to this in the data collected by the Task Force on Religious Life. See especially the *LCWR Synthesis* for the Fifth Inter-American, Appendix, p. 176: "When our commitment to the poor discloses that the majority of the poor are women, we become aware of ourselves as women who are oppressed and marginalized, within our church as well as in our society." See also p. 174: "A spirit of kinship with all women prompts special concern for women who are abused, deprived of opportunities to achieve their potential or victims of the 'feminization of poverty' phenomenon in American society."

REFLECTION QUESTIONS

1. What are my names for God and what experiences have led me to know God by these names? What is at stake in surfacing our own names for God?

2. How can Gospel-centered women, committed to a collaborative and inclusive approach, minister in and relate to the Church as they experience it?

3. What is the responsibility of women religious insofar as the Church is patriarchal? Are there particular issues and concerns that women religious have a special responsibility to address?

4. The authors state that women religious are naming ourselves *women* and because we do, we image God differently. These experiences then yield political consequences in our relationship to the institutional Church. The authors suggest that the political interaction will yield new

ecclesial patterns. What might the characteristics and the values of these new patterns/ structures be?

RECOMMENDED READING

Brueggemann, Walter. *The Prophetic Imagination.* Philadelphia: Fortress Press, 1985.

Cameron, Anne. *Daughters of Copper Woman.* Vancouver, British Columbia: Press Gang Publishers, 1981.

Christ, Carol and Judith Plaskow, eds. *Women Spirit Rising: A Feminist Reader in Religion.* San Francisco: Harper & Row, 1979.

Daly, Mary. *Beyond God the Father: Toward a Philosophy of Women's Liberation.* Original Reintroduction by the Author. Boston: Beacon Press, 1973.

Fiorenza, Elisabeth Schüssler. *In Memory of Her: A Feminist Reconstruction of Christian Origins.* New York: The Crossroad Publishing Company, 1984.

Gage, Matilda Joslyn. *Women, Church and State: The Original Expose of Male Collaboration Against the Female Sex.* Watertown, Mass.: Persephone Press, 1980, c. 1893.

Gutierrez, Gustavo. *We Drink From Our Own Wells: The Spiritual Journey of a People.* trans. Matthew J. O'Connell. Maryknoll, NY: Orbis Books, 1984.

Hooks, Bell. *Feminist Theory: From Margin to Center.* Boston: South End Press, 1984.

Kolbenschlag, Madonna, ed. *Between God and Caesar: Priests, Sisters and Political Office in the United States.* New York: Paulist Press, 1985.

Lerner, Gerda. *The Creation of Patriarchy.* New York: Oxford University Press, 1986.

Lorde, Audre. *Sister Outsider: Essays and Speeches.* Trumansburg, NY: Crossing Press, 1984.

Morton, Nelle. *The Journey Is Home.* Boston: Beacon Press, 1985.

Mud Flower Collective. *God's Fierce Whimsy: Christian Feminism and Theological Education.* New York: Pilgrim Press, 1985.

Ruether, Rosemary Radford. *Sexism and God-Talk: Toward a Feminist Theology.* Boston: Beacon Press, 1983.

Schneiders, Sandra M. *Women and the Word.* New York: Paulist Press, 1986.

Spender, Dale. *Man Made Language*. 2nd edition. London: Routledge and Kegan Paul, 1980.

Spretnak, Charlene. *The Politics of Women's Spirituality: Essays on the Rise of Spiritual Power Within the Feminist Movement*. Garden City, NY: Anchor Press/Doubleday, 1982.

Walker, Barbara G. *The Crone: Woman of Age, Wisdom, and Power*. San Francisco, Harper & Row, 1985.

Welch, Sharon D. *Communities of Resistance and Solidarity: A Feminist Theology of Liberation*. Maryknoll, NY: Orbis Books, 1985.

A Story of Creation

Kathy Galloway
The Iona Community, Scotland

Once upon a time, in the beginning, a labour of love was undertaken.

It started with a sign, to show that something was about to happen. Light came forth from the deep darkness, bright, clear and unmistakable.
And it was very good.

At the second time, the waters were broken. At first, they gushed, then they dried to a trickle, and a space was created. It was exactly the right size. By now, the creation was well under way.
And it was very good.

At the third time, a cradle was made ready. It was comfortable and beautiful and waiting. And food was prepared, issuing sweetly and warmly and in precisely the right measure from the being of the labourer.
And it was very good.

At the fourth time, rhythm was established. Ebbing and flowing, contracting and expanding, pain and joy, sun and moon, beginning and ending. The labour of love progressed.
And it was very good.

At the fifth time, there was ceaseless activity. Fluttering like the wings of the dove, humming like the murmur of the dragonfly, swimming like the darting golden fish, wriggling like the lithe serpent, leaping like the flashing deer, surging like the mighty lion.
And it was very good.

At the sixth time, there was a momentary, endless hesitation. Then a child was born. And the child looked just like the one who had given it life. The child too was born with the power to create and to make decisions, and to love.
The labourer looked at all that had been accomplished, and rejoiced, for it was very good.

At the seventh time, the labour was finished. The task was complete.
And the labourer rested, for she was very, very tired.

Contributors

Sheila Carney, RSM, is President of the Sisters of Mercy, County of Allegheny, Pittsburgh, Pennsylvania, and a former lecturer in Religious Studies at Saint Vincent College in Latrobe, Pennsylvania, with emphasis on courses in social justice and the role of women in the Church. In addition to teaching at the college level, she has been involved in adult education and in the ministry of spiritual direction.

Anne Clifford, CSJ, is a doctoral candidate in the Theology Department of the School of Religious Studies at the Catholic University of America. Among her many interests is the interrelationship of culture, particularly that of the United States, and religion/ theology. Currently she is teaching religious studies and theology courses at the Catholic University and at Trinity College in Washington, D.C.

Mary Elsbernd, OSF, is an Associate Professor of Theology at Briar Cliff College in Sioux City, Iowa, and a member of the Sisters of St. Francis, Dubuque, Iowa. She has a Ph.D. and a S.T.D. from Katholiek Universiteit, Leuven, in Social Morality. Her current areas of academic interest include peace studies, human rights in the encyclical tradition, women in ministry and introducing the Scriptures to young adults.

Nadine Foley, OP, is Prioress of the Adrian Dominican Congregation. She holds advanced degrees in science, philosophy and Scripture (The Catholic University of America, Union Theological Seminary) and has taught at Barry University, Siena Heights College, Drake University and Marist College, where she was also Chair of the Humanities Division. She edited *Preaching and the Non-Ordained* and has written on women in the Church, issues related to mission and ministry, and on contemporary women's apostolic religious life.

Margaret Gannon, IHM, is professor of history at Marywood College in Scranton, Pennsylvania. Her teaching and research interests are in the areas of peace, development and women's studies. She is also active in U.S. ethnic and minorities studies. Her doctoral degree in history is from St. John's University.

Patricia Jean Manion, SL, is a human development consultant on the Growth, Community and Education Staff of the Sisters of Loretto. She also works with individual clients using dreams as a resource. She has taught at the elementary, secondary and graduate levels and was a college administrator for ten years. She holds a Ph.D. from the University of Denver and has done post graduate work at the C. G. Jung Institute in Zurich.

Anne Munley, IHM, currently serves as Director of Apostolic Planning for the Congregation of the Sisters, Servants of the Immaculate Heart of Mary, Scranton, Pennsylvania. Prior to assuming this position, she was an Assistant Professor of Sociology at Marywood College. She received her doctoral degree from Boston College.

Catherine Osimo, CSC, has been involved in adult catechesis at the parish level in the Diocese of San Diego for the last three years. She also teaches theology for the Institute of Christian Ministries at the University of San Diego and is engaged in the formation of men for the permanent diaconate. She received her Doctor of Ministry degree from San Francisco Theological Seminary.

Elaine M. Prevallet, SL, is currently director of Knobs Haven Retreat Center on the grounds of the Loretto Motherhouse at Nerinx, Kentucky. Prior to taking this position in 1978, she had taught at Pendle Hill, a Quaker learning community in Wallingford, Pennsylvania, and at Loretto Heights College in Denver, Colorado. Her doctoral degree in religious studies is from Marquette University.

Marilyn Thie, SC, is Associate Professor of Philosophy and Religion at Colgate University in Hamilton, New York, where she also teaches courses in Women's Studies. She is currently working on a feminist political spirituality, drawing on her involvement with women in Latin America and her study of nineteenth century feminist theorists. Her Ph.D. in philosophy is from Georgetown University.

Patricia Wittberg, SC, is an Assistant Professor of Sociology at Fordham University in New York. She is interested in the study of church organizations and is co-director of Fordham's summer graduate program in pastoral planning and research.

Reflections Upon the Religious Life of U.S. Women Religious

A Paper Prepared by LCWR for the Fifth Inter-American Conference on Religious Life, 1985

(This paper is part of an unpublished document, entitled *Apostolic Religious Life in a Changing World and Church,* that contains other papers contributed by the Confederation of Latin American Religious, the Conference of Major Superiors of Men of the USA, and the Canadian Religious Conference.)

QUESTION 1
From your experience, how have changes in the church and society over the past twenty years influenced apostolic religious life?

Over the last twenty years, American life and culture has experienced an unprecedented rate of change. Developments in apostolic religious life during this period are *part of* or a *reaction to* broader social and cultural trends. The capacity to create technology capable of massive violence and destruction; the forging of a world order in which greed, power, and coercion determine the distribution of resources and the achievement of human potential; the promotion of unjust social, economic and political systems that perpetuate oppression of women, the poor, the uneducated, the homeless, the frail, the dispossessed, the powerless; a growing tendency to use media to shape opinion and control information; and growth of various self-help, consciousness-raising and solidarity movements have converged with trends in the post Vatican II church to prompt in American religious the emergence of a shifting consciousness of the contemporary meaning of a call to participate in the redemptive mission of Jesus.

This shift in consciousness is influencing apostolic religious life in various ways:

1. There is among American religious an increased identification with incarnational theology.
    The kingdom is here and now and it is still to come. The call to apostolic religious life includes being vulnerable to God's presence in all of reality. Creation is good; the human is a sacred place. This world is to be brought to love, wholeness and holiness in accordance with the plan of the Creator.

2. American religious are keenly aware that the call to apostolic religious life includes sharing in the movement of God in concrete circumstances of society, history and culture.

    Through mission, apostolic religious offer witness to the presence of God in this world and in these times. Apostolic religious are to be leaven, agents of change, catalytic and counter-cultural forces for conversion and cultural transformation in the light of Gospel values.

3. There is among American religious a growing tendency to reject dichotomies such as sacred/profane, faith/action, consecration/mission.

    Apostolic spirituality is a dynamic spirituality that involves continuous efforts to integrate contemplation and action, commitment to a religious life style and to practical deeds of compassionate love. Apostolic religious are to be healers of the breach, reconcilers, unifiers. It is by being immersed in culture and living an integrated life of prayer and service that one encounters and is led to deeper experience of the sacred.

4. A heightened sense of mission and awareness of unmet survival needs of suffering brothers and sisters are leading American religious to critique social structures, institutions and systems from a Gospel perspective.

    Social sin results from a distortion of Gospel values. American religious are experiencing a re-awakening to the need for continuous personal, communal, societal, and global conversion to values that promote life, hope, dignity, justice and self-determination. Radical conversion demands a prophetic stance toward economic, political and social systems that contribute to the exploitation and dehumanization of persons. Apostolic religious are drawn increasingly to stand with and for the poor.

5. American women religious are coming to believe in and deeply value their experience as women; it is as women that they perceive, think, act, feel and experience the revelation of God.

    Sensitive to the needs of hurting humanity and aware of forces that threaten life, create hostilities, crush potential and sack the earth of its resources, apostolic women religious identify with Jesus as "the suffering servant" and see in their womanhood a capacity to participate in the painful process of birthing a future in which all life is reverenced. A spirit of kinship with all women ·prompts special concern for women who are abused, deprived of opportunities to achieve their potential or victims of the "feminization of poverty" phenomenon in American society.

6. Grounded in the experience of women as givers and tenders of life, apostolic religious recognize that values traditionally characterized as feminine have vast potential for transforming culture and developing modes of relating that lead to wholeness, healing love, and enablement of persons.

Life-giving modes of relating emerge from willingness to use gifts for the sake of the human community and from valuing interdependence, integration, cooperation, collaboration, bonding, reconciliation, compassion, hospitality, healing, altruism, stewardship, simplicity of life style, collective responsibility and conflict resolution based on prayer, negotiation, and non-violence. Together and as individuals American religious are assuming the challenge to be women of prayer, women of presence, messengers of joy and prophets of hope.

QUESTION 2

How has the new consciousness of the oppressed and marginalized groups impacted your understanding of the following of Christ, your images of God, and your understanding of apostolic religious life?

The first section is longer, not because we judge it more important than the other topics, but because in the first section we establish the parameters shaping and informing discussions of our images of God and our understanding of apostolic religious life.

A. Following of Christ
   1. Like Jesus, the paradigm of religious life, who hears the cries of the anguished and poor, we are invited to learn with and from the poor and marginalized, to become poor and marginalized ourselves.
       a. The charisms of many communities of women religious were born out of an awareness of and identification with a particular need in society. Women, bonded through the inspiration of the Holy Spirit, were led to see life from a perspective that compelled us to be with those in need. This identification with our marginated sisters and brothers united us in such a way that little by little, all began to be drawn into the mainstream of society.
       b. Vatican II's call for renewal began a process in women religious that has consistently drawn us into deeper and deeper dispossession . . . a dispossession of security, of status, of clear and safe answers. This dynamism of dispossession gives us a unique experience of being both bonded and marginalized in relationship to all peoples. We know what it is to possess and we know what it is to be dispossessed.
       c. In an attempt to stand in solidarity with the poor and oppressed, we have

the experience of being misunderstood; we know a more conscious oppression and marginalization.

d. Entering into this profound faith moment, we follow Jesus who did not cling to his divinity, but out of desire to be with us, became human. We walk with a Christ who walked with the poor, who identified with the marginated. We are consoled, challenged, and strengthened by a companionship that is transforming and liberating.

e. We begin more and more to hear, like Jesus, the cry of the anguished.

2. Following Christ calls for social responsibility that flows out of a social spirituality.

a. As religious women we follow Christ in identifying with the poor and marginated, the dispossessed and outsiders. Like Christ, we recognize that religious commitment is embodied in the world, thereby involving us with the specific social, political, economic, and intellectual realities shaping people's lives.

b. When our commitment to the poor discloses that the majority of the poor are women, we become aware of ourselves as women who are oppressed and marginalized, within our church as well as in our society.

c. Initially committed to serve those marginalized, this understanding changes as we discover that standing with the marginalized and oppressed means we become additionally marginalized. We learn that in standing for and with the marginalized, we counter societal values. The more conscienticized we become, the more marginated we become.

d. These understandings impel us to social action that liberates and transforms.

e. Women religious increasingly live in the world acting with a new consciousness: seeing the world in women-centered ways; bonded as women with all the powerless; rejecting dualistic patterns of thinking that separate what we know to be interconnected; knowing oppression through working with the poor and marginalized; seeing oppressions as interrelated and systemic; aware of God's presence incarnated in all reality, but especially manifested in activity that transforms and liberates from oppressions; developing a global awareness; bonding with others seeking to liberate all people and the earth from oppressive relations, institutions, and technologies; creating patterns of empowerment and strategies of creative resistance to counter powers that dominate.

f. A social spirituality means we are called to risk, to give public witness, to develop a mature conscience, to shape a new vision, develop new values, to speak and act for peace and justice.

3. Our following of Christ is embodied in a specific cultural context.

    a. Bonding with the oppressed and marginalized groups, especially those persons and groups rendered powerless in and by U.S. society, develops in U.S. women religious ways of seeing their world and themselves differently.

    b. Our society has myths which welcome and include but has, at the same time, a history which divides peoples from each other and the earth: native Americans, people of color, and immigrants; the homeless, battered, and imprisoned; the unemployed, unemployable, and retired; third world peoples; women, children, elderly, sick; victims of violence—military, domestic, sexual, structural.

    c. Identifying with these peoples in our society places us with them on the margin, often placing us at odds with some aspects of church and society.

B. Images of God

1. In the manner of Jesus, U.S. women religious live faithful to our image of God. The following of Jesus strengthens our convictions to own our experiences as women.

2. With a woman's consciousness, we image God. God is mother and father; creator and nourisher; patient and compassionate; a woman clothed and unclothed; a woman struggling to give birth.

3. Justice becomes the cry of God's being. Jesus is the Sacrament of God, disclosing the Spirit as the suffering servant.

4. God is immanent in creation, in the midst of the web of life. As we bond with the oppressed and marginalized, we know God standing on the side of the poor and oppressed, seeing with the eyes of the poor, leading the oppressed by alleviating oppression.

    In this context, we see God angry, sad, suffering, marginalized; we see God incarnated in peoples of color, in women, in the homeless and battered, the victims of violence and oppression of all kinds.

5. Religious find themselves in a "Dark Night." The painful and intense moments of disintegration which carry the hope for what can break through characterize our living in this in-between.

C. Understanding of Apostolic Religious Life

1. The secular world has become the place to encounter and to reveal the sacred. Theological reflection on human experience and just relationships in the world

have given flesh to an incarnational theology in which we experience God-with-us.

2. Religious perceive the Mission of Jesus as creating a human dwelling place befitting the sacredness of the world and its human family. The needs of the poor cry out for a more human, just world in which to live. Religious see the labor to create such a world integral to the Mission of Jesus.
3. In standing in solidarity with the marginalized of our society, we become marginalized ourselves; therein lies the possibility to be prophetic.
4. An emerging understanding of religious life sees us *as* church, rather than being in relation *to* church.
    a. Increasingly women religious see ourselves less as women running church institutions and more as church women.
    b. We see ourselves moving from maintaining existing structures to creating alternatives.
    c. We see connections between direct service and systemic change.
5. With a consciousness of women, of ourselves, as responsible mature persons, we seek new patterns of relating to church hierarchy.
    a. We seek to name ourselves, to collaborate with other women, and to further the empowerment of laity in the church.
    b. We expect dialogue as peers to replace parent-child relationships.
    c. We work for patterns of mutual accountability with structures for responsible dissent.
6. Our understanding of apostolic religious life is shaped by our rootedness in U.S. culture, the liberating effects of dispossession, and our experience of standing with the marginalized.
7. These impel us to labor for the ongoing conversion and continual transformation of our society and our church.
8. Effecting conversion and transformation requires public articulation and lived witness of value, often putting us in conflict with established centers of power in society and church.
9. Fidelity to society and church may, at times, mean loyal dissent.

QUESTION 3
What are the elements which characterize apostolic religious life?

1. Mission
    Mission, in its aspect of service, outgoing response to the needs of the world, is a central defining characteristic.
    Mission is the fundamental charge of Jesus to the whole church and, as a conse-

quence, to apostolic women religious who are within the church. They share the character of being agents of change and cultural transformation in the world in concert with all others in the church who are baptized into mission. Justice, as a constitutive dimension of the preaching of the Gospel, is integral to mission that is co-creative and incarnational. It implies further a special identification with the poor.

2. Community

Community is essential to apostolic religious life as an expression of mission and as a support to ministry.

As a requisite element of mission, religious community reflects the values of the Gospel in simplicity of life style, exemplification of the Beatitudes, Eucharistic centering and promotion of the freedom of true Christian disciples.

3. Freedom

Religious life is a medium within which the individual woman is facilitated in personal growth toward freedom, an activity which in itself exemplifies the liberating activity of the Gospel.

The person is not facilitated to personal growth *for the sake of the mission* in an instrumental sense but as a manifestation of the freedom with which Christ has made us free.

Freedom similarly is a characteristic of the religious institute as a whole, comprised as it is of mature women who have freely entered into it. The freedom of the institute is expressed uniquely in its apostolic ministries carried out in response to the needs of the time.

4. Ministry

Ministries are carried out as a result of an ongoing reading of the signs of the times by the members of the religious institute.

The institute bears corporate witness as a result of communal discernment.

— as expressing a prophetic voice calling itself and the larger church to Gospel fidelity.

— as deriving its authority for mission through participation in that of the universal church.

— as a leavening agent embodying a sacramental presence in the world.

QUESTION 4
How do you understand the gospel paradox "to be in the world but not of the world"?

Introduction: As American women religious bonded together in the following of Jesus Christ, we experience the world in which we are rooted as essentially holy. This world is the locus of God's revelation and activity, the place in which God's truth of justice, mercy, and love is to be incarnated. We recognize that the reign of God has not yet fully come and that the powers of personal sin and structural evil permeate cultures. We are called by our very humanity to live out our immersion in the world by witnessing to the goodness of this creation and resisting the forces of sin.

1. A dualistic interpretation of the secular/sacred is transformed.

    We resist the interpretation of this Gospel text as support for a lack of immersion in our world. Such an interpretation, which separates the sacred from the profane, violates our experience of ourselves and even our experience of Jesus, who was so immersed in this world that he embraced in his flesh both the essential goodness of our humanity and the burden of its sin. Therefore, we stand with Jesus Christ in identification with the goodness, holiness and beauty of this world and with him against the powers of sin even to death.

2. Mission is a call to the transformation of culture.

    The structures of evil that permeate our world order are those of oppression, exploitation, domination, and violence. The call to witness to the goodness of creation and the fullness of the reign of Jesus places us in a confrontational stance toward these evils in our society and world. Therefore, a dominant expression of our mission today is to transform this very culture in which we ourselves are inseparably immersed. If we are to be a healing and prophetic presence and, ultimately, a sign/sacrament of freedom and hope in our church and world, this transformation must begin with our own conversion.

3. Personal and communal conversion is integral to effecting salvation history in our times.

    Conversion is before all else a question of consciousness. A movement of God's Spirit in our times is a growing consciousness of the ecclesiastical, social, economic, and political structures that perpetuate the oppression and dehumanization of world peoples. In turn, this emerging consciousness demands that we, individually and as church, create lifestyles and structures that fit us to be a leaven of transformation and a witness to the values of Jesus's gospel. These values include the option for the poor, the liberation of all peoples, the equality of women and men in our church and society.

QUESTION 5
What is the image of church which has the most meaning for you?

Introduction: The reflections of women religious indicate that certain traditional images of church retain their power, that is, people of God, community, pilgrim people. Even in the continuity, however, there are new awarenesses of qualities which are inherent in the traditional images but which we have not emphasized in the past. Another category of images is made up of new images, some of these reflecting a distinctively feminine mode of perception.

1. There are emerging nuances of traditional images of church. In reference to the image of church as community, there is great emphasis on the church in relationship in which the full equality of all members is valued, thereby releasing for mission the full diversity of gifts. Inclusivity—the embracing of peoples, cultures, male-female, the poor—is a marked quality of this community.

2. The church as prophetic, as herald, as transforming of cultures is imaged in a relationship of mutuality; as it transforms, it is in itself transformed by incorporating all that is good, just, beautiful in human and cosmic experience. In the transforming process the church listens to and is taught by the poor, the suffering, the marginalized and itself becomes a poor, marginalized community. The church becomes a critical voice of judgment of those values which are not in harmony with the Gospel.

3. The church as suffering servant is imaged in particular relationship with the religious and social outcasts of our times, the poor, the marginalized and the oppressed. The contemporary question for our era is not, "Why does God allow so much suffering in our world?", rather, "Why does God suffer so much in our world?"; God incarnated and immersed in our world makes justice the very cry of God. The church is perceived as participating in the mission of Jesus and therefore given over to creating a dwelling place on earth characterized by justice, mercy and love. This building up of the reign of God in our world demands a posture of personal and communal conversion of the church.

4. The church as imaging new forms that are beyond present boundaries is emerging. These images reflect a feminine mode of perception and experience. The church is like a woman struggling to give birth; the church is like a web of life embedded in the world; the church is like a parent, one who is nourishing, forgiving, prodigal and compassionate. These images will continue to evolve as women reflect on their experience.

An Exploratory Content Analysis of Major Themes Present in Selected Documents of United States Women Religious

Anne Munley, IHM

In the years since Vatican II, perhaps no segment of the Church in the United States has changed more than apostolic women religious. Faith-filled movement from a monastic mode of life and service to insertion in a society replete with complex historical, economic, political, cultural and social realities has triggered a need for a new articulation of the nature of apostolic religious life. Sensational press accounts and fragmented or superficial outside observations about the lives of women religious are inadequate and sometimes counter-productive expressions of *what it means* to be a woman religious committed to furthering the mission of Jesus in this world at this time. The time has come to look at apostolic women religious and to ask of them the question: "Who do *you* say that you are?"

Early in the work of the LCWR Task Force on Religious Life it was decided that one way to glean a sense of "who apostolic women religious say that they are" was to analyze objectively documents written by them and flowing from the concrete realities of their day-to-day experience. The method selected for this process was content analysis. A description of the methodology, some general observations and an analysis of the findings are as follows.

Methodology

Three random samples were drawn from the 1985 LCWR Directory. Of the 224 general superiors of United States congregations listed, two samples of 45 cases each were selected. Each of these samples represents 20% of the general superiors or their equivalents of United States congregations who hold membership in LCWR. Congregations in Sample A were contacted by letter and asked to forward documents emerging from their most recent chapter as well as administrative reports of the general government for the last completed term. Congregations in Sample B were asked to submit mission statements, goal or priority statements, vow formulae or formulae for corporate renewal of vows. A third sample of 35 cases was selected from the 96 provincial superiors of United

States provinces of international congregations listed in the Directory. Provinces in Sample C were requested to send any or all of the documents specified in Samples A and B.

Of the 45 congregations in Sample A, 31 responded to the Task Force's request for materials (a return rate of 69%). Thirty-five of the 45 congregations in Sample B forwarded documents (a 78% return rate). Of the 35 provinces in Sample C, 22 sent materials (a return rate of 63%). Of the 125 cases in Samples A, B, and C, a total of 88 responded for an overall return rate of 70%.

Of the 31 respondents in Sample A, 28 (90%) submitted chapter outcomes/reports and 23 (74%) submitted administrative reports. Of the 35 respondents in Sample B, 28 (80%) submitted mission statements, 32 (91%) submitted goals/priorities or philosophy/ objective statements, 33 (94%) vow formulae, 1 (3%) constitution only, and 4 (11%) sections of constitutions. Of the 22 respondents in Sample C, 3 (14%) submitted constitutions, 12 (55%) mission statements, 18 (82%) vow formulae, 14 (64%) general chapter documents, 10 (45%) provincial chapter documents and 12 (55%) provincial reports.

Three teams of women religious were selected to surface and quantify the major themes present in the documents. Micheleen Barragy, CDP, and Jane Coles, CDP, of Our Lady of the Lake University, San Antonio, Texas, analyzed the contents of Sample A. Susan Hadzima, IHM, and Christine Mihelich, IHM, of Marywood College, Scranton, Pennsylvania, worked on Sample B and Mary Hayes, SNDdeN, and Helen James John, SNDdeN, of Trinity College, Washington, D.C., focused on the themes present in Sample C. After a phase one report from each team, a more detailed analysis of theme, congregation, date and type of document was requested. All documents were then reviewed by the writer so that general observations and an across-sample content analysis of themes could be prepared.

General Observations

A dominant impression arising from systematic review of all the documents submitted is a remarkable sense of the dynamism present in United States congregations of women religious. The built-in structure of periodic general or provincial chapters, collegial decision-making processes and constitutional provision for ongoing changes in leadership are functional means for organizational revitalization. Chapter reports, goal and priority statements and administrative reports reveal much more than the written word. They evidence collaborative group process and a high degree of accountability to the membership. Goal and priority statements as well as chapter reports are mission-oriented, Gospel-oriented, value-oriented, future-oriented, action-oriented and evaluation-oriented. Mission statements and in many cases vow formulae are inspirational and set forth a corporate vision of shared purpose, discipleship and commitment to participation in the transformation of the world. Scattered throughout all the documents are references to the charism of the founder/foundress which suggest appreciation of the original inspiration that sparked the establishment of the institute as well as a sense of charism as continuously unfolding and dynamic in time and in history.

Administrative reports and chapter documents are frank and suggest a realistic grasp of the problems and challenges that are part of the contemporary experience of United States women religious. This is evidenced by statistics about declining numbers, rising median ages and ministry shifts and by information about fiscal and retirement needs and projections. While the documents contain evidence of the poignancy of change that involves "letting go," some grief and some dying, there are also many indications of hope, a willingness to risk, faith-filled reaching out and a desire to share in the bringing to birth of a just social order. Another significant characteristic of the documents that constitute the data for the study is their affective or experiential quality. Beliefs, goals, dreams, priorities, hopes and even problems as stated in the documents reflect feeling as well as clarity of thought.

A sense of life and movement is present in the major themes that emerge from the documents. Even though the themes are interconnected at various levels of reality—personal, interpersonal, societal, structural, for the purposes of analysis it is possible to separate them into those that are primarily external in focus or primarily internal in focus.

Themes across the three samples that are primarily external in focus are: solidarity with the poor, a strong sense of apostolic calling that involves a spirituality of insertion in the world as leaven, an incarnational theology based on the realization that the kingdom is here and now and yet to come, awareness that social justice is a constitutive element of apostolic religious life, emphasis on responsible stewardship and investment policies, renewed commitment to the witness of community and simplicity of life-style, a prophetic stance manifested in many cases by corporate stands on justice and peace issues, a global focus and grasp of the interdependent consequences of maldistribution of wealth and resources and of infringements on human dignity, concern for women in church and society, a perception of power and influence as something to be used on behalf of the oppressed, a desire to contribute to the development of the laity and a valuing of collaboration as a means to building a healed, reconciled and redeemed world.

Themes across the three samples that are primarily internal in focus are: ongoing congregational or provincial planning, ongoing spiritual renewal and development, discernment of ministries, revitalization of community, life planning, leadership development, team models of leadership, participatory government, health and wellness of members, responsible stewardship and fiscal planning, providing for the needs of aging members, vocation ministry and alternate forms of membership, e.g., lay associates.

Since Sample C includes both congregational and provincial documents, an additional observation is in order. Documents developed at the province level tend to be more specific than those at the general level and give more evidence of the concrete issues, involvements and action plans of women religious. While it is true that constitutions, vow formulae, mission statements, general chapter reports, administrative reports and provincial documents tend to address different kinds of concerns with different degrees of specificity, definite patterns of overlapping exist with respect to dominant themes.

Analysis of Themes

EXTERNAL THEMES

The theme of being *called to justice and peacemaking* is present in documents of 78% of the congregations selected in Samples A, B and C. Twenty-seven (87%) of the 31 congregations in Sample A included this theme in chapter documents, administrative reports, constitutions and/or goal and priority statements. Twenty-seven (77%) of the 35 congregations in Sample B expressed this theme in mission statements, goal and priority statements and/or in chapter statements on such issues as peace and justice, solidarity with the poor, opposition to proliferation of nuclear weapons and alternative investments. Fifteen (68%) of the 22 United States provinces of international congregations in Sample C reflected this theme in constitutions, general or provincial chapter documents, and/or in province goals, administrative reports, mission statements or action plans.

Additional justice-related themes emerged in content analysis of Samples A and C. In Sample A, the theme of the need for *empowerment of the politically oppressed* appeared in documents of 32% of the congregations, *peacemaking* as a separate theme in 61% of the congregations, *corporate stance process* regarding justice in 29% of the congregations, and programs for *social justice awareness education* in 45% of the congregations. In Sample C, the theme of *corporate stances on peace and the arms race* was present in documents of 18% of the congregations and the theme of *conflict within the Church* as a justice and peace issue in 14% of the congregations.

Solidarity with the poor is a major theme in general chapter documents, administrative reports, constitutions, vow formulae, goal and priority statements, mission statements, and/or provincial administrative reports and document of 75% of the congregations. Solidarity with the poor and a thrust to serve the poor appeared in 24 (77%) of the 31 congregations in Sample A, 22 (63%) of the 35 congregations in Sample B and 20 (86%) of the 22 congregations in Sample C.

Clearly related to solidarity with the poor is the theme of *simplicity of life*. Although not analyzed as a separate theme in Sample A, the emphasis on the preferential option, sharing of resources with the poor, investing to benefit the poor, non-consumerism and conservation of resources in the analysis of solidarity with the poor indicates that the theme of simplicity of life was indeed present in Sample A documents. In the analysis of Sample B, 14 (40%) of the congregations elaborated on the theme of simplicity of life in their documents. In Sample C, simplicity was treated by 18% of the congregations in the context of asceticism.

Forty-five percent of the congregations in Samples A, B and C included the theme of *responsible stewardship and sharing with the poor* in their various congregational and/or provincial documents. This theme was present in 19 (61%) of the congregations in Sample A, 12 (34%) of Sample B and 9 (41%) of Sample C.

Concern for women in the church and society appeared in general chapter documents, administrative reports, constitutions, goal, mission and priority statements or provincial documents, mission statements or administrative reports of 30 (34%) of the 88 congregations that were respondents in Samples A, B and C. In Sample A, 16 (52%) of the congregations included this theme, in Sample B, 7 (20%) and in Sample C, 7 (32%). Particular ways in which the theme of women in the church and society was expressed reflect consciousness of many facets of the present day women's issue, e.g. the feminization of poverty, economic inequity, domestic violence, development of the role of women in the church. Expressions of this theme indicate commitment to collaborate with other women to promote consciousness raising, greater self-understanding of women, and sharing of feminine spirituality and values. They also suggest a willingness to offer leadership in working with women and in enabling them and calling them to leadership as well as a dedication to transforming social structures that contribute to victimization, exploitation and discrimination.

Though not explicitly labeled as "witness," various themes surfacing in the documents lend themselves to analysis as forms of *public witness*. Each of the 9 external themes emerging from Sample A (call to justice, solidarity with the poor, women in church and society, need for empowerment of the politically oppressed, peacemaking, stewardship, collaboration, corporate stance process and social justice awareness education) involves an action dimension at interpersonal, institutional or social structural levels. In Sample C, themes of solidarity with the poor, internationality and global awareness, concrete actions for peace and justice and interpretation of the vow of chastity in relation to the human community, the vow of obedience in relation to mission and the vow of poverty in relation to solidarity with the poor and asceticism are expressions of the theme of public witness.

In Sample B, various themes cluster around the broad concept of witness. The theme of *being a sign of Christ's presence in the world* was present in 26 (74%) of the congregations in this Sample. The theme of *embodiment of Gospel values* surfaced in documents of 25 (71%) of the congregations and that of countercultural witness in 9 (26%). *Hospitality* as a form of witness appeared in 4 (11%) of the congregations and *community life* as witness in 19 (54%) of the 35 congregations that were Sample B respondents.

The theme of *apostolic spirituality* was developed in the analysis of Sample B. Eleven (31%) of the congregations in this Sample included the concept of apostolic spirituality in goal/priority/philosophy/objective statements, mission statements or constitutions. The notions of being "called" and "sent" central to apostolic spirituality were also part of the Sample B analysis. The theme of *responding to God's call* was present in documents of 21 (60%) of the congregations and that of *being missioned in the midst of the people of God* in 21 (60%) of the respondents in Sample B.

Though not specifically analyzed in Sample A, the theme of an *incarnational theology* is prominent in the analysis of Samples B and C. Twelve (34%) of the 35 congregations in Sample B define apostolic mission as witnessing the kingdom in the here and now and heralding the yet to come. Documents of seventeen (77%) of the 22 United States provinces of international congregations in Sample C also reflect an incarnational theology.

Two final external themes surfacing from content analysis of various documents are *global consciousness* and *collaboration as a means to building the kingdom*. Forty-nine percent of the congregations in Sample B and 64% of the congregations in Sample C reveal a global perspective in chapter or province documents, mission, goal and priority statements, or in positions on specific justice issues. Documents of 17 (55%) of the congregations in Sample A promote collaboration with bishops, clergy, laity and with other ministering groups. Seven (20%) of the congregations in Sample B related the collaboration theme to enablement of the laity in mission statements and in goal and planning documents.

INTERNAL THEMES

Besides the ten external themes that were most dominant in content analysis of Samples A, B and C, seven internal themes were also apparent. The notion of *evolutionary change in ministry trends* was evident in administrative reports, chapter documents or constitutions of 14 (45%) of the congregations in Sample A. Both change and continuity appeared in the analysis of Sample B. While mission, goal and priority statements of 13 (37%) of the congregations in Sample B reaffirmed present ministries, 16 (46%) of the congregations described trends of movement to new ministerial options. It is significant to note that of the 13 congregations in Sample B that reaffirmed present ministries, all but 2 also reflected the theme of new ministerial options.

A commitment to *ongoing spiritual renewal* is a second internal theme present in each of the three Samples. This theme appeared in chapter documents and administrative reports of 29% of the congregations in Sample A. The content analysis of Sample B dealt with the topic of spiritual renewal by noting three themes. Four (11%) of the congregations in Sample B included in their documents the specific goal of working toward the spiritual renewal of each member. Seventeen (49%) of the congregations in Sample B emphasized the need for renewal in the context of conversion/transformation of heart and 19 (54%) related renewal to discernment and listening to the Spirit. For 18 (82%) of the provinces in Sample C, the renewal theme emerged in the context of focus on the spirit of the foundress/founder.

A third internal theme emerging from analysis of the documents is that of *quality of community life*. In chapter documents, and administrative reports of Sample A, 9 (29%) of the congregations affirmed the value of healthy local community. Documents of 16 (46%) of the congregations in Sample B also highlighted the need for renewed emphasis on building warm, prayerful, faith-sharing, supportive and interdependent local communities. Nine (29%) of the congregations in Sample A developed the theme of *diversity and unity* in local community life. The sub-theme of respect for diversity of life-style also surfaced in documents of 10 (45%) of the United States provinces of international congregations in Sample C.

Though not developed as a theme in the content analysis of Sample A, the theme of *co-responsibility, accountability and collegiality in government* was prominent in the analyses of Samples B and C. Fifteen (43%) of the congregations in Sample B and 15 (68%) of the United States provinces of international congregations in Sample C emphasize the theme in mission, goal and priority statements, administrative reports, action plans, vow renewal formulae and/or chapter and province documents. Characteristics of the administrative reports in all three Samples were a team approach in leadership, a sharing of responsibility in the roles of general or provincial superiors and their councils and accountability to the membership.

In each of the samples there was substantial evidence of an emphasis on *planning*. In chapter documents and administrative reports of 52% of the congregations in Sample A, this theme centered on fiscal planning and accountability. Nine (26%) of the congregations in Sample B included the theme of long range ministry planning. In Sample C, a planning thrust was evidenced by 77% of the United States provinces in the study.

The themes of *aging and retirement, vocation ministry* and *alternate forms of membership* are interrelated in that each is concerned with the issue of membership and the capacity of congregations to carry their ministries and way of life into the future. Chapter documents and administrative reports of 39% of the congregations in Sample A included the theme of aging and retirement. This theme also appeared in documents of 36% of the provinces in Sample C. Vocation ministry and alternate forms of membership were internal themes in 59% of the provinces in Sample C.

Conclusion

Who do United States apostolic women religious say that they are? This exploratory content analysis of documents emerging from collegial process and based on the concrete world of experience suggests some components of an answer to this question.

UNITED STATES APOSTOLIC WOMEN RELIGIOUS ARE:

WOMEN CALLED TO JUSTICE AND PEACE

WOMEN WHO STAND IN SOLIDARITY WITH THE POOR

WOMEN COMMITTED TO SIMPLICITY OF LIFE, RESPONSIBLE STEWARDSHIP AND SHARING WITH THE POOR

WOMEN WITH A CONCERN FOR WOMEN IN CHURCH AND SOCIETY

WOMEN WHOSE LIVES RENDER PUBLIC WITNESS TO GOSPEL VALUES AND TO THE PRESENCE OF A LOVING AND COMPASSIONATE GOD IN THIS WORLD

WOMEN GROWING IN THEIR UNDERSTANDING OF APOSTOLIC SPIRITUALITY

WOMEN WHO BELIEVE THAT THE KINGDOM OF GOD IS HERE AND NOW AND YET TO COME

WOMEN WHO DESIRE GLOBAL VISION AND CONSCIOUSNESS

WOMEN WHO VALUE COLLABORATION AS A MEANS TO CREATING A CIVILIZATION OF LOVE

WOMEN EXPERIENCING EVOLUTIONARY CHANGES IN MINISTRY

WOMEN COMMITTED TO ONGOING SPIRITUAL RENEWAL, CONVERSION AND TRANSFORMATION OF HEART

WOMEN EMBRACING THE CHALLENGE OF BUILDING HEALTHY LIFE IN
COMMUNITY

WOMEN MODELING CO-RESPONSIBLE, ACCOUNTABLE AND COLLEGIAL
GOVERNANCE PROCESS

WOMEN WHO SEE PLANNING AS A FORM OF RESPONSIBLE STEWARDSHIP

WOMEN WHO VALUE AND CARE FOR THEIR ELDER MEMBERS

WOMEN WHOSE DISCIPLESHIP CALLS THEM TO RISK AND TO FAITH IN
THE FUTURE

WOMEN WHOSE TOTAL WAY OF LIFE PROFESSES BELIEF THAT JESUS IS
THE CHRIST, THE SON OF THE LIVING GOD!

RECOMMENDED READING

Woodward, Evelyn, *Poets, Prophets & Pragmatists. A New Challenge to Religious Life.* Notre Dame: Ave Maria Press, 1987.

Images of God

The responses listed in the columns below represent a summary of discussions held in the LCWR Regions in the Spring of 1986. Following a videotape that modeled a similar dialogue, members engaged in discussions around the questions—"what is our world . . . who do we say God is . . . who do we say we are?" The responses were collated into the two categories identified as "images" and "experiences." They do not constitute scientific data or analysis in this form.

REGIONAL REFLECTIONS ON THE COMMUNITARIAN "FACE OF GOD"

Images

Experiences

REGION 1

God is multifaceted. God is: surprise, mystery, life, energy, spirit, love, creator, liberator, provider, sustainer, paradox.

God is revealed through: relationships, daily realities, struggles, pain, doubt, absence, suffering, laughter. For us, "God is eternal discovery and eternal growth" Teilhard.

REGION 2

God is Creator, life-giver, energy force, dynamic mystery, the source of cosmic unity, hope and joy; God is companion, presence, the gentle spirit; God is the crucified, lover, clown. In contrast and paradox, we see the God of wrath giving way to the God of mercy; the unchanging and the changing; the concrete and the abstract; a presence and an absence, male and female image.

Like a strobe light, God is reflected in energy and light as she/he moves through our lives at different moments. We experience God as indwelling Spirit and are opened to God's own revelation through our own reflection and prayer. We experience God in a relational way through human interactions and life experiences, in our times of joy and peace as well as in times of trauma, emptiness, change, powerlessness, letting go and death. We experience the enabler and energizer, sustaining us even when God is absent from our lives. Through all of life's experiences, we trust the revelation of God and the call to wholeness.

Images   *Experiences*

REGION 5

We find that our God is *personal.* No longer having proscriptions about our God-images, we are free to know God uniquely—and God is uniquely known by each one. In all of this, our sense is that our God-image is in change, is *dynamic.* It is not now what it has been; it is growing even yet. We sense the change is developmental and the fruit of our aging is found in our prayer. The sense of God is as a process, a movement within us to wholeness and growth—a life-force toward goodness. We see the "livingness" of God, this changing face of God as multifaceted *mystery*—a mystery which we seem to grasp at fleeting moments. We see these faces of God as we see the changing images in a kaleidoscope. We see God as on-going creation, always integrating all areas of life—the focal point of Christian unity.

Our God-images are rooted in our *experiences.* This includes both inner and relational experiences. Our God rises within from deep experiences of prayer, from Scripture meditation; God is also revealed in the communal "breaking of bread" experiences. As each one shares her moment with the sacred, new faces of the sacred are made available to the community. Some of our experiences of God surprise us, break over us unprepared; others are sought experiences wherein we are led by Scripture guides or communal guides to find God among the poor and marginated, the suffering and dying, the young and old, the searching. God is constant presence, promise, relationship, fidelity—the source of our life and mission. Our experiences name God as a God of love, freedom, justice, and risk.

REGION 6

Our sharing confirmed that God cannot be confined to a specific image. We acknowledge development and ambiguity in our image of God. We experience a certain comfortableness with the ambiguity and with the struggle to know who God is as our perceptions of ourselves and our world change.

However, expressions of our experience say that God is: pervading presence, within-ness, encompassing totality, active, dynamic, energizing power, transforming life, response-elicitor, sustaining, unconditional love, no-thing, neither male nor female, one-ing-ness, delight-full, co-creator with us. We find God revealed in storytelling the stuff of life: situations, events, people.

Images	Experiences

REGION 7

God is being imaged in new expressions because of the conviction that our personal and communal experiences are loci of God's revelation. Cannot "name" God for that is to have power over God (Old Testament notion of naming) but our words are conveying new images/descriptions of God; we seem to find God in experience, *in life*—God *in life* (rather than intellectual, theoretical.)

Our God is: presence, fidelity, love, caring, accepting, compassionate, life-giving, ever-changing, energy, freedom itself. Communitarian, relational and cannot be reduced to privatism. Immanent, experienced in relationships and events of our lives. Permeates all created reality. Paradox, ambiguity, mystery (one often sees only the back of God). Feminine: birthing, nurturing, caring, leading us toward integration, wholeness. Found in life; in our struggles toward wholeness, in struggles of peers, in our fragile brokenness we see death/resurrection. Urgent, quickening awareness that God is doing something new in our time! The wineskins are bursting. We need a new expression of our worship. We are beginning to trust the experience we have of God.

REGION 8

Constant, enduring, comfortable presence. Mystery, so unchanging, but always a surprise. God easily found in nature, in history and culture, in conflict and dissent (these are scenes of God's revelation and activity), best combination of masculine/feminine, no concrete image but presence sensed by qualities, our God is one who liberates and frees us from all forms of oppression, exploitation and dominance and calls us to integrated

Communitarian "face of God" revealed in our experience. Intimately involved in struggles and joys of his people, dynamic presence deepening as our lives go on; momentary and profound feelings and revelations of presence; presence of power and creativity; identifying with and calling us to identify with poor and powerless—compassionate; acts in the midst of his people, and not from without; expression and sense of

Images	Experiences

REGION 8 (continued)

and integral development and freedom, our stance has changed—contemplative relationship with God.

relationship comes from who we are—(our existential situation and the many factors which shape our faith: family, education, culture). We find God's presence in other people, in groups, in relationships.

REGION 9

God is: life-giving, energizing presence, changing, evolving, cosmic energy, friend and companion.

. . . I am with you.

REGION 10

Intimate presence within; creator/nourisher/sustainer (mother/father); enduring faithfulness; mystery/inexpressible; person/incarnational presence. Within, yet totally other; awesome, yet intimate/folksy; *mutual* presence; breath of life; abiding peace in quietness; hidden, waiting. Trustworthiness; always; waiting; incomprehensible; unknown; surprise; can't name, don't try, let God be God. Others' images of God will be quite different from ours, given different experiences and different settings. "Mid-life" images differ from "young" images of God. We can't assume that others' images will be different, need to be open to learn from others. How can we learn from others' images without imposing ours? Problematic of masculine/feminine images and at what

Dynamic; in process; active. How to name, important to try to name what is experienced. Initiated/experienced more than named. Expressed in other media: sound/music, color/art, touch/gesture. With me/us as friend, companion walking with. Present to and with me. Knowing me better than myself. Calling me by name, inviting me. Giving, touching, strengthening, healing hands. Dancing with me. God *is* (we believe this and experience it); God is one, the center, cosmic, all-inclusive. God is discovered/experienced: a) in suffering, brokenness, sinfulness, powerlessness; b) in others, in the sharing of relationships; c) perhaps differently for individuals as contrasted to groups, nations, cultures, historical moments (i.e., God's manifestation to groups may differ from how God is experienced by individuals).

Images	Experiences

REGION 10 (continued)

point to share with males our images of God.

God is experienced more often than imaged.

REGION 11

Communitarian 'face of God' is: inclusive, not exclusive; limitless, expansive, pervasive, not limited; everywhere is the locus of God, not limited to 'sacred'; dynamic, not static; transcendent, immanent, not mostly separated; intimate, not remote or distant; experienced, not theoretical/rational; feminine as well as masculine; horizontal, circular, not vertical; creator as well as challenger to co-creation with us; unconditional lover/supporter, not judger; a God-life experience inside me, not one who needs me to empty self. *Images:* compassionate one; faithful; present in the poor; present in all of life (pain, joy); joy; strength; wonder; spouse; friend; protector; life-giver; loving mother, father; source; source of all BE-ing; source of life, all good; creator; present in all of life, persons, events; person, care and gift-giver; connection, connector; presence, living and source of security; great Spirit; loving; calling forth; challenging; personal; intimate; energy, power; without, within, around; all-present; all-pervasive; presence, cloud; transparent; dynamic, surprising; more human than I.

Events/Experiences which shaped new 'face of God': Chapters; Vatican II; Experience of God in what is human; trusting one's inner authority; experiences of weakness/limits; experiencing love and loving; retreat experiences; study/praying Scriptures (OT and NT); impact of feminism, a new consciousness; inclusive language; in the poor; creation spirituality; receiving, giving, sharing; struggling with poor of Third World for liberation; deepening of personal prayer; living, praying, reading Scripture in a Third World culture; women mystics; experiences with persons/groups of multiple faiths/religions. No one has a 'corner' on God.

Changes in Image of God: judge; power; control; provider; same; sterile; old; I do something for God; God is up; male; good; limited; punisher; loving Father; God as parent; watching for good, bad; God was *out* there; presence, mostly in Sacraments; hide 'n seek; separated from secular; static; competitive: all-perfect, etc.

REGION 12

It is very difficult, if not impossible, to get at an image of God. Some conceptualize God as wind, lover, surprise, energy, movement. Although most people said that they most frequently refer to God as "he" and "him," they do not visualize God as masculine. Rather, the qualities which best describe God are those which are perceived as feminine. Our concepts/images of God keep on evolving and that is as it must be if we are open to a God who will not be "boxed in." How we perceive God is very dependent on what is going on in our lives at the moment and how open we are to the persons and events around us. Our language and words are just not adequate to us as we attempt to articulate our God. Totally useless is the pious God-talk of our past.

However, we do find it possible to share our experiences of God. The most common experience is that of PRESENCE. God is always there in our most ordinary experiences—compassionate, loving, accepting, faithful, peace-loving. We never fail to meet God among the poor and suffering—those who are being deprived of justice and their rights. We feel called to continue to share our experiences and insights in processes like this one. God is the best of the best and is extraordinarily present in our ordinary events!

REGION 13

God's revealing presence is imaged and experienced in relationship with people (cultures, men/women, creed, race, masculine/feminine) and life experiences (light/darkness, joy/sorrow, love, compassion, wholeness, unity, communion) and creation (relationship).

Communitarian face of God is our universe as experienced in our world by us in humanity, in nature, in the poor. God, an active, nurturing, personal presence—life. Feminine: constant, encouraging, compassionate God, not "out there" but "within." A redeeming God who is in the chaos, absurdity and waiting the "now" moment. *I AM.* God is a loving presence in persons and events in one's life and within each—a cosmic

| Images | Experiences |

force and energy. God permeates all that is and is discoverable/reflectable in every face. (The totality of creation.) God is loving, concerned, yet pained. God is an intimate God involved in all that happens. God is creative and challenging energy and presence who bonds us together, liberates us and calls us to new life and wholeness.

REGION 14

What needs to be stated first is that the experience of God, the "grasp" of God shifts. It is a concept of God in transition. Anytime we locate God as absolutely one or another reality, we are limiting God. Our image of God is evolving and it (the image, experience) has particularly evolved from a God who is "outside" "judge" "non-relational" to a God who is energy, the wellspring within . . .

God is experienced as personal, as loving, as one who abides within and among. God is with us as the loving compassionate one. The experience of God as loving, faithful friend came often through a sense of powerlessness, a need to relinquish security and the getting in touch with one's brokenness. This experience of God invites us to be creators and co-responsible as we develop a global and cultural awareness. This experience of God is of the heart. There has been a shift from God of the intellect to a God of the heart.

REGION 15

Loving presence—faithful; sustainer of life; inner sense of peace; inclusive being (male and female realities); creative strength; a living, active force of creative movement; a faithful friend; compassionate listener; caring, personal providence; an inclusive lover; an ever-present freshness and newness; the vision/reality of future life.

Shared/communal prayer is an important part of the feminine growth in the spiritual life. God is understood and discovered in his/her absence as well as his/her presence. As a faithful God, his/her presence is recognized and experienced in both conflict and serenity. God in certain experiences of life cannot be described in words, but is the

199

all-present peace that fills the human spirit. The deepening of one's understanding of God is often revealed in surprising and unexpected ways. God's face is seen in the experiences of one's own human process and in the lives of those with whom we openly share our faith journey. We are, in fact, converted by and through our experiences of prayer which touch our hearts amidst conflict, disorder, and a lack of harmony. Sharing and reflecting are important components of the feminine discovery of a personal God. Women's "relational" qualities are a significant part of a feminine spirituality. The beauty and wonder of God is for the women a part of all creation—of all nature—of all humanity.

DATE DUE

JAN 10 '90			